Er. D.C. Gupta

Current Electricity
for JEE Main & Advanced
(Study Package for Physics)

Fully Solved

disha
Nurturing Ambitions

Includes Past JEE & KVPY Questions

Useful for Class 12, KVPY & Olympiads

- Head Office : B-32, Shivalik Main Road, Malviya Nagar, New Delhi-110017
- Sales Office : B-48, Shivalik Main Road, Malviya Nagar, New Delhi-110017
  Tel. : 011-26691021 / 26691713

Page Layout : Prakash Chandra Sahoo

Typeset by Disha DTP Team

Printed at: **Repro Knowledgecast Limited, Thane**

DISHA PUBLICATION
ALL RIGHTS RESERVED

© Copyright Author

No part of this publication may be reproduced in any form without prior permission of the publisher. The author and the publisher do not take any legal responsibility for any errors or misrepresentations that might have crept in. We have tried and made our best efforts to provide accurate up-to-date information in this book.

For further information about the books from DISHA,
Log on to **www.dishapublication.com** or email to **info@dishapublication.com**

Booklet No.	Title	Chapter Nos.	Page Nos.
	STUDY PACKAGE IN PHYSICS FOR JEE MAIN & ADVANCED		
1	Units, Measurements & Motion	Ch 0. Mathematics Used in Physics Ch 1. Units and Measurements Ch 2. Vectors Ch 3. Motion in a Straight Line Ch 4. Motion in a Plane	1-202
2	Laws of Motion and Circular Motion	Ch 5. Laws of Motion and Equilibrium Ch 6. Circular Motion	203-318
3	Work Energy, Power & Gravitation	Ch 7. Work, Energy and Power Ch 8. Collisions and Centre of Mass Ch 9. Gravitation	319-480
4	Rotational Motion	Ch 1. Rotational Mechanics	1-120
5	Properties of Matter & SHM	Ch 2. Properties of Matter Ch 3. Fluid Mechanics Ch 4. Simple Harmonic Motion	121-364
6	Heat & Thermodynamics	Ch 5. Thermometry, Expansion & Calorimetry Ch 6. Kinetic Theory of Gases Ch 7. Laws of Thermodynamics Ch 8. Heat Transfer	365-570
7	Waves	Ch 9. Wave – I Ch 10. Wave –II	571-698
8	Electrostatics	Ch 0. Mathematics Used in Physics Ch 1. Electrostatics Ch 2. Capacitance & Capacitors	1-216
9	Current Electricity	Ch 3. DC and DC circuits Ch 4. Thermal and Chemical effects of Current"	217-338
10	Magnetism, EMI & AC	Ch 5. Magnetic Force on Moving Charges & Conductor Ch 6. Magnetic Effects of Current Ch 7. Permanent Magnet & Magnetic Properties of Substance Ch 8. Electromagnetic Induction Ch 9. AC and EM Waves	339-618
11	Ray & Wave Optics	Ch 1. Reflection of Light Ch 2. Refraction and Dispersion Ch 3. Refraction at Spherical Surface, Lenses and Photometry Ch 4. Wave optics	1-244
12	Modern Physics	Ch 5. Electron, Photon, Atoms, Photoelectric Effect and X-rays Ch 6. Nuclear Physics Ch 7. Electronics & Communication	245-384

Contents

Study Package Booklet 9 - Current Electricity

3. DC and DC Circuits   217-306

3.1 Introduction	218
3.2 Ohm's law	221
3.3 Electricity from chemicals : cell	226
3.4 Electromotive force (emf)	227
3.5 Circuit analysis	229
3.6 Electrical instruments	250
Review of formulae and important points	256
Exercise 3.1- 3.6	258-286
Hints & solutions	287-306

4. Thermal & Chemical Effects of Current   307-338

4.1 Thermal effect of current : joule's law	308
4.2 Electrical appliances	310
4.3 Seebeck effect	315
4.4 Peltier effect	317
4.5 Thomson effect	318
4.6 Chemical effect of current	318
4.7 Faraday's law of electrolysis	319
Review of formulae and important points	320
Exercise 4.1-4.6	322-332
Hints & solutions	333-338

CHAPTER 3

DC & DC Circuits
(217-306)

- Positive terminal
- Steel top plate
- Positive electrode
- Separator
- Negative electrode
- Negative terminal

3.1 INTRODUCTION
3.2 OHM'S LAW
3.3 ELECTRICITY FROM CHEMICALS : CELL
3.4 ELECTROMOTIVE FORCE (EMF)
3.5 CIRCUIT ANALYSIS
3.6 ELECTRICAL INSTRUMENTS
REVIEW OF FORMULAE AND IMPORTANT POINTS
EXERCISE 3.1
EXERCISE 3.2
EXERCISE 3.3
EXERCISE 3.4
EXERCISE 3.5
EXERCISE 3.6
HINTS & SOLUTIONS

3.1 Introduction

When you turn on a light, you are using the sort of electricity that flows along the wires, like water flows along pipes. This is called current electricity. It is usually made up of billions of electrons flowing along a wire. These electrons do not move along a wire by themselves. They have to be pushed by potential difference, produced by the battery.

Inside a wire

An electric current consists of billions of free electrons, flowing along a wire. The electrons "hop" from one atom to the next travelling in short bursts. Individual electrons move only fractions of a milimetre each second.
But like pushing a row of railway wagons, they at the speed of light, 300,000 kilometres per second.

Direct current, DC

In DC, all the electrons moves in the same direction, in all the time that the electricity flows. This type of current is produced by the batteries in torches cars and similar devices.

Alternating current, AC

In AC, the direction of electron movement changes many times each second. The electrons move one way, then the other, and so on.

Electric current

In an isolated metallic conductor, the free electrons move randomly like the molecules of a gas and so the net rate of flow of charge through any hypothetical plane is zero. If potential difference is applied across the ends of the conductor, an electric field is set up at every point within the conductor. This field exerts force on free electrons in opposite to direction of field and will give them a resultant motion. This flow of electrons constitutes an electric current. It can be defined as the rate at which charge passes through any specified surface area. Thus

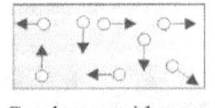

Conductor without p.d.

Fig. 3.1

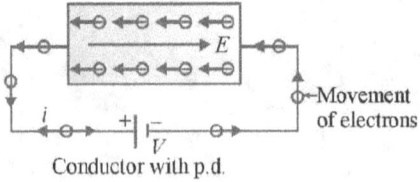

Conductor with p.d.

Fig. 3.2

$$i = \frac{dq}{dt}.$$

SI unit of electric current is C/s. 1 C/s = 1A.
We can get the charge that passes through any cross-section of the wire in time interval from t_1 to t_2 by integration. i.e.,

$$q = \int_{t_1}^{t_2} i\, dt.$$

More about electric current

1. The current is the same for all cross-sections of a conductor of non-uniform cross-sections. It is similar to the water flow. Charge flows faster where the conductor is smaller in cross-section and slower where the conductor has larger cross-section.

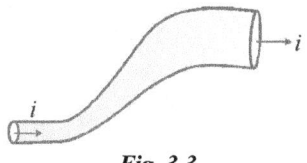

Fig. 3.3

2. As electrons move faster than positive ions, so the net current is due to electrons. This type of current is known as conduction current.

3. In liquids the flow of current occur due to both types of ions. In gases it is due to positive ions and electrons. In semiconductors, it is due to flow of holes and electrons.

$$1A = \frac{1C}{s} = \left(\frac{1}{1.6 \times 10^{-19}}\right) \text{ electrons/s}$$

$$= 6.25 \times 10^{18} \text{ electron/s}$$

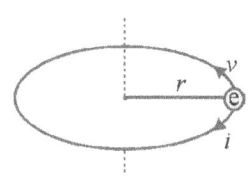

Fig. 3.4

4. Current constitutes by an electron: Let an electron is moving on a circular path of radius r with a speed v. The current due to its motion at any section of path,

$$i = \frac{q}{t}$$

$$= \frac{e}{\frac{2\pi r}{v}} = \frac{ev}{2\pi r}$$

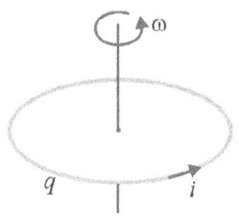

Fig. 3.5

5. If charge q is distributed over the ring uniformly or non-uniformly, current at any section of ring

$$i = \frac{q}{t} = \frac{q}{2\pi/\omega}$$

$$= \frac{q\omega}{2\pi}$$

6. Direct current (dc) and alternating current (ac):

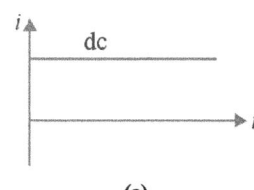

(a)

Current density ($\vec{J}$)

It is a characteristic of a point inside a conductor rather than the conductor as a whole. It is defined as the current per unit area through an infinitesimal area normal to the direction of current flow.

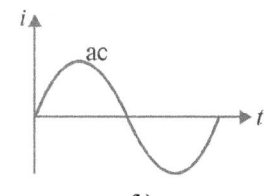

(b)

Fig. 3.6

1. The current density at a point P is given by

$$\vec{J} = \frac{di}{dA}\hat{n}$$

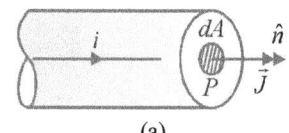

(a)

2. If cross-sectional area is not normal to the current, then

$$J = \frac{di}{dA\cos\theta} \text{ or } i = \int \vec{J} \cdot d\vec{A}$$

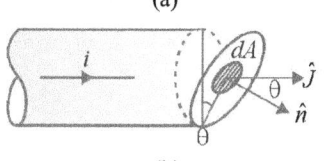

(b)

Fig. 3.7

3. For uniform distribution of current

$$J = \frac{i}{A}.$$

4. It is a vector quantity. Its SI unit is A/m².

220 ELECTRICITY & MAGNETISM

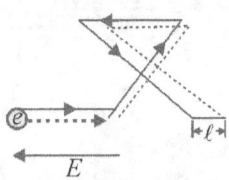

Fig. 3.8 Dotted path represents the motion of electron with field $\vec{E}$.

Drift velocity

When an electric field is applied in an conductor, a force acts on each electron in the direction opposite to the field. The electrons get bised in their random motion in favour of the force. As a result, the electrons drift slowly in this direction. If the electron drifts a distance ℓ in a long time t, we can define drift velocity (average velocity) as :

$$v_d = \frac{\ell}{t}$$

If τ is the average time between two successive collisions, then the distance drifted in this time

$$\ell = \frac{1}{2}a t^2 = \frac{1}{2}\left(\frac{Ee}{m}\right)\tau^2$$

∴ Drift velocity $\quad v_d = at = \dfrac{eE\tau}{m}$

The order of drift velocity is 10^{-4} m/s. It is very small in comparison to thermal speed ($\approx 10^5$ m/s) of electron at room temperature.

Now consider a cylindrical conductor of cross-sectional area A placed in electric field $\vec{E}$. Take a small length $v_d \Delta t$ of the conductor. The volume of this portion is $A v_d \Delta t$. Let n is the number of free electrons per unit volume of the wire, then total free electrons in this volume is $n A v_d \Delta t$.

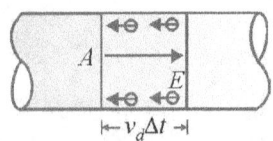

Fig. 3.9

The charge crossing this area $\quad \Delta q = n A v_d \Delta t \, e$

or $\quad i = \dfrac{\Delta q}{\Delta t} = n e A v_d$

and $\quad J = \dfrac{i}{A} = n e v_d$

More about drift velocity

We can write $v_d = \dfrac{i}{neA}$.

(i) If a constant current flows through a conductor of non-uniform cross-section, then $v_d \propto \dfrac{1}{A}$

(ii) Also, $\quad v_d = \dfrac{i}{neA} = \dfrac{V/R}{neA}$

$$= \dfrac{V}{\left(\dfrac{\rho\ell}{A}\right)neA} = \dfrac{V}{\rho\ell n e}$$

Clearly if conductors of different cross-sectional area are connected with same p.d., the drift velocity is independent of cross-sectional area.

Microscopic view of Ohm's law $\vec{E} = \rho \vec{J}$:

We have got $\quad v_d = \dfrac{eE\tau}{2m}$

and $\quad J = n e v_d$

From above equations, we get $\quad J = \left(\dfrac{ne^2\tau}{2m}\right) E$

or $\quad E = \left(\dfrac{2m}{ne^2\tau}\right) J$

or $\quad E = \rho J \quad$ Ohm's law

where $\rho = \dfrac{2m}{ne^2\tau}$, is called resistivity of the material.

The conductivity of material is defined as $\sigma = \dfrac{1}{\rho}$.

The quantity $\dfrac{1}{R}$ is called conductance.

3.2 Ohm's Law

If the physical conditions of conductor (temperature, length etc.) do not change, then the current in the conductor is directly proportional to the potential difference across the conductor.

Resistivity (ρ)

It can be defined as the ratio of electric field applied to current density. Thus

$$\rho = \dfrac{E}{J}.$$

Resistivity is the property of material which does not depend on size and shape of the conductor. SI unit of resistivity is Ohm-meter (Ω-m). A perfect conductor would have zero resistivity and a perfect insulator have infinite resistivity. Metals and alloys have the lowest resistivities and hence they are the best conductors. It is a familiar fact that good electrical conductors, such as metals, are good conductors of heat, while poor electrical conductors such as plastics are also poor thermal conductor.

Variation of resistivity with temperature

The resistivity of metallic conductors increases with increasing temperature as

$$\rho_t = \rho_0[1+\alpha t+\beta t^2]$$

where ρ_0 = resistivity of conductor at $0°$ C

ρ_t = resistivity of conductor at $t°$ C

t = is the temperature difference between t and $0°$ C,

and $\alpha \ \& \ \beta$ are temperature coefficients of resistance

$\alpha > \beta$, and positive for metals and negative for non-metals.

Note: The resistivity of the alloy manganin is practically independent of the temperature.

Resistance

In the relation $\vec{E} = \rho \vec{J}$, it is difficult to measure $\vec{E}$ and $\vec{J}$ directly. It is, therefore very convenient to put this relation in macro parameters like current and potential difference. To do this let us consider a conductor of length ℓ and cross-sectional area A as shown in *fig. 3.11*.

We can write $\quad \vec{E} = \rho \vec{J}$

As $\quad E = \dfrac{V}{\ell}$ and $J = \dfrac{i}{A}$

$\therefore \quad \dfrac{V}{\ell} = \rho \dfrac{i}{A}$

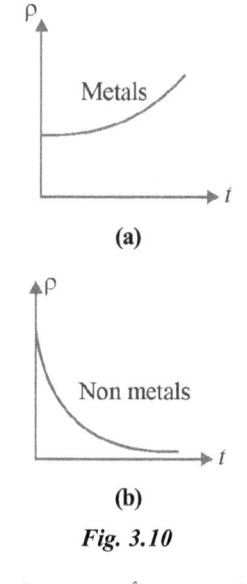

Fig. 3.10

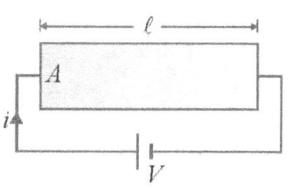

Fig. 3.11

ELECTRICITY & MAGNETISM

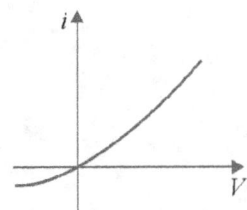

(a) Ohmic conductor

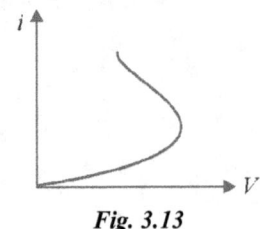

(b) Non-ohmic conductor
Fig. 3.12

or
$$V = i\left(\frac{\rho \ell}{A}\right) = iR$$

This relation is often referred to as Ohm's law.

where R is called resistance of the specimen and is equal to $R = \frac{\rho \ell}{A}$.

The SI unit of R is ohm (Ω). Its symbol is —⋁⋁⋁—.
The material obeying Ohm's law is called ohmic conductor or a linear conductor. If ohm's law is not obeyed, then the conductor is non-ohmic or non linear.
Fig 3.12 (a) is a curve for metalic conductor. The straight line shows that the resistance of conductor is the same no matter what applied voltage is used to measure it. fig.3.12 (b) is not straight line and the resistance depends on voltage applied, the resistance is called dynamic resistance and the conductor is called non-ohmic conductor.

Thermistor

Thermistor is the heat sensitive resistor. It is usually made by semiconducting material for which $V-i$ plot is not linear. The temperature coefficient of thermistor is negative and usually large. It is of the order of $-0.04/\,°C$.

Thermistors are used for making resistance thermometers which can measure very low temperature.

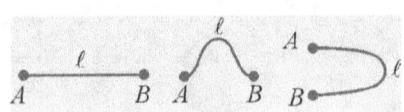

Fig. 3.13

Fig. 3.14

Note:

1. Resistance depends on length of wire not on the shape of the wire.

   All the wires have same resistance between A & B. ℓ is the straight length of wire between its ends.

2. $V = iR$ is the general relation between i and V which is applicable to both type of conductors, ohmic as well as non-ohmic.

Variation of resistance with temperature

As the resistance of any specimen is proportional to its resistivity, which varies with temperature, and also resistance varies with temperature. Therefore we have

$$R_t = R_0(1+\alpha t + \beta t^2)$$

for small t,
$$R_t \simeq R_0(1+\alpha t)$$

Temperature coefficient of resistance (α)

If R_1 and R_2 are the values of resistance at temperature t_1 and t_2 respectively, then
$$R_1 = R_0(1+\alpha t_1) \text{ and } R_2 = R_0(1+\alpha t_2)$$

$\therefore$
$$\frac{R_1}{R_2} = \frac{1+\alpha t_1}{1+\alpha t_2}$$

or
$$\alpha = \frac{R_2 - R_1}{R_1 t_2 - R_2 t_1}.$$

Note:

We have assumed α to be constant for all temperature. But actually it varies with temp. If R_t is the resistance at any temperature, then $R_t = R_0(1+\alpha t)$, differentiating above equation w.r.t. temp, we get

$$\alpha = \frac{1}{R_0}\left(\frac{dR_t}{dt}\right).$$

Resistance of conductor of non-uniform cross-section

Consider a conductor of length ℓ and radius at its ends are r_1 and r_2. The resistance of element under consideration

$$dR = \frac{\rho\, dx}{\pi r^2}$$

where,

$$r = r_1 + \left(\frac{r_2 - r_1}{\ell}\right) x$$

$\therefore$

$$dR = \frac{\rho\, dx}{\pi \left[r_1 + \left(\frac{r_2 - r_1}{\ell}\right) x\right]^2}$$

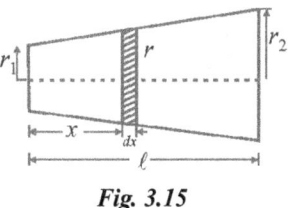

Fig. 3.15

Resistance of whole conductor

$$R = \int_0^\ell dR = \int_0^\ell \frac{\rho\, dx}{\pi \left[r_1 + \left(\frac{r_2 - r_1}{\ell}\right) x\right]^2}$$

or

$$R = \frac{\rho \ell}{\pi\, r_1 r_2}.$$

Why conductor offers resistance?

Resistance means the hinderance offered to the flow of charge. Electrons in their motion collide with the positive ions and themselves, due to which resistance in motion occurs. The resistance mainly occurs due to collisions of electrons with the positive ions.

Super conductors

Kamerlingh found that mercury offers zero resistance at 4.2 K. This phenomenon is called super conductivity and the metal is called superconductor. Certain alloys become superconductors at rather high temperature. The resistance of material in the superconducting state is zero and the currents once established in closed superconducting circuits persist for weeks, even though there is no battery in the circuit.

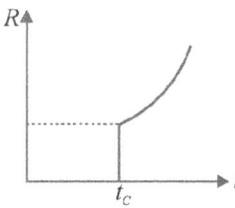

Stretching a wire

Consider a wire of length ℓ, radius of cross-section r and is of resistance R. It is stretched to length ℓ'. Let its resistance becomes R'. Assuming volume of material remains constant after stretching or compression, and so

Fig. 3.16 Resistance-temperature graph for superconductor

$$\pi r^2 \ell = \pi r'^2 \ell'$$

or

$$\frac{\ell'}{\ell} = \frac{r^2}{r'^2}$$

We have,

$$R = \frac{\rho \ell}{\pi r^2} \quad \text{and} \quad R' = \frac{\rho \ell'}{\pi r'^2}$$

$\therefore$

$$R' = R \frac{\ell'}{\ell} \times \frac{r^2}{r'^2}$$

$$= R \frac{\ell'}{\ell} \times \frac{\ell'}{\ell}$$

or
$$R' = R\left(\frac{\ell'}{\ell}\right)^2$$

Also
$$R' = R\frac{r^2}{r'^2} \times \frac{r^2}{r'^2}$$

or
$$R' = R\left(\frac{r}{r'}\right)^4$$

% change in resistance, if there is small change in length
$$\frac{\Delta R}{R} \times 100 = 2\frac{\Delta \ell}{\ell} \times 100$$

Resistors in series and parallel

Series : The resistors are said to be in series, if they provide a single path between the points. The current is same in each resistor in series, but p.d. across resistor is proportional to its resistance. Let us consider two resistances R_1 and R_2 connected in series. For series connection
$$V = V_1 + V_2$$
Since i is same in both the resistors,
$$\therefore \quad iR = iR_1 + iR_2$$
or
$$R = R_1 + R_2$$
The above equation is true for any number of resistors in series. Thus for n-resistors
$$R = R_1 + R_2 + \ldots + R_n$$

Parallel : The resistors are said to be in parallel between the points, if each provides an alternative path between the points. The potential difference is the same across each resistor, but current divide in inverse ratio of their resistances. For parallel connection of resistors
$$i = i_1 + i_2$$
$$\frac{V}{R} = \frac{V}{R_1} + \frac{V}{R_2}$$
or
$$\frac{1}{R} = \frac{1}{R_1} + \frac{1}{R_2}$$

For n-resistors in parallel
$$\frac{1}{R} = \frac{1}{R_1} + \frac{1}{R_2} + \ldots + \frac{1}{R_n}$$

Effective value of α

(i) **In series :** Suppose α_1 and α_2 are the temperature coefficient of resistance of the resistors R_1 and R_2 respectively. Let α be their effective value.

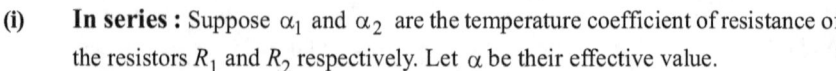

At 0°C $\quad R_{01} \quad\quad\quad R_{02} \quad\quad\quad\quad\quad\quad R_0 = R_{01} + R_{02}$
At t°C $\quad R_{01}(1+\alpha_1 t) \quad R_{02}(1+\alpha_2 t) \quad\quad R_0(1+\alpha t)$

Their equivalent resistance at any temperature in series is
$$R_t = R_{1t} + R_{2t}$$

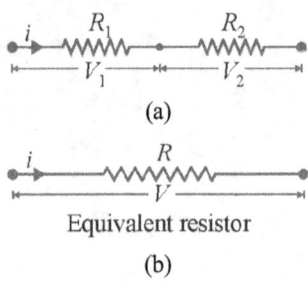

(a)

Equivalent resistor
(b)

Fig. 3.17

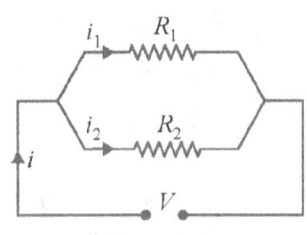

Fig. 3.18

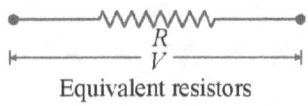

Equivalent resistors

Fig. 3.19

or $R_0(1+\alpha t) = R_{01}(1+\alpha_1 t) + R_{02}(1+\alpha_2 t)$

or $(R_{01}+R_{02})(1+\alpha t) = (R_{01}+R_{02}) + (R_{01}\alpha_1 + R_{02}\alpha_2)t$

or $(R_{01}+R_{02}) + (R_{01}+R_{02})\alpha t = (R_{01}+R_{02}) + (R_{01}\alpha_1 + R_{02}\alpha_2)t$

After solving, we get $\alpha = \left(\dfrac{R_{01}\alpha_1 + R_{02}\alpha_2}{R_{01}+R_{02}}\right)$

(ii) In parallel :

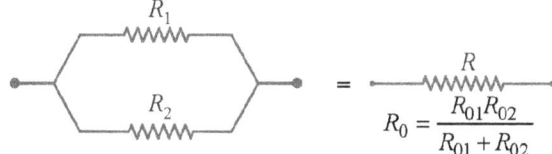

At any temperature $t°C$ **Fig. 3.20** $R_0 = \dfrac{R_{01}R_{02}}{R_{01}+R_{02}}$

$$\dfrac{1}{R_t} = \dfrac{1}{R_{1t}} + \dfrac{1}{R_{2t}}$$

or $\dfrac{1}{R_0(1+\alpha t)} = \dfrac{1}{R_{01}(1+\alpha_1 t)} + \dfrac{1}{R_{02}(1+\alpha_2 t)}$

or $\dfrac{1}{\left(\dfrac{R_{01}R_{02}}{R_{01}+R_{02}}\right)(1+\alpha t)} = \dfrac{1}{R_{01}(1+\alpha_1 t)} + \dfrac{1}{R_{02}(1+\alpha_2 t)}$

or $\dfrac{R_{01}+R_{02}}{R_{01}R_{02}(1+\alpha t)} = \dfrac{1}{R_{01}(1+\alpha_1 t)} + \dfrac{1}{R_{02}(1+\alpha_2 t)}$

$\dfrac{(R_{01}+R_{02})(1+\alpha t)^{-1}}{R_{01}R_{02}} = \dfrac{1}{R_{01}}(1+\alpha_1 t)^{-1} + \dfrac{1}{R_{02}}(1+\alpha_2 t)^{-1}$

Solving by Binomial theorem, we have

$\dfrac{1}{R_{01}}(1-\alpha t) + \dfrac{1}{R_{02}}(1-\alpha t) = \dfrac{1}{R_{01}}(1-\alpha_1 t) + \dfrac{1}{R_{02}}(1-\alpha_2 t)$

or $\alpha t\left(\dfrac{1}{R_{01}} + \dfrac{1}{R_{02}}\right) = \left(\dfrac{\alpha_1}{R_{01}} + \dfrac{\alpha_2}{R_{02}}\right)t$

or $\alpha = \left(\dfrac{\alpha_1 R_{02} + \alpha_2 R_{01}}{R_{01}+R_{02}}\right)$

Ex. 1 The region between two concentric spheres of radii r_1 and r_2 is filled with a conducting material of conductivity σ. Find resistance between the spheres.

Sol.

Choose an element of thickness dr at a distance r from the centre. Its resistance

$dR = \rho\dfrac{dr}{4\pi r^2} = \left(\dfrac{1}{\sigma}\right)\dfrac{dr}{4\pi r^2}$

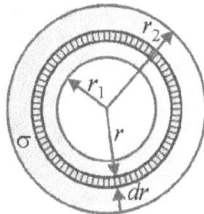

Fig. 3.21

The resistance between the spheres

$$R = \int_{r_1}^{r_2} dR = \dfrac{1}{4\pi\sigma}\int_{r_1}^{r_2}\dfrac{dr}{r^2}$$

$$= \dfrac{(r_2 - r_1)}{\sigma 4\pi r_1 r_2} \quad \text{Ans.}$$

Ex. 2 Find resistance of the annular disc between centre and periphery of the disc. The inner and outer radius of the disc is a and b respectively. The thickness of the disc is t and conductivity of its material is σ.

Sol.

The resistance of a cross-section perpendicular to the current flow on any radius r and thus of area $2\pi rt$ is given by

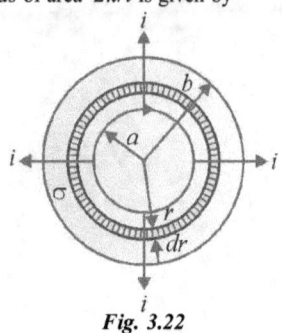

Fig. 3.22

$$dR = \rho\frac{dr}{2\pi rt} = \frac{1}{\sigma}\frac{dr}{2\pi rt}$$

Total resistance

$$R = \int_a^b \frac{1}{\sigma}\frac{dr}{2\pi rt}$$

or $$R = \frac{1}{2\pi\sigma t}\ell n\left(\frac{b}{a}\right) \quad \text{Ans.}$$

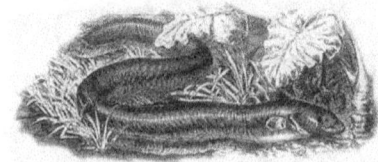

Fig. 3.23

3.3 Electricity from chemicals : Cell

If we want to flow the charge through a resistor, we must set-up a potential difference across it. Let us connect each end of the resistor to a conducting sphere, with one sphere charged positively and other negatively as in *fig. 3.23*.

The problem with such a device is that charge flows till their potential become equal. When that happens, the flow of charge stops. Therefore, to maintain a steady flow of charge we need a device which can maintain potential difference between the terminals of the resistor. Such a device is called emf device. It may be a battery, electric generator or solar cells etc.

The simplest unit for making electricity is called a cell. It makes electricity for chemical reactions and works like a pump to push electrons along wires. A battery has two or more cells and some types, such as car batteries, are rows or "batteries" of single cells, hence our common name "battery" for single and multiple cells. In a primary cell, as electricity is produced, the chemicals are slowly used up. Eventually, the chemicals run out and the battery can not make electricity any more. In a secondary cells, the chemicals can be replenished or reformed by recharging the cell with electricity.

Electric animal
Muscles produce tiny electrical signals as they work. In the electric eel, these muscles form large blocks along the body. They produce powerful surges of electricity, hundreds of volts, like a "living battery"

Car batteries

Also called an accumulator, a vehicle batteries can be recharged. The chemical reaction which has taken place to make electricity can be reversed by putting electricity back in, so the battery can be used again. In a vehicle the recharging is carried out by an alternator, which is driven by the engine. Most car batteries have six linked cells, each with an output of about two volts. Each cell consists of lead plates, lead dioxide plates and sulphuric acid. Electricity is produced in the reactions between the plates and the sulphuric acid.

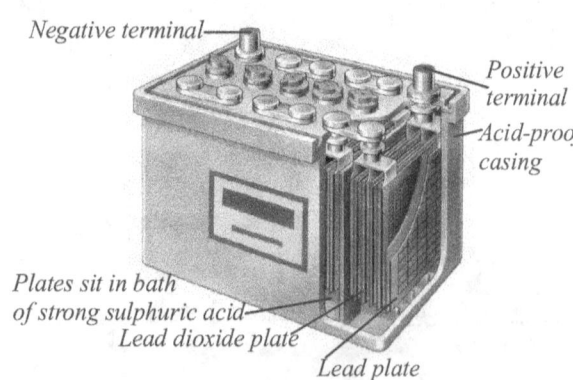

Substances such as acids dissolve in water to form charged particles, ions – positive cations (red) and negative anions (blue). In a cell, these form the electrolyte. When other materials, such as metal roads, are put in the electrolyte, they act as electrodes. They attract opposite-charged ions and cause an electric current to flow.

How a cell works

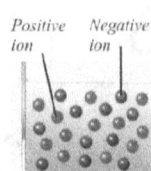

The electrolyte consists of charge particles called ions, positive and negative.

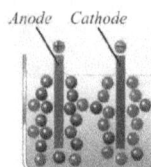

The electrodes are the positive anode and the negative cathode.

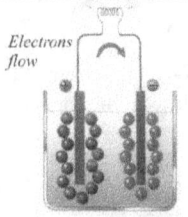

Opposite electrical charges attract and electrons move, making the current.

3.4 Electromotive force (EMF)

Emf of a source is defined as the workdone per unit charge that the source does in moving charges from its lower potential terminal to its high potential terminal. i.e.,

$$\xi = \frac{dW}{dq}.$$

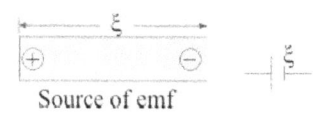

Source of emf
Fig. 3.24

The term electromotive force is somewhat confusing in that concept to which it refers as not a force, but a work per unit charge.

For a source in open circuit, the potential difference V, is equal to the electromotive force. Thus

$$V = \xi$$

Under closed circuit condition, the source offers some resistance to the flow of charge. This resistance is called internal resistance. Because of this internal resistance the potential across the terminals of source is decreased by ir.

∴ p.d across the terminals of the cell

$$V = \xi - ir$$

Now consider the case in which source is being charged by an other source like alternator. When this is the case, the current within the source is from positive terminal to negative terminal. The terminal voltage is then greater than the emf ξ and so p.d. across the terminals of the source

$$V = \xi + ir.$$

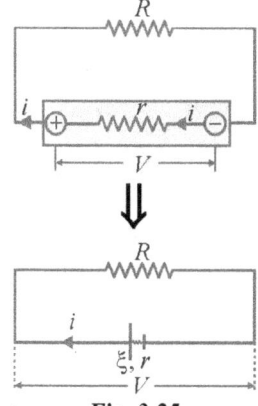

Fig. 3.25

Fig. 3.26

What happens inside a source of emf ?

1. Consider a source of emf which maintains a potential difference across its terminals. Let us consider the charges inside the source. In an open circuit, the charges are in equilibrium, therefore the net force on each charge must be zero. i.e.,

$$\vec{F} = 0 = \vec{F}_e + \vec{F}_n$$

where $\vec{F}_e$ is the force exerted by field produced by the terminals of the source. This field is electrostatic in nature. The other force ($\vec{F}_n$) which is equal in magnitude to $\vec{F}_e$ is the force exerted by field, is of nonelectrostatic in nature, whatever its origin is. Thus we can write

$$\vec{E}_e + \vec{E}_n = 0$$

or $$\vec{E}_e = -\vec{E}_n$$

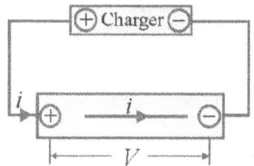

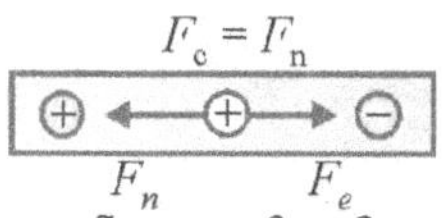

Source of emf
Fig. 3.27

2. The electrostatic potential difference V is defined as the work done per unit charge done by the electrostatic field $\vec{E}_e$ on a charge moving from positive terminal to negative terminal of the source. And the work done by $\vec{E}_n$, per unit charge, when a charge moves from negative terminal to positive terminal of the source, is called electromotive force ξ of the source.

When $\vec{E}_e = -\vec{E}_n$, we have $V = \xi$.

3. Now suppose that the terminals of a source are connected by a conducting wire forming a complete circuit. The driving force on the free charges in the wire is due to the electrostatic field $\vec{E}_e$ field set up by the charged terminals of the source. This set up a current in the wire from positive terminal to negative terminal of the source. The charges on the terminals decreases slightly and hence the electrostatic

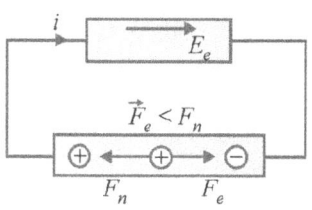

Fig. 3.28

228 ELECTRICITY & MAGNETISM

fields both within the wire and source decrease also. As a result $\vec{E}_e$ becomes smaller than $\vec{E}_n$. Hence positive charges within the source are driven towards the positive terminals, and there is a current within the source from negative to positive terminal of the source. As $\vec{E}_e$ is some what less than $\vec{E}_n$ in closed circuit condition, correspondingly V is less than ξ. The difference is equal to the work per unit charge done by the resultant field, which is simply ir.

$$\therefore \quad V = \xi - ir$$

Short circuit : If the terminals of a source are connected by a conductor of zero resistance (practically negligible resistance), the source is said to be short circuited.

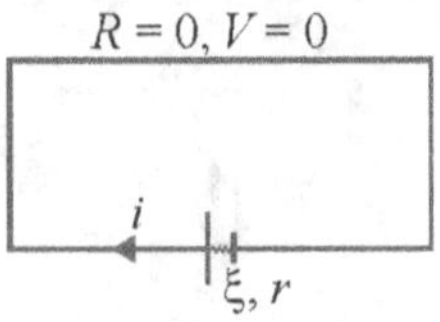

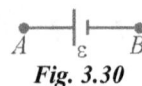

Fig. 3.29

The short circuit current can be obtained as

$$V = 0 = \xi - ir$$

or

$$i = \frac{\xi}{r}$$

Open circuit : When no current is drawn from the source, it is said to be an open circuit. Thus

$$i = 0$$

$$\therefore \quad V = \xi - ir = \xi - 0 \times r$$

or

$$V = \xi$$

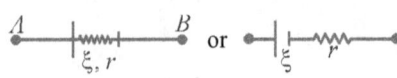

Fig. 3.30

At a glance

1. For an ideal source of emf (cell) whose internal resistance (r) is zero, $V_{AB} = \xi$
2. A practical cell which has some internal resistance (r).

$$V_{AB} = \xi$$

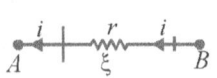

Fig. 3.31

3. When cell is discharging :

$$V_{AB} = \xi - ir$$

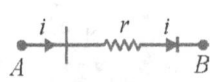

Fig. 3.32

4. When cell is charging :

$$V_{AB} = \xi + ir$$

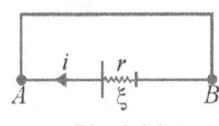

Fig. 3.33

5. Short circuit : $V_{AB} = 0$

or

$$0 = \xi - ir \Rightarrow i = \frac{\xi}{r}$$

6. Open circuit :

$$i = 0$$

$$\therefore \quad V_{AB} = \xi - ir = \xi - 0 = \xi$$

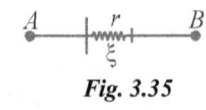

Fig. 3.34

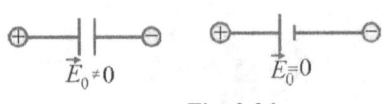

Fig. 3.35

Difference between a cell and a capacitor

1. Capacitor can provide variable (decreasing) potential in a circuit for short time. While cell can provide constant potential for a long time (many years).
2. The energy stored between plates of capacitor is electrical while energy stored between terminals of cell is chemical.
3. The plates of capacitors are usually made of same material. The terminals of cell always be of different materials.
4. The electric field between the plates of capacitor is non zero. But electric field between the terminals of cell is zero in open circuit.

Fig. 3.36

3.5 Circuit analysis

Ohm's law can give the solution of the circuit which has one loop or circuit with many loops which can be reduced to a single loop. To analyse complicated circuits Kirchhoff developed a method which is based on two laws. These are :

Kirchhoff's first law or junction rule

According to it, the algebraic sum of currents at any junction is equal to zero. i.e., $\Sigma i = 0$.

or

The sum of currents entering at any junction is equal to the sum of currents leaving the junction.

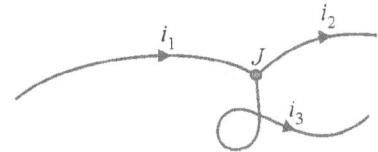

Fig. 3.37

Kirchhoff's first law is based on conservation of charge; the magnitudes of the currents in the branches must add to give the magnitude of the current in the original conductor, so that $i_1 = i_2 + i_3$.

Kirchhoff's second law or loop rule

According to it the algebraic sum of potential drop across all circuit elements in a closed loop is equal to zero. i.e., $\Sigma V = 0$.

Second law is based on conservation of energy.

(a) For a circuit having cells and resistors, we can wirte

$$\Sigma iR + \Sigma \xi = 0.$$

(b) For a circuit having cells, capacitors and resistors, we have

$$\Sigma iR + \Sigma \frac{q}{C} + \Sigma \xi = 0.$$

Guidelines and sign conventions

The guidelines and sign conventions, we have used in previous chapter can also be used here also.

1. Assume the currents in each branch of the circuit. At each junction, they must satisfy junction rule. The current in any resistor is due to the net response of all the sources present in the circuit.
2. You may choose any close loop, which may have cell or not. But for a circuit having only one cell, choose a close loop, which include this cell.
3. (a) The potential drop across any resistor in the direction of flow of current can be taken as negative and positive for reverse direction of current.
   (b) The potential drop across the capacitor is taken as negative from its positive plate to its negative plate and positive for reverse sense.

Note: See the sign of charge of first coming plate of the capacitor. In the above case, the first coming plate when moves from left to right across the capacitor is positive which has charge (q).

(c) The emf of the cell is taken as negative from positive terminal to negative terminal of the cell and positive for reverse sence.

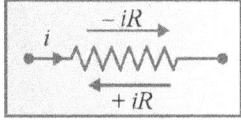

Fig. 3.38

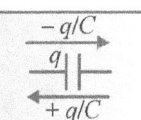

Fig. 3.39

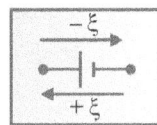

Fig. 3.40

Note: In the final calculations, some of the currents/all currents may be of negative sign. Do'nt be bother about their sign. The negative sign indicate that the actual direction of current will be opposite of assumed direction of current. In further calculations you have to use the value of current with the negative sign.

Grouping of cells : Battery

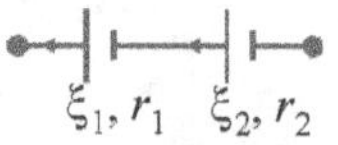

1. **Series grouping :**

   (a) **Right grouping of cells :** When each cell in series delivers the current in same direction.

   The equivalent emf $\xi_{eq} = \xi_1 + \xi_2$

   The equivalent resistance $r_{eq} = r_1 + r_2$

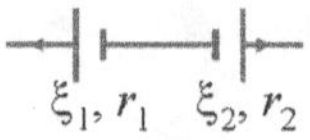

   Fig. 3.41

   (b) **Wrong grouping of cells :** When cells deliver current in opposite directions.

   The equivalent emf $\xi_{eq} = \xi_1 - \xi_2 \quad (\xi_1 > \xi_2)$

   The equivalent resistance $r_{eq} = r_1 + r_2$

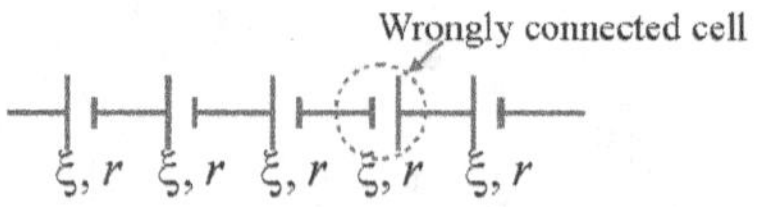

   Fig. 3.42

   In a series of 5 identical cells, if one of the cells is wrongly connected :

   The net emf of rightly connected cells $= 4\xi$

   The net emf of wrongly connected cell $= -\xi$

   The equivalent emf of all cells in series $= 4\xi - \xi$

   or $\xi_{eq} = 3\xi$

   The equivalent internal resistance $r_{eq} = 5r$

   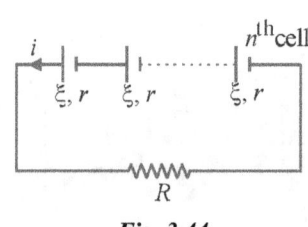

   Fig. 3.43 — Wrongly connected cell

   Thus when one cell is wrongly connected, the net or equivalent emf is decreased by 2ξ. But internal resistance is always be additive.

   For a battery of n-identical cells, if m cells are wrongly connected then effective emf

   $$\xi_{eq} = (n-2m)\xi$$
   $$r_{eq} = nr$$

   (c) **For a battery of n-identical cells :**

   Net or equivalent emf $\xi_{eq} = n\xi$

   and equivalent resistance $R_{eq} = nr + R$

   $\therefore$ Net current $i = \dfrac{\xi_{eq}}{R_{eq}}$

   $= \dfrac{n\xi}{nr + R}$

   Fig. 3.44

   (i) If $R \ll nr$, then $i \simeq \dfrac{\xi}{r}$. This is the current in the resistor due to only one cell.

   Therefore series grouping of cells in such a case when external resistance is very small in comparison to internal resistance is of no use.

   (ii) If $R \gg nr$, $i_{max} \simeq n\dfrac{\xi}{R}$. This time the current in resistor R is n times the current due to one cell. Therefore series grouping of cells is useful in this case.

2. **Parallel grouping**
   (a) For a battery of n-identical cells, all are rightly connected

   Equivalent emf $\xi_{eq} = \xi$

   and equivalent resistance $R_{eq} = \dfrac{r}{n} + R$

   $\therefore \quad i = \dfrac{\xi_{eq}}{R_{eq}}$

   $= \dfrac{\xi}{\dfrac{r}{n} + R}$

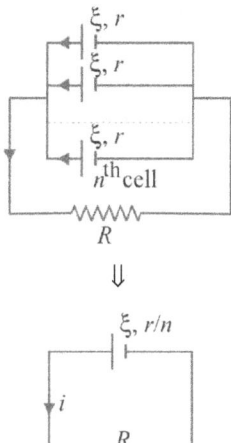

   (i) If $R \gg \dfrac{r}{n}$, $i = \dfrac{\xi}{R}$. This is the current in the resistor due to only one cell. Therefore such grouping of cells is of no use.

   (ii) If $R \ll \dfrac{r}{n}$, $i_{max} = n\dfrac{\xi}{r}$. That time the current in resistor R is n times the current due to one cell. In such a case parallel grouping of cells is useful.

Fig. 3.45

(b) **Battery having cells of different emf**
(i) Two cells are rightly connected : Both the cells delivering currents in same sence.

Method I :
In closed loop $ACDBHGA$

$$-\xi_1 + i_1 r_1 + iR = 0$$

or $\quad i_1 = \dfrac{\xi_1}{r_1} - i\dfrac{R}{r_1}$

Similarly $\quad i_2 = \dfrac{\xi_2}{r_2} - i\dfrac{R}{r_2}$

and $\quad i_1 + i_2 = \dfrac{\xi_1}{r_1} + \dfrac{\xi_2}{r_2} - iR\left(\dfrac{1}{r_1} + \dfrac{1}{r_2}\right)$

or $\quad i = \dfrac{\xi_1}{r_1} + \dfrac{\xi_2}{r_2} - iR\left(\dfrac{1}{r_1} + \dfrac{1}{r_2}\right)$

or $\quad i = \dfrac{\left(\dfrac{\xi_1}{r_1} + \dfrac{\xi_2}{r_2}\right)}{1 + R\left(\dfrac{1}{r_1} + \dfrac{1}{r_2}\right)}$

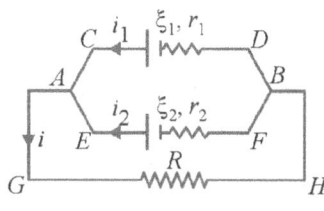

Fig. 3.46

$= \dfrac{\left(\dfrac{\xi_1 r_2 + \xi_2 r_1}{r_1 r_2}\right)}{\left(\dfrac{r_1 r_2 + R(r_1 + r_2)}{r_1 r_2}\right)}$

$= \dfrac{\xi_1 r_2 + \xi_2 r_1}{(r_1 + r_2)\left[\dfrac{r_1 r_2}{r_1 + r_2} + R\right]}$

$= \dfrac{\xi_1 r_2 + \xi_2 r_1 / (r_1 + r_2)}{\left[\dfrac{r_1 r_2}{r_1 + r_2} + R\right]} = \dfrac{\xi_{eq}}{R_{eq}}$

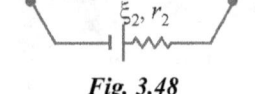

Fig. 3.47

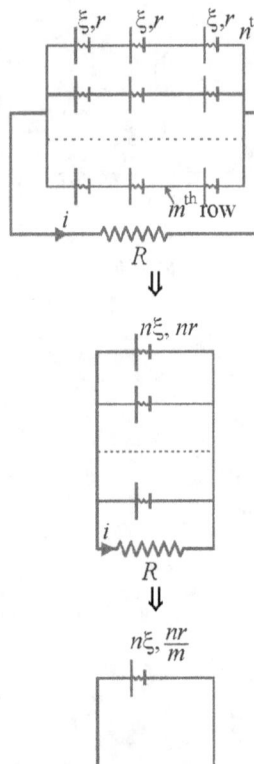

Fig. 3.48

Fig. 3.49

$$\therefore \quad \xi_{eq} = \frac{\xi_1 r_2 + \xi_2 r_1}{r_1 + r_2}$$

Method II :
(i) In closed loop $ACDBFEA$
$$-\xi_1 + i r_1 + i r_2 + \xi_2 = 0$$
or
$$i = \frac{\xi_1 - \xi_2}{r_1 + r_2}$$
Now
$$V_{AB} = \xi_1 - i r_1$$
$$= \xi_1 - \left(\frac{\xi_1 - \xi_2}{r_1 + r_2}\right) r_1$$
or
$$\xi_{eq} = V_{AB} = \frac{\xi_1 r_2 + \xi_2 r_1}{r_1 + r_2}, \text{ and } r_{eq} = \frac{r_1 r_2}{r_1 + r_2}$$

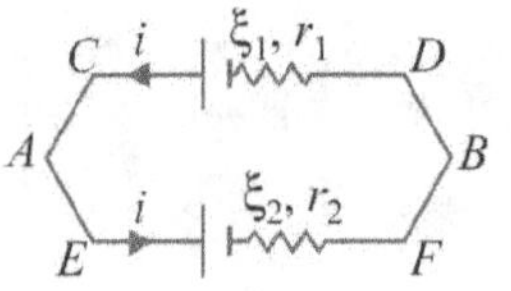

(ii) If cells are wrongly connected : The equivalent emf of them can be easily obtained by any of the methods discussed above. Or otherwise putting $-\xi_2$ is place of ξ_2, so we have

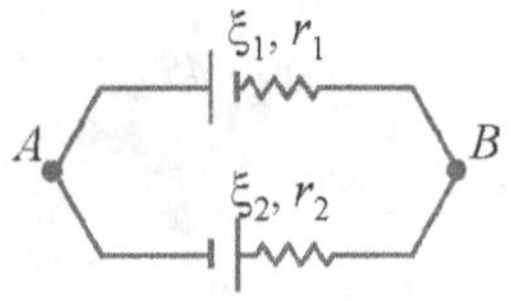

$$\xi_{eq} = \frac{\xi_1 r_2 - \xi_2 r_1}{r_1 + r_2}$$

$$r_{eq} = \frac{r_1 r_2}{r_1 + r_2}.$$

3. **Mixed Grouping :**
Let there are n-identical cells in a row and m such rows are in parallel. The total number of cells in the circuit is mn.
Equivalent emf
$$\xi_{eq} = n\xi$$
and equivalent resistance
$$R_{eq} = \frac{nr}{m} + R$$

$\therefore$ Net current
$$i = \frac{\xi_{eq}}{R_{eq}}$$
$$= \frac{n\xi}{\frac{nr}{m} + R}$$
$$= \frac{mn\xi}{nr + mR}$$
$$= \frac{mn\xi}{\left(\sqrt{nr} - \sqrt{mR}\right)^2 + 2\sqrt{nr}\sqrt{mR}}$$

The current i will be maximum, when denominator in above expression is minimum. It to be minimum when
$$\sqrt{nr} - \sqrt{mR} = 0$$
or
$$\frac{nr}{m} = R$$
or total internal resistance = total external resistance
then
$$i_{max} = \frac{mn\xi}{2\sqrt{nr}\sqrt{mR}} = \frac{\xi}{2}\sqrt{\frac{mn}{rR}}.$$

Ex. 3 Find the equivalent emf of the three cells which are connected as shown in *fig. 3.50*

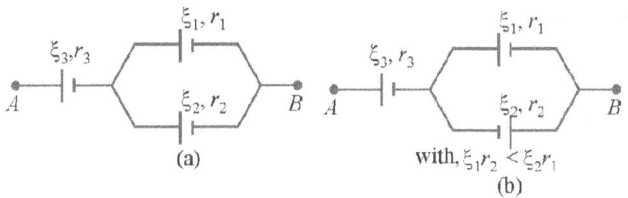

Fig. 3.50

Sol.
(a) The equivalent emf of cells ξ_1 and ξ_2 is

$$\xi = \frac{\xi_1 r_2 + \xi_2 r_1}{r_1 + r_2}$$

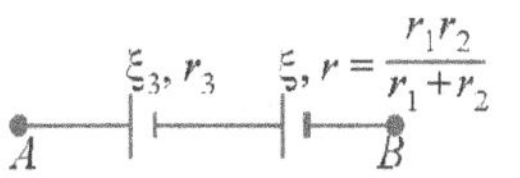

Fig. 3.51

$$\therefore \quad \xi_{eq} = V_{AB} = \xi_3 + \xi$$

$$= \xi_3 + \frac{\xi_1 r_2 + \xi_2 r_1}{r_1 + r_2}$$

and $\quad R_{eq} = r_3 + \dfrac{r_1 r_2}{r_1 + r_2}$

(b) The equivalent emf of cells ξ_1 and ξ_2 is

$$\xi = \frac{\xi_1 r_2 - \xi_2 r_1}{r_1 + r_2}$$

$$= -\frac{(\xi_2 r_1 - \xi_1 r_2)}{r_1 + r_2}$$

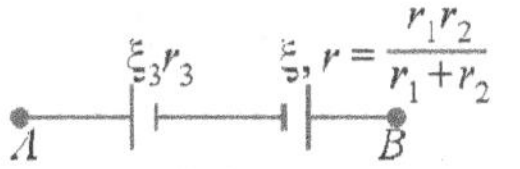

Fig. 3.52

$$\therefore \quad \xi_{eq} = V_{AB} = \xi_3 + \xi$$

$$= \xi_3 - \left(\frac{\xi_2 r_1 - \xi_1 r_2}{r_1 + r_2}\right)$$

and $\quad R_{eq} = r_3 + \dfrac{r_1 r_2}{r_1 + r_2}$.

Ex. 4 Find equivalent emf of four different cells are connected in parallel. Their emfs and internal resistances are shown in *fig. 3.53*.

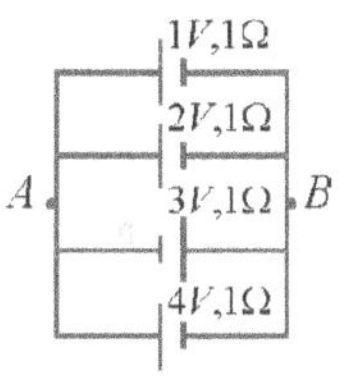

Fig. 3.53

Sol.

The cells can be connected in the following manner

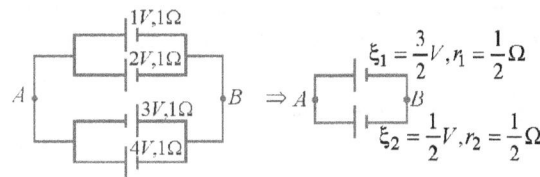

Fig. 3.54

$$\xi_1 = \frac{1 \times 1 + 2 \times 1}{1 + 1} = \frac{3}{2} V, r_1 = \frac{1}{2} \Omega$$

$$\xi_2 = \frac{4 \times 1 - 3 \times 1}{1 + 1} = \frac{1}{2} V, r_2 = \frac{1}{2} \Omega$$

Now $\quad \xi = \dfrac{\xi_1 r_2 + \xi_2 r_1}{r_1 + r_2}$

$$= \frac{\frac{3}{2} \times \frac{1}{2} + \frac{1}{2} \times \frac{1}{2}}{\frac{1}{2} + \frac{1}{2}}$$

$$= 1 V \qquad \text{Ans.}$$

Ex. 5 Two sources of current of equal emf are connected in series and have different internal resistances r_1 and r_2 ($r_2 > r_1$). Find the external resistance R at which the potential difference across the terminals of one of the sources (which one in particular) become equal to zero.

Sol.

The current in the circuit is

$$i = \frac{2\xi}{r_1 + r_2 + R}$$

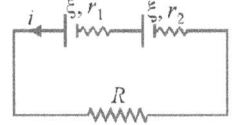

Fig. 3.55

Since i is same in both the cells

$$\therefore \quad V_1 = \xi - ir_1 \quad \text{and} \quad V_2 = \xi - ir_2$$

Since both the cells are giving the currents therefore V_1 and V_2 can not be negative.

Since $r_2 > r_1$, therefore firstly V_2 can be zero

$$\therefore \quad 0 = \xi - \left(\frac{2\xi}{r_1 + r_2 + R}\right) r_2$$

or $\quad R = (r_2 - r_1)$. $\qquad$ **Ans.**

The method of principle of superposition

Complicated circuit can be solved by using the principle of superposition. According to this principle, when a number of cells are present in a circuit, the current in any resistor is same as the superposition of the currents due to all the cells, acting one at a time, the others being absent.

Ex. 6 Analyse the following electrical circuit.

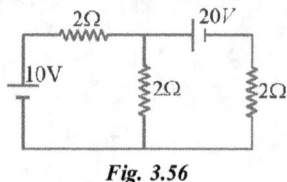

Fig. 3.56

Sol.

Method I:

Assuming first only 10V is present in the circuit, and then only 20V is present in the circuit. Find current in each case. Finally superpose the currents due to both the cells. It can be understand from the *fig. 3.55*.

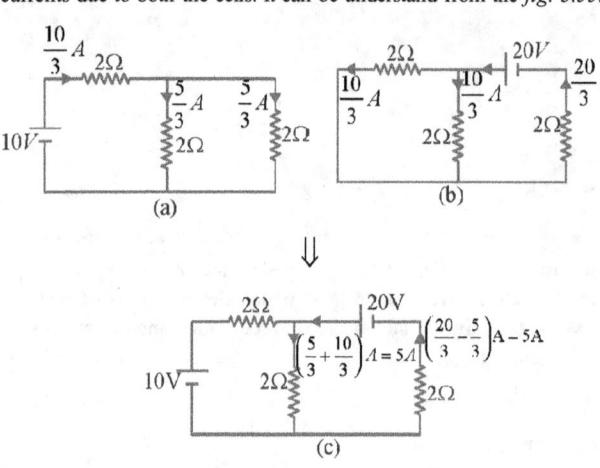

Fig. 3.57

Method II:

By using Kirchhoff's method.

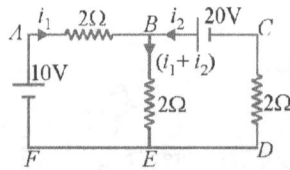

Fig. 3.58

Assuming the currents in resistors as shown in *fig. 3.59*. In closed loop ABEFA, we have

$$-2i_1 - 2(i_1+i_2) + 10 = 0$$

or $\quad 2i_1 + i_2 = 5 \quad$ ....(i)

In closed loop BCDEB, we have

$$-20 + 2i_2 + 2(i_1+i_2) = 0$$

or $\quad i_1 + 2i_2 = 10 \quad$ ...(ii)

Solving equations (i) and (ii), we get

$$i_1 = 0, \text{ and } i_2 = 5A$$

Finding the potential difference :

Ex. 7 Consider the following circuit and find potential difference $V_A - V_B$.

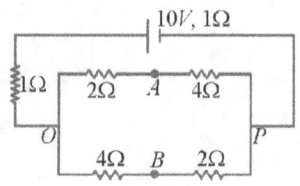

Fig. 3.59

Sol.

The currents in different resistors can be obtained as follows: The net current drawn from the source

$$i = \frac{10}{\left[1+1+\frac{6\times 6}{6+6}\right]} = 2A.$$

This current will divide equally in branches OAP and OBP because they have equal resistances.

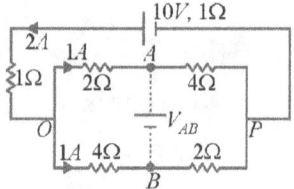

Fig. 3.60

Method I: $\quad V_A - V_B = (V_O - V_B) - (V_O - V_A)$

$$= 4 \times 1 - 2 \times 1 = 2V \quad \textbf{Ans.}$$

Method II:

Connect a hypothetical cell between A and B, taking A as positive terminal. Now apply loop rule in close loop OABO, to get $V_{AB} = V_A - V_B$. Thus

$$-2\times 1 - V_{AB} + 4 \times 1 = 0$$

or $\quad V_{AB} = 2V \quad \textbf{Ans.}$

Ex. 8 See the circuit shown in *fig. 3.61*. Find the current through the switch S when it is closed.

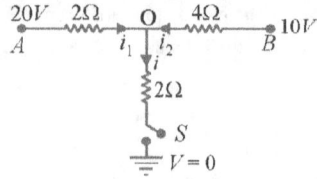

Fig. 3.61

Sol.

Let i_1 and i_2 be the currents in the branches A O and B O respectively. By junction rule the current in switch S is

$$i = i_1 + i_2$$

or $\quad\dfrac{V_O - 0}{2} = \dfrac{20 - V_O}{2} + \dfrac{10 - V_O}{4}$

or $\quad V_O = 10\,V$

∴ Current, $i = \dfrac{V_O - 0}{2}$

$= \dfrac{10 - 0}{2} = 5A.$ Ans.

Ex. 9 Find out the value of current through $2\,\Omega$ resistance for the given circuit. Also find the potential difference between A and B.

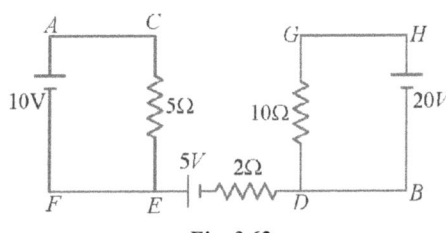

Fig. 3.62

Sol.

Let i_1 and i_2 be the currents in $5\,\Omega$ and $10\,\Omega$ resistors respectively.

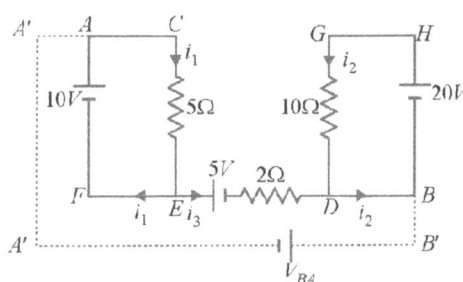

Fig. 3.63

In close loop $ACEFA$,
$\quad -5i_1 + 10 = 0$
or $\quad i_1 = 2A$
In close loop $GHBDG$
$\quad -20 + 10 i_2 = 0$
or $\quad i_2 = 2A$

Let i_3 is the current in $2\,\Omega$ resistor. At junction E,

$\quad i_1 = i_1 + i_3$
which gives $\quad i_3 = 0$

($2\,\Omega$ resistor is in open circuit, therefore current in it will be zero)

To get the potential difference $V_{BA} = V_B - V_A$, connect a hypothetical cell between A and B keeping B as positive terminal.

Now in close loop $A\,A'\,B'\,B\,D\,E\,F\,A$, we have
$\quad +V_{BA} + 5 + 5 i_1 = 0$

or $\quad V_{BA} = -5 - 5 i_1$
$\quad = -5 - 5 \times 2$
$\quad = -15\,V.$ Ans.

Ex. 10 Find the reading of the ammeter A as shown in *fig. 3.64*.

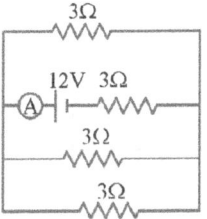

Fig. 3.64

Sol.

The above circuit can be reduced as follows.

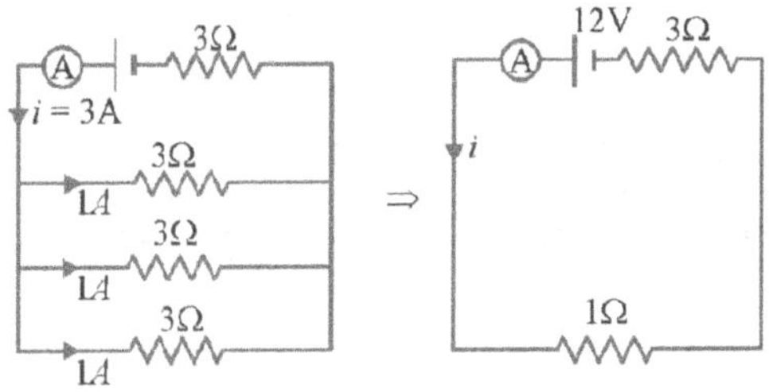

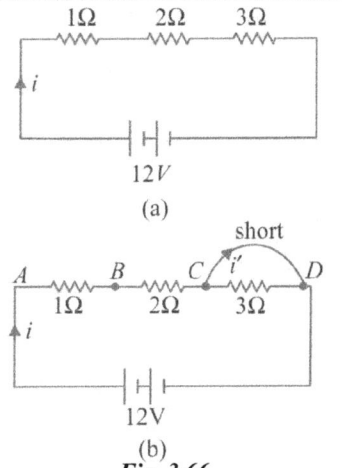

Fig. 3.65

The reading of ammeter A is i, where

$$i = \dfrac{12}{3+1} = 3A$$

The current distribution in all the resistors is also shown in the *fig. 3.65*.

More about short

When two points of a circuit are connected together by a resistanceless wire, they are said to be short-circuited. Since 'short' has theoretically zero resistance, so it gives rise to two important facts :

(i) no voltage can exist across it because $V = ir = i \times 0 = 0$,
(ii) current through it is very large, theoretically infinity.

Short in series circuit

Consider a circuit with three resistors in series with a source of emf as shown in *fig. 3.66* (a) The equivalent resistance of the circuit $R = 1 + 2 + 3 = 6\,\Omega$ and resultant current

$i = \dfrac{12}{6} = 2A$ which is same in all the resistors.

Now $3\,\Omega$ resistor has been shorted out by a wire CD as shown in *fig. 3.66* (b) so that $R_{CD} = 0$.

Fig. 3.66

The equivalent resistance of circuit $R' = 1 + 2 = 3\Omega$ and current in the resistors

$$i' = \frac{12}{3} = 4A \text{ in } 1\Omega \text{ and } 2\Omega \text{ resistors, but no current in } 3\Omega \text{ resistor.}$$

Short in parallel circuit

Consider a circuit as shown in *fig. 3.67* (a).
The equivalent resistance of circuit

$$\frac{1}{R} = \frac{1}{1} + \frac{1}{2} + \frac{1}{3}$$

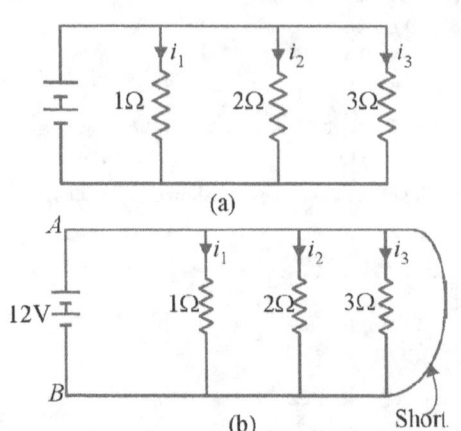

which gives $\qquad R = \frac{6}{11}\Omega$

currents in resistors are
$$i_1 = \frac{12}{1} = 12A$$
$$i_2 = \frac{12}{2} = 6A$$
$$i_3 = \frac{12}{3} = 4A$$

Fig. 3.67

Now suppose a short is placed across 3Ω resistor as shwon in *fig. 3.67* (b). The entire current will pass through the short.

$$\therefore \quad R_{AB} = 0$$
$$i_1 = i_2 = i_3 = 0.$$

But short draws infinite current.

Ex. 11 In the circuit shown in *fig. 3.68* E, F, G and H are cells of emf 2, 1, 3 and 1 V respectively. The resistances 2, 1, 3 and 1 Ω are their respective internal resistances. Calculate (a) the potential difference between B and D and (b) the potential differences across the terminals of each of the cells G and H.

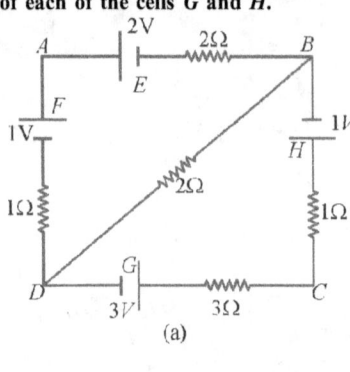

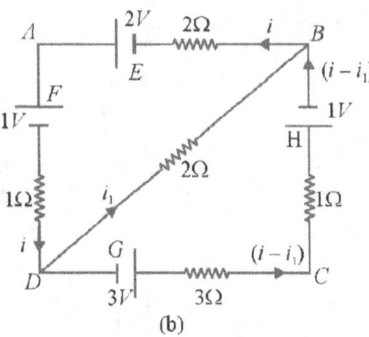

Fig. 3.68

Sol.
The proposed currents are shown in *fig. 3.68* (b)
In close loop $ABDA$, we have
$$-2 + 2i + 2i_1 + 1i + 1 = 0$$
or $\qquad 3i + 2i_1 = 1 \qquad$ ...(i)
In close loop $BCDB$, we have
$$1 + 1(i - i_1) + 3(i - i_1) - 3 - 2i_1 = 0$$
or $\qquad 2i - 3i_1 = 1 \qquad$ ...(ii)
After solving equations (i) and (ii), we get

$$i_1 = -\frac{1}{13} A$$

and $\qquad i = \frac{5}{13} A$

(a) The potential difference
$$V_D - V_B = 2i_1$$
$$= 2\left(-\frac{1}{13}\right) = -\frac{2}{13}V$$

or $\qquad V_B - V_D = \frac{2}{13}V$

(b) The current in the cell is
$$i - i_1 = \frac{5}{13} - \left(-\frac{1}{13}\right) = \frac{6}{13}A$$

Since cell G is discharging and H is charging

$$\therefore \quad V_G = \xi - ir = 3 - \frac{6}{13} \times 3$$

$$= \frac{21}{13}V \qquad \textbf{Ans.}$$

DC and DC Circuits

and $V_H = \xi + ir = 1 + \dfrac{6}{13} \times 1$

$= \dfrac{19}{13} V$. **Ans.**

Ex. 12 A part of a circuit in steady state along with the currents flowing in the branches, the values of resistances etc. is shown in *fig. 3.69*. Calculate the energy stored in the capacitor.

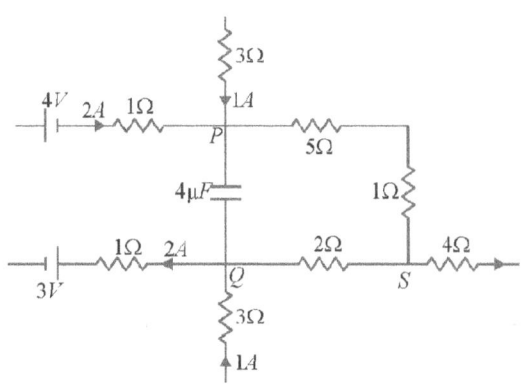

Fig. 3.69

Sol.
After charging fully there is no current in arm of capacitor. By using junction rule the currents in the resistors are shown in *fig. 3.69*.

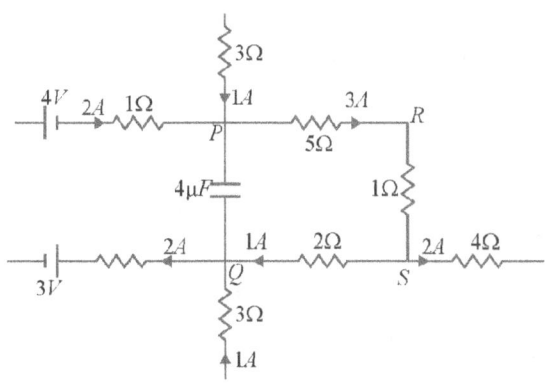

Fig. 3.70

The p.d. across the capacitor is
$V_P - V_Q = (V_P - V_R) + (V_R - V_S) + (V_S - V_Q)$
$= 5 \times 3 + 1 \times 3 + 2 \times 1$
$= 20 \, V$

The energy stored in the capacitor is
$U = \dfrac{1}{2} C V^2$
$= \dfrac{1}{2} \times 4 \times 10^{-6} \times 20^2$
$= 800 \, \mu J$. **Ans.**

Ex. 13 Twelve cells each having the same emf are connected in series and are kept in a closed box. Some of the cells are wrongly connected. This battery is connected in series with an ammeter and two cells identical with each others. The current is $3A$ when the cells and battery aid each other and $2A$ when the cells and battery oppose each other. How many cells are wrongly connected ?

Sol.
Let m cells are wrongly connected in the battery and ξ is the emf of each cell, then
$\xi_{net} = (12 - 2m) \xi$
When two cells aid the battery, then current

$$3 = \dfrac{(12 - 2m)\xi + 2\xi}{R} \quad ...(i)$$

where R is the total resistance of the circuit.
When two cells opposes the battery, then

$$2 = \dfrac{(12 - 2m) \xi - 2\xi}{R} \quad ...(ii)$$

Solving above equations, we get
$m = 1$
Hence one cell is wrongly connected in the battery.

Ex. 14 Find the charges on the four capacitors of capacitances $1\mu F$, $2\mu F$, $3\mu F$ and $4\mu F$ shown in *fig. 3.71*.

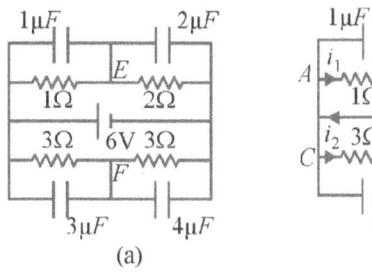 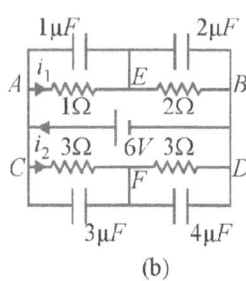

(a) (b)

Fig. 3.71

Sol.
The current will flow through the resistors only. Let i_1 and i_2 be the currents in branches AB and CD respectively, then

$$i_1 = \dfrac{6}{1+2} = 2A$$

and $$i_2 = \dfrac{6}{3+3} = 1A$$

(i) p.d. across $1\mu F$ capacitor
$V_{AE} = 1 \times 2 = 2V$
charge on the capacitor $= 1 \times V_{AE} = 2\mu C$

(ii) p.d. across $2\mu F$ capacitor
$V_{EB} = 2 \times 2 = 4V$
charge on the capacitor $= 2 \times V_{EB} = 8\mu C$

(iii) p.d. across $3\mu F$ capacitor
$V_{CF} = 3 \times 1 = 3V$
charge on the capacitor $= 3 \times V_{CF} = 9\mu C$

(iv) p.d. across $4\mu F$ capacitor
$V_{FD} = 4 \times 1 = 4V$
charge on the capacitor $= 4 \times V_{FD} = 16\mu C$. **Ans.**

Ex. 15
A long round conductor of cross-sectional area S is made of material whose resistivity depends only on a distance r from the axis of the conductor $\rho = \dfrac{\alpha}{r^2}$, where α is a constant. Find

(a) the resistance per unit length of such a conductor
(b) the electric field strength in the conductor due to which a current i flows through it.

Sol.
(a) Consider a cylindrical element of radii between r and $(r + dr)$. Its resistance

$$dR = \frac{\rho \ell}{2\pi r\, dr}$$

or $$\frac{1}{dR} = \frac{2\pi r\, dr}{\rho \ell} \qquad \text{...(i)}$$

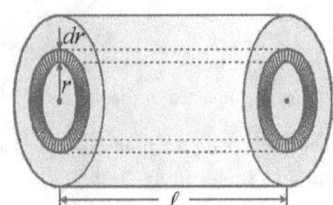

Fig. 3.72

Since all such resistance are in parallel

$$\therefore \quad \frac{1}{R} = \int_0^a \frac{1}{dR} = \int_0^a \frac{2\pi}{\rho \ell} r\, dr$$

(where a is the radius of conductor)

$$= \int_0^a \frac{2\pi r\, dr}{\left(\dfrac{\alpha}{r^2}\right)\ell} = \frac{2\pi}{\alpha \ell}\int_0^a r^3\, dr = \frac{2\pi}{\alpha \ell}\left(\frac{a^4}{4}\right) = \frac{(\pi a^2)^2}{2\pi \alpha \ell}$$

$$= \frac{S^2}{2\pi \alpha \ell}$$

Thus $$R = \frac{2\pi \alpha \ell}{S^2} \qquad \text{... (ii)}$$

The resistance per unit length of wire $R = \dfrac{2\pi \alpha}{S^2}$

(b) Equation (ii) can be written as $R = \left(\dfrac{2\pi\alpha}{S}\right)\left(\dfrac{\ell}{S}\right)$. Compare with $R = \dfrac{\rho \ell}{S}$, we get $\rho = \dfrac{2\pi \alpha}{S}$.

By Ohm's law $E = j\rho = \dfrac{i}{S} \times \dfrac{2\pi\alpha}{S} = \dfrac{2\pi\alpha i}{S^2}$.

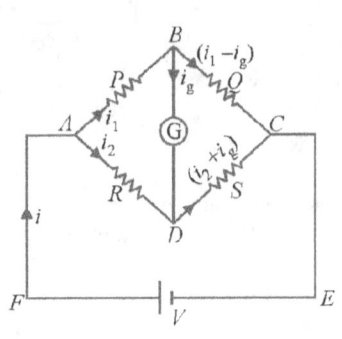

Fig. 3.73

Wheatstone bridge

It is a special type of resistance network, commonly used for comparing resistances or unknown resistance can be measured in terms of three known resistances. It consists of four resistances connected in the form of a bridge.

Analysis

Let four resistors P, Q, R and S are connected as in *fig. 3.74*.
The proposed currents are as shown in *fig. 3.74*.
At junction A $\quad i = i_1 + i_2 \qquad \text{...(i)}$
In close loop $A B D A$;
$$-P i_1 - G i_g + R i_2 = 0 \qquad \text{...(ii)}$$
and in close loop $B C D B$;
$$-Q(i_1 - i_g) + S(i_2 + i_g) + G i_g = 0 \qquad \text{...(iii)}$$
In close loop $A B C E F A$;
$$-P i_1 - Q(i_1 - i_g) + V = 0 \qquad \text{...(iv)}$$
After solving above equations we can get i_1, i_2 and i_g. The equivalent resistance between A and C is

$$R_{AC} = \frac{V}{i} = \frac{V}{i_1 + i_2}$$

On substituting the values of i_1 and i_2, we can get R_{AC}.

Balanced Wheatstone bridge

For balanced bridge; $V_B = V_D$, and so no current flows through the galvanometer ($i_g = 0$), the equations (ii) and (iii) reduce to
$$-P i_1 + R i_2 = 0$$

DC and DC Circuits 239

or $\qquad \dfrac{i_1}{i_2} = \dfrac{R}{P}$ ...(v)

and $\qquad -Q i_1 + S i_2 = 0$

or $\qquad \dfrac{i_1}{i_2} = \dfrac{S}{Q}$ ...(vi)

Now from equations (v) and (vi), we have

$$\dfrac{R}{P} = \dfrac{S}{Q}$$

or $\qquad \dfrac{P}{Q} = \dfrac{R}{S}$

The balanced bridge now effectively reduces as :
The equivalent resistance between A and C

$$\dfrac{1}{R_{AC}} = \dfrac{1}{(P+Q)} + \dfrac{1}{(R+S)}$$

The relation $\qquad \dfrac{P}{Q} = \dfrac{R}{S}$ can be written as

$$\dfrac{P}{R} = \dfrac{Q}{S}.$$

That is if positions of the galvanometer and battery are interchanged, then there will still no deflection in the galvanometer.

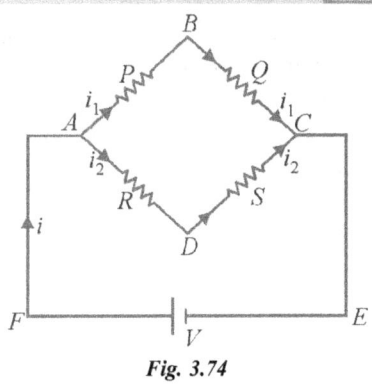

Fig. 3.74

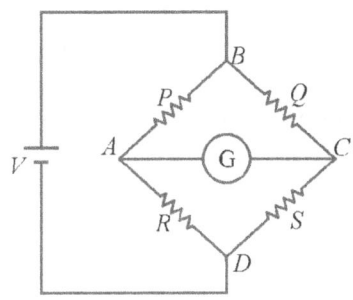

Fig. 3.75

Ex. 16
Find the equivalent resistance between the points A and B of the circuit shown in *fig. 3.76*.

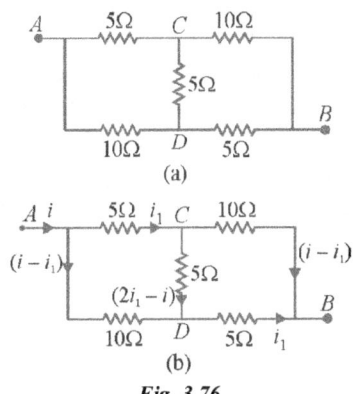

Fig. 3.76

Sol.
Method I :
The given circuit is not balanced bridge therefore we have to find the equivalent resistance either by circuit analysis by Kirchoff's law or by other method.

Suppose current i enters through the junction A into the circuit. Let i_1 goes to the $5\,\Omega$ resistor and the rest $i - i_1$ goes to $10\,\Omega$ resistor. By symmetry, the current i, coming out from the junction B will be composed of a part i_1 from $5\,\Omega$ resistor and $i - i_1$, from $10\,\Omega$ resistor. By junction rule the current in middle $5\,\Omega$ resistor is $(2i_1 - i)$ as shown in *fig. 3.76 (b)*.

We have
$$V_A - V_B = (V_A - V_C) + (V_C - V_B)$$
$$= 5 i_1 + 10(i - i_1) = 10 i - 5 i_1 \quad ...(i)$$

Also
$$V_A - V_B = (V_A - V_C) + (V_C - V_D) + (V_D - V_B)$$
$$= 5 i_1 + 5(2 i_1 - i) + 5 i_1$$
$$= 20 i_1 - 5i \quad ...(ii)$$

From equations (i) and (ii), we get

$$i_1 = \dfrac{3}{5} i$$

Substituting this value in equation (i), we get

$$V_A - V_B = 10 i - 5 \times \dfrac{3i}{5}$$
$$= 7 i$$

or $\qquad \dfrac{V_A - V_B}{i} = 7$

or $\qquad R_{AB} = 7.$

Method II :

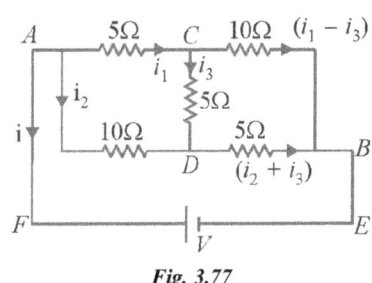

Fig. 3.77

240 ELECTRICITY & MAGNETISM

Supposing a source is connected between the terminals A and B. The current distribution is shown in fig. 3.77.

At junction A, $\quad i = i_1 + i_2$

Resistance between A and B, $R_{AB} = \dfrac{V}{i} = \dfrac{V}{i_1 + i_2}$

In close loop $A\ C\ D\ A$,
$$-5 i_1 - 5 i_3 + 10 i_2 = 0 \quad \ldots(i)$$
or $\quad -i_1 - i_3 + 2 i_2 = 0$

In close loop $C\ B\ D\ C$,
$$-10 (i_1 - i_3) + 5 (i_2 + i_3) + 5 i_3 = 0$$
or $\quad -2 i_1 + i_2 + 4 i_3 = 0 \quad \ldots(ii)$

Now in close loop $A\ C\ B\ E\ F\ A$
$$-5 i_1 - 10 (i_1 - i_3) + V = 0$$
or $\quad -3 i_1 + 2 i_3 = -\dfrac{V}{5} \quad \ldots(iii)$

From equations (i) and (iii), we get
$$-5 i_1 + 4 i_2 = -\dfrac{V}{5} \quad \ldots(iv)$$

From equations (ii) and (iii), we get
$$4 i_1 + i_2 = \dfrac{2V}{5} \quad \ldots(v)$$

Solving equations (iv) and (v), we get
$$i_1 = \dfrac{9V}{105}$$
$$i_2 = \dfrac{6V}{105}$$

Also $\quad i_3 = \dfrac{V}{35}$

$\therefore \quad R_{AB} = \dfrac{V}{i_1 + i_2} = \dfrac{V}{\left(\dfrac{9V}{105} + \dfrac{6V}{105}\right)}$

$= 7\,\Omega.$

Note:
$$i_1 - i_3 = \dfrac{6V}{105} = i \text{ and } i_2 + i_3 = \dfrac{9V}{105} =$$

Thus the current in $5\,\Omega$ resistor connected symmetrically is same and currents in $10\,\Omega$ resistors also remains same.

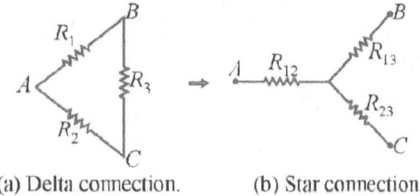

(a) Delta connection.   (b) Star connection.
Fig. 3.78

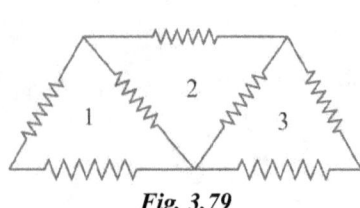
Fig. 3.79

Delta-star transformation

In solving networks, having many loops by the applications of Kirchhoff's method, one sometimes experiences great difficulty due to large number of simultaneous equations that have to be solved. However, such complicated networks can be simplified by successively replacing delta meshes by equivalent star system and vice versa. Suppose we have three resistances R_1, R_2 and R_3 connected in the form of delta as shown in fig. 3.78

(a) These three resistances can be replaced by three resistances R_{12}, R_{23} and R_{13} in the form of delta between the same terminals as shown in fig. 3.78 (b).

where $\quad R_{12} = \dfrac{R_1 R_2}{R_1 + R_2 + R_3}$.

$R_{13} = \dfrac{R_1 R_3}{R_1 + R_2 + R_3}$

and $\quad R_{23} = \dfrac{R_2 R_3}{R_1 + R_2 + R_3}$.

Note: In any network there may be many deltas. Students are advised to transform the delta into star which has symmetry. For example in a network of three deltas, transform middle delta into star.

Ex. 17 Take the previous problem and find its equivalent resistance between the terminals *A* and *B* by using delta-star transformation method.

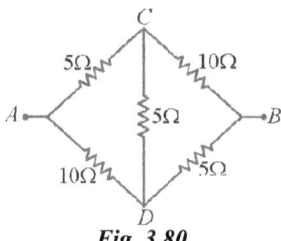

Fig. 3.80

Sol.

We can simplify the circuit by transforming delta *A C D* into star as follows.

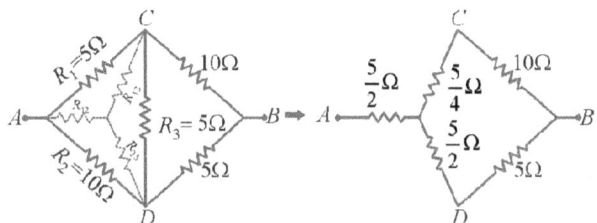

Fig. 3.81

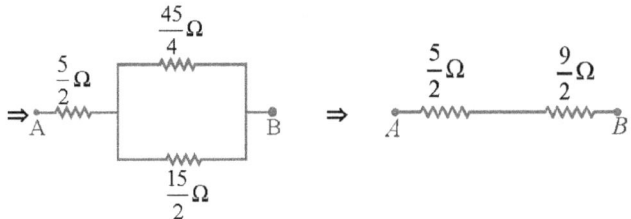

Fig. 3.82

$$R_{12} = \frac{R_1 R_2}{R_1 + R_2 + R_3} = \frac{5 \times 10}{5 + 10 + 5} = \frac{5}{2} \Omega,$$

$$R_{13} = \frac{R_1 R_3}{R_1 + R_2 + R_3} = \frac{5 \times 5}{5 + 10 + 5} = \frac{5}{4} \Omega,$$

$$R_{23} = \frac{R_2 R_3}{R_1 + R_2 + R_3} = \frac{10 \times 5}{5 + 10 + 5} = \frac{5}{2} \Omega,$$

$$R_{AB} = \frac{5}{2} + \frac{9}{2} = 7 \, \Omega$$

Ex. 18 Find the equivalent resistance of the circuit shown in *fig. 3.83* between the points *A* and *B*. Each resistor has a resistance 1Ω.

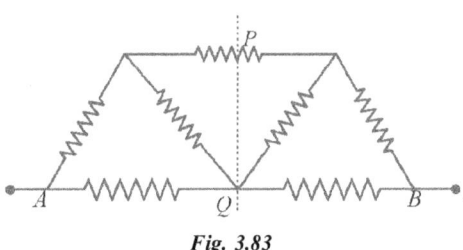

Fig. 3.83

Sol.   Method I : By junction removal method

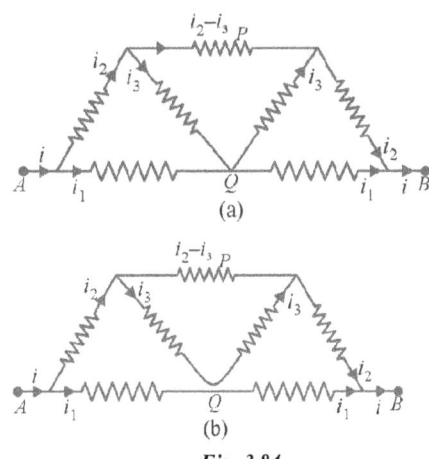

Fig. 3.84

Because of symmetry about dotted line *PQ*, the currents in left part of circuit are same as the right part of the circuit. The current distribution in the resistors may be as in *fig. 3.84* (b). It is very clear from the figure that resistors having current i_3 can be removed from the junction *Q* without affecting the currents in other resistors as shown in *fig. 3.84* (b). The resulting circuit can be simplified as :

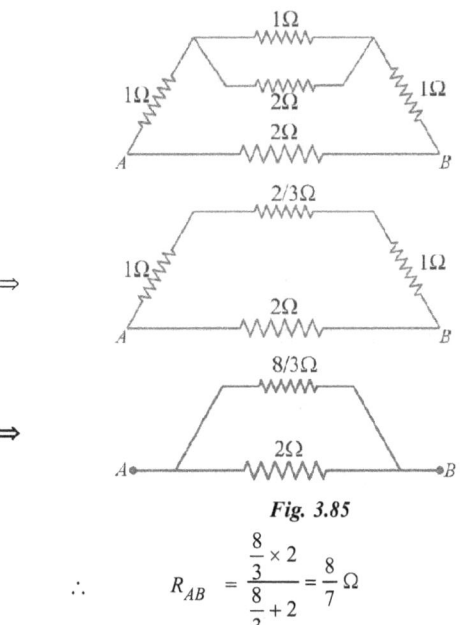

Fig. 3.85

$$\therefore \quad R_{AB} = \frac{\frac{8}{3} \times 2}{\frac{8}{3} + 2} = \frac{8}{7} \Omega$$

Method II :

Since network of resistors is symmetrical about dotted line *PQ*, therefore it has equal resistances about *PQ*. We can break it into two equal parts as:

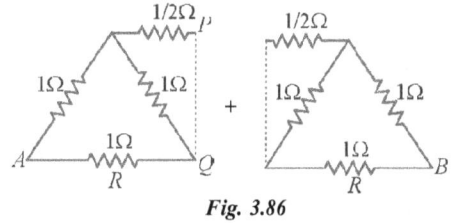

Fig. 3.86

242 ELECTRICITY & MAGNETISM

The resistance of each half $= R$, which is equal to

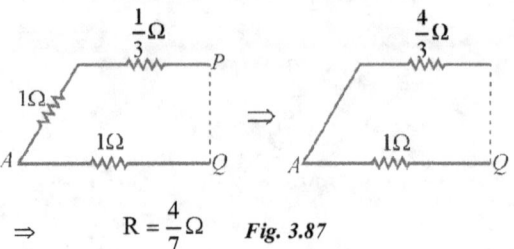

$$\Rightarrow \quad R = \frac{4}{7}\Omega \quad \text{Fig. 3.87}$$

The equivalent resistance between A and B

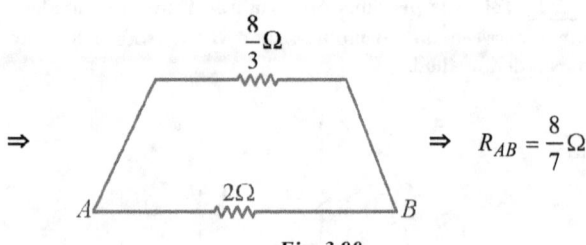

Fig. 3.88

$$R_{AB} = 2R = 2 \times \frac{4}{7} = \frac{8}{7}\Omega$$

Method III : By delta-star transformation :

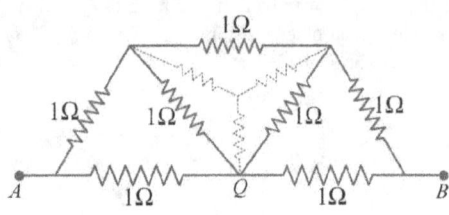

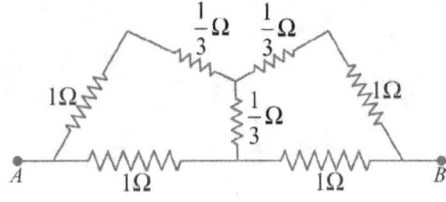

Fig. 3.89

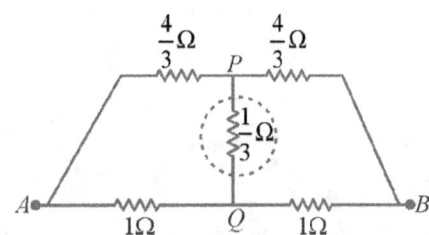

$$\boxed{\frac{P}{Q} = \frac{R}{S}}$$

$\Rightarrow$

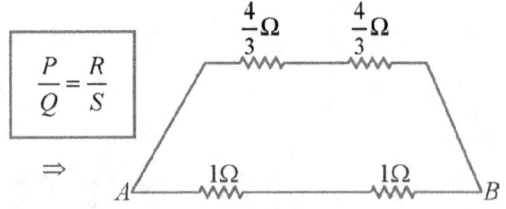

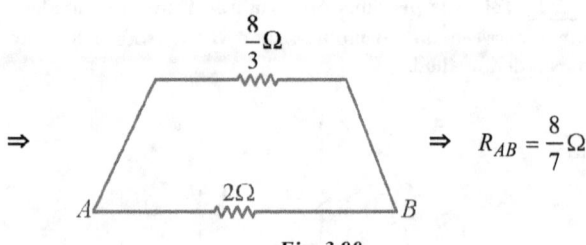

Fig. 3.90

Ex. 19 Find resistance between A and B in the following networks of resistances. Each resistance is equal to r.

Sol.
Solution in brief are:
1.

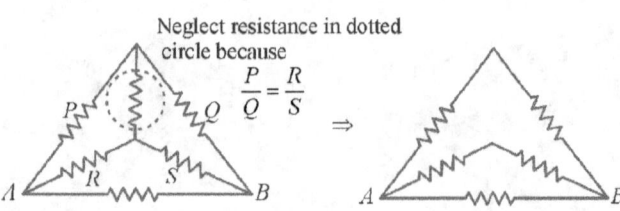

Fig. 3.91

Ans : $\dfrac{r}{2}$

2.

Fig. 3.92

Ans : $\dfrac{4r}{5}$

3.

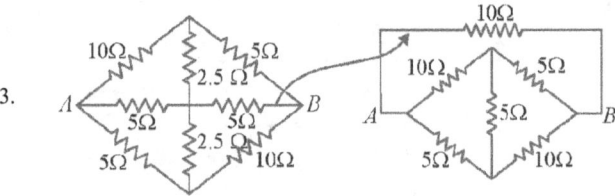

Fig. 3.93

Ans : $R_{AB} = 4.1\ \Omega$

4. $\quad R_{AB} = ?$. Each resistance is r

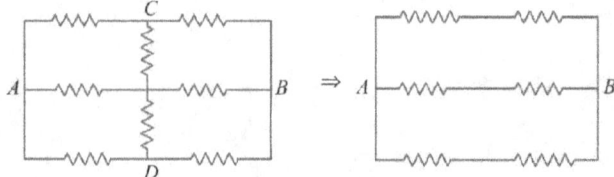

Fig. 3.94

Ans. $\dfrac{2r}{3}$.

5.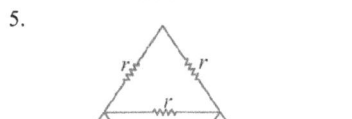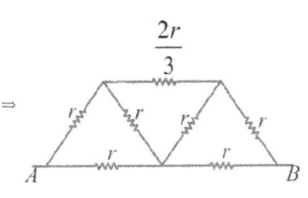

Fig. 3.95

Ans. $\dfrac{10r}{9}$.

6. The circuit now can be simplified by delta-star transformation. Balanced Wheatstone bridge :

(i)
(ii)
(iii)

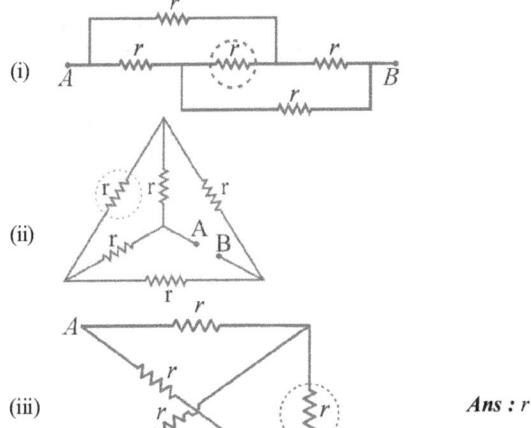

Fig. 3.96

Incircle resistor can be neglected.

Ans : r

7.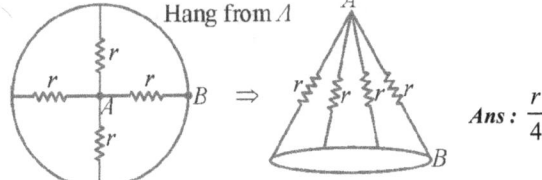

Fig. 3.97

Ans : $\dfrac{r}{4}$

8.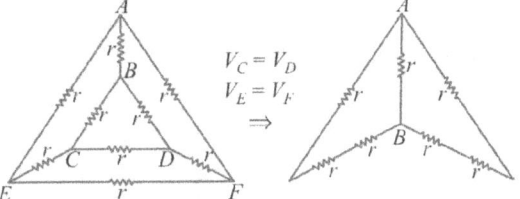

Fig. 3.98

Ans : $\dfrac{4r}{3}$

9.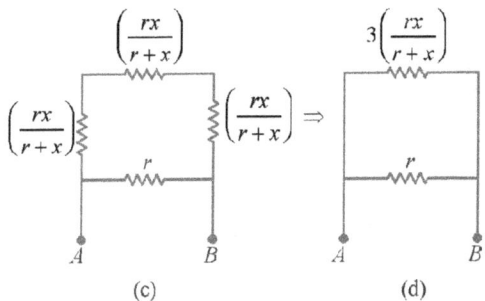

Fig. 3.99   Ans. $R = \dfrac{3}{5}r$

Ex. 20 Find the equivalent resistance of the given network of resistors between the points A and B.

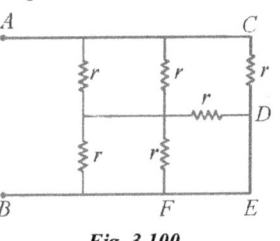

Fig. 3.100

Sol. Junctions D and F are equipotential and so they can be connected together without affecting the circuit. The simplified circuit is shown in *fig. 3.101*.

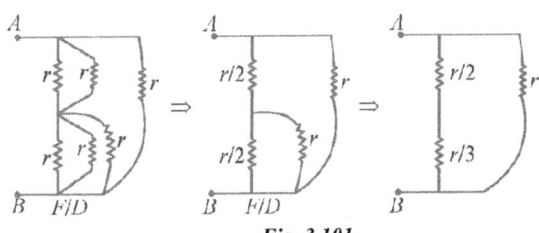

Fig. 3.101

Ans. $R_{AB} = \dfrac{5}{11}r$

Ex. 21 There is an infinite wire grid with square cells as shown in *fig. 3.102*. The resistance of each side is r. Find the equivalent resistance of the whole grid between any two neighbouring points such as A and B.

(a)   (b)

Fig. 3.102

Sol. Let x is the resistance between A and B. The circuit now can be reduced as shown in *fig. 3.103* (c) and (d). The resistance between A and B is also r, so

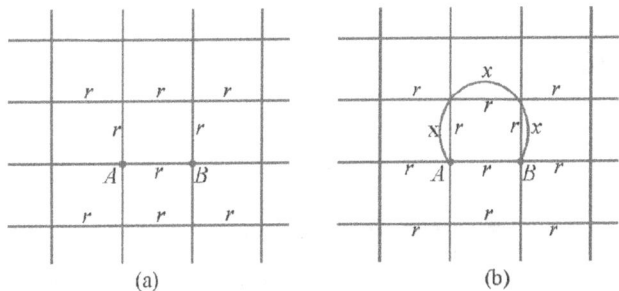

(c)   (d)

Fig. 3.103

$$\frac{1}{x} = \frac{1}{3\left(\frac{rx}{r+x}\right)} + \frac{1}{r}$$

After solving, we get $x = \dfrac{r}{2}$.

Ex. 22 A five pointed regular star has been soldered together form of a uniform wire. The resistance of the section CL is r;
(a) Find the resistance of the section FL.
(b) What is the equivalent resistance across the terminals A and F?

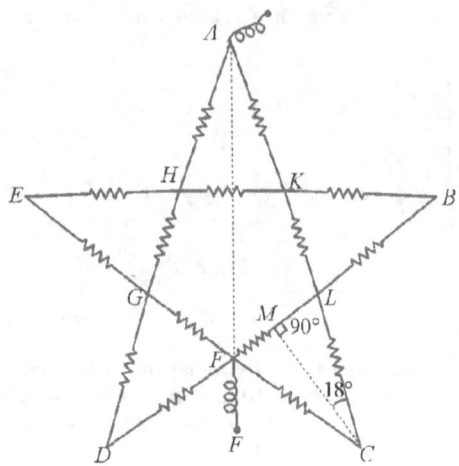

Fig. 3.104

Sol.
Suppose length of $ALC = \ell$
The length of the section $FL = 2\,ML$
$= 2\,LC \sin 18°$
$= 2\,\ell \sin 18°$
$= 0.62\,\ell$

(a) Since resistance of wire is proportional to its length, therefore resistance of section FL, $r' = 0.62\,r$.
(b) The given network of resistors is symmetrical about AF, so it can be break into two identical parts, each with a resistance R. HK has no current because $V_H = V_K$. Therefore its resistance can be neglected. The resistance of left part R can be obtained as :

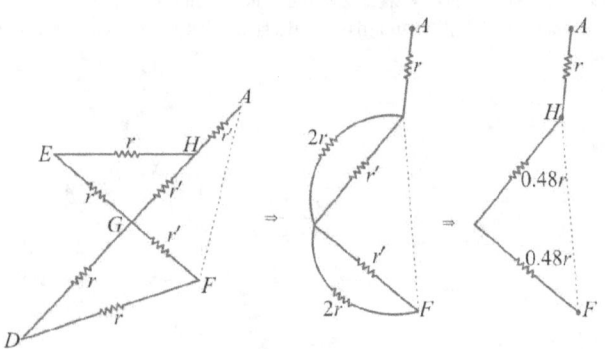

Fig. 3.105

$R = r + 0.48\,r + 0.48\,r = 1.96\,r$
$\therefore\ R_{AF} = \dfrac{R}{2} = \dfrac{1.96\,r}{2}$
$= 0.98\,r$ **Ans.**

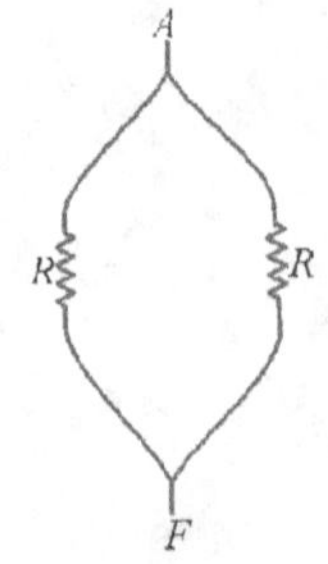

Fig. 3.106

Ex. 23 Twelve equal wires, each of resistance r ohm are connected so as to form a skeleton cube. Find the equivalent resistance between the diagonally opposite points 1 and 7.

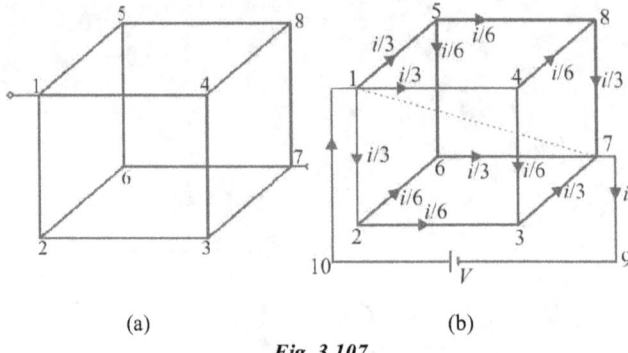

(a) (b)
Fig. 3.107

Sol.
Connect a source between points 1 and 7.
The network is symmetrical about the diagonal 1-7. Therefore current in resistors are distributed symmetrically about the diagonal. The current distribution is shown in *fig. 3.107* (b).
Choose a close loop 1-2-3-7-9-10-1, we have

$$-r\frac{i}{3} - r\frac{i}{6} - r\frac{i}{3} + V = 0$$

or $\quad \dfrac{V}{i} = \dfrac{5}{6}r$

or $\quad R_{17} = \dfrac{V}{i} = \dfrac{5}{6}r$ **Ans.**

Ex. 24 Twelve equal wires each of resistance r are joined to form a skeleton cube. Find the equivalent resistance between two corners on the same edge of the cube.

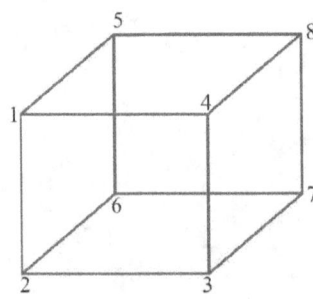

Fig. 3.108

DC AND DC CIRCUITS

Sol. Method I:

Connect a source between points 1 and 2. Let current i enters through point 1 into the network. The network is symmetrical about dotted line. The currents above and below dotted line are symmetrically distributed as shown in *fig. 3.109*.

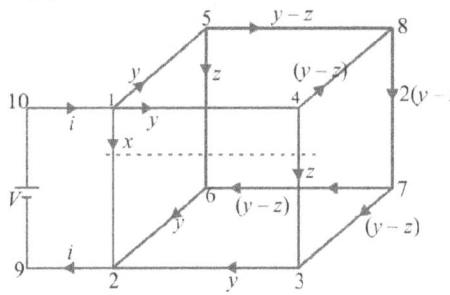

Fig. 3.109

By junction rule at 1, we have
$$i = x + 2y$$

$$\therefore \quad R_{12} = \frac{V}{i} = \frac{V}{x+2y} \quad \ldots(i)$$

In close loop 1–2–9–10–1, we have
$$-rx + V = 0 \text{ or } x = \frac{V}{r} \quad \ldots(ii)$$

In close loop 1–4–3–2–1
$$-ry - rz - ry + rx = 0$$
$$\text{or} \quad x - 2y - z = 0 \quad \ldots(iii)$$

In close loop 4-8-7-3-4
$$-r(y-z) - r \times 2(y-z) - r(y-z) + rz = 0$$
$$\text{or} \quad -4(y-z) + z = 0$$
$$\text{or} \quad -4y + 5z = 0 \quad \ldots(iv)$$

From equations (iii) and (iv), we get
$$-4y + 5(x-2y) = 0$$
$$\text{or} \quad 5x = 14y$$

Since $x = \dfrac{V}{r}$

$$\therefore \quad y = \frac{5}{14} \times \frac{V}{r}$$

Now
$$R_{12} = \frac{V}{x+2y} = \frac{V}{\dfrac{V}{r} + 2 \times \dfrac{5V}{14r}}$$

$$= \frac{7}{12}r \quad \text{Ans.}$$

Method II:

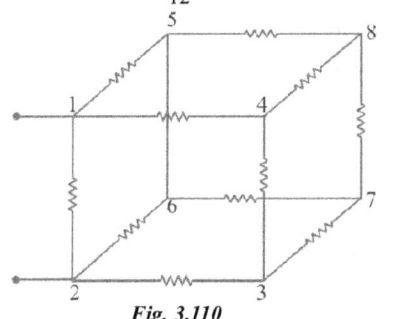

Fig. 3.110

Our previous knowledge reveals that points 3 and 6 must be at the same potential. So must be 4 and 5. If points of equal potential are joint by a wire, the currents in the circuit do not change. The given network of resistors can be reduced successively as shown in *fig. 3111*.

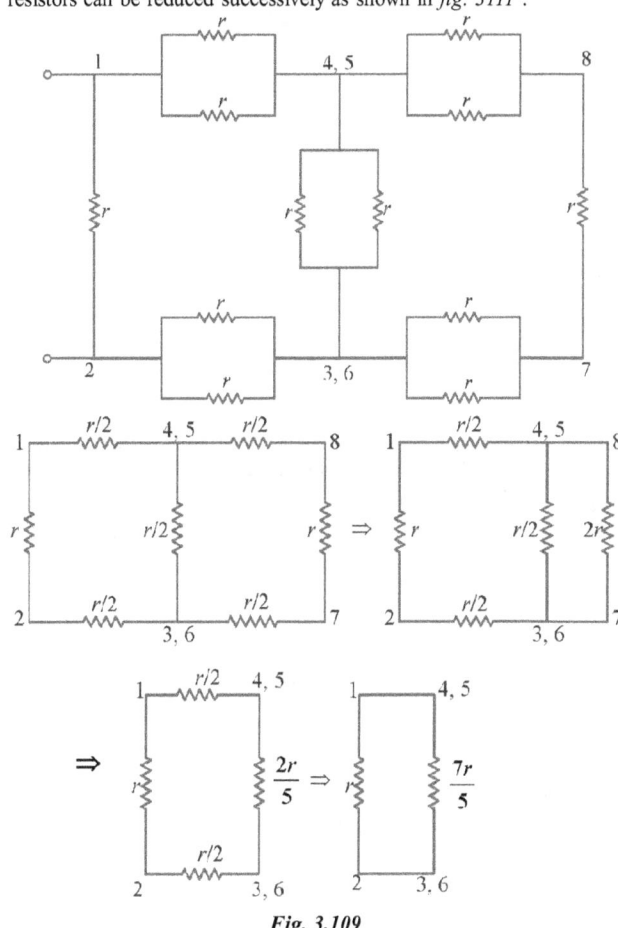

Fig. 3.109

$$R_{12} = \frac{r \times \dfrac{7r}{5}}{r + \dfrac{7r}{5}} = \frac{7}{12}r \quad \text{Ans.}$$

Ex. 25 Twelve wires, each having resistance r, are joined to form a cube as shown in *fig. 3.112*. Find the equivalent resistance between the ends of a face diagonal such as 1 and 8.

Sol.

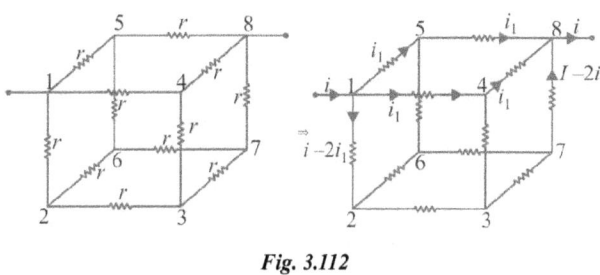

Fig. 3.112

$$V_5 = V_6$$
$$V_3 = V_4$$

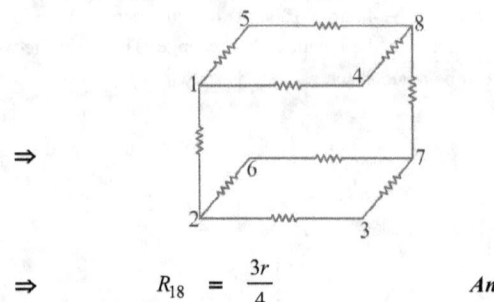

$\Rightarrow \qquad R_{18} = \dfrac{3r}{4}$ **Ans.**

Infinite ladder : Find the equivalent resistance of the infinite network as shown in *fig. 3.113*.

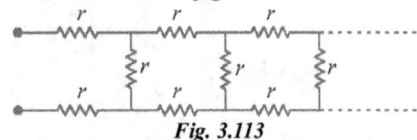

Fig. 3.113

Let equivalent resistance between the points is R. The equivalent between the points remain R if one more cell is connected with the network. i.e.,

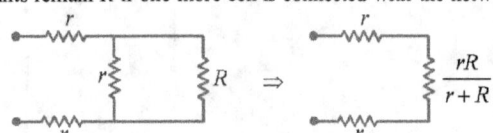

Fig. 3.114

$$\Rightarrow \qquad R = r + \dfrac{rR}{r+R} + r$$

$$= 2r + \dfrac{rR}{r+R}$$

or $\qquad Rr + R^2 = 2r^2 + 2Rr + Rr$

or $\qquad R^2 - 2Rr - 2r^2 = 0$

$$\therefore \qquad R = \dfrac{2r \pm \sqrt{(2r)^2 + 4 \times 2r^2}}{2}$$

$$= r \pm \sqrt{3}\, r$$

Retain only positive sign, because R always positive.

$$\therefore \qquad R = (\sqrt{3} + 1)\, r. \qquad \textbf{Ans.}$$

Ex. 26 (a) What is the potential difference between points A and B in *fig. 3.115* when switch S is open ?
(b) Which point, A or B, is at the higher potential ?
(c) What is the final potential of point B when switch S is closed ?
(d) How much does the charge on each capacitor change when S is closed?

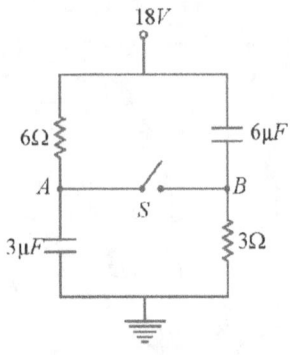

Fig. 3.115

Sol.
(a) In open circuit, there is no current in the resistors. Therefore,
$V_A = 18\,V$ and $V_B = 0$
$\therefore \qquad V_A - V_B = 18 - 0 = 18\,V$ **Ans.**
(b) It is clear from (a), that A is at higher potential.

(c)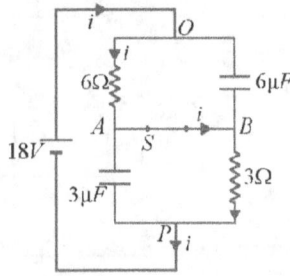

Fig. 3.116

When switch is closed, the current starts flowing in the resistors. The circuit can be realised as in *fig. 3.116*

$$i = \dfrac{18}{6+3} = 2\,A$$

We have $\quad V_O - V_P = 6 \times 2 = 12\,V$
and $\quad V_B - V_P = 3 \times 2 = 6\,V$
Since $V_P = 0$, $\quad \therefore V_B = 6V$ **Ans.**

(d) With the switch S open each capacitor is charged with potential 18 V. Therefore charge on them :
Charge on $3\mu F$ capacitor $= 3 \times 18 = 54\,\mu C$
Charge on $6\mu F$ capacitor $= 6 \times 18 = 108\,\mu C$
When switch S is closed, the p.d. across $3\mu F$ capacitor
$= 3 \times 2 = 6V$
and charge stored $= 3 \times 6 = 18\,\mu C$
The p.d. across $6\mu F$ capacitor
$= 6 \times 2 = 12V$
and charge stored $= 6 \times 12 = 72\,\mu C$
Now change in charge on $3\mu F$ capacitor
$= 18 - 54$
$= -36\mu C$
and change in charge on $6\mu F$ capacitor
$= 72 - 108$
$= -36\mu F$

Ex. 27 A dc source with internal resistance R_0 is loaded with three identical resistances R interconnected as shown in *fig. 3.117*. At what value of R will the thermal power generated in the circuit be the highest?

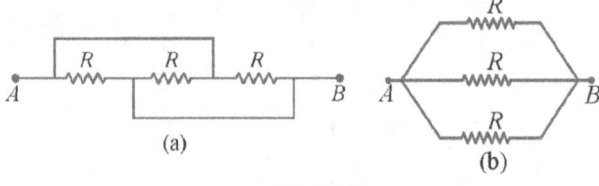

Fig. 3.117

Sol.
The given arrangement of the resistors is equivalent to the three resistors in parallel (fig. b). Thus equivalent resistance between the terminals

$$R_{AB} = \dfrac{R}{3}$$

For the maximum thermal power, the net external resistance of the circuit is equal to the internal resistance. Thus

$$\frac{R}{3} = R_0$$

or $R = 3R_0$ **Ans.**

Ex. 28 Find the equivalent resistance across the terminals A and B of a tetrahedron $ADCB$ shown in *fig. 3.118*. The resistances of all the edges of the tetrahedron are equal.

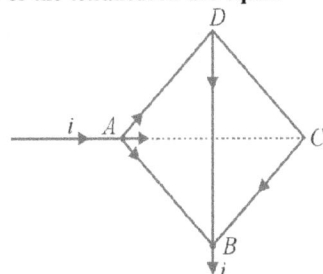

Fig. 3.118

Sol.
From symmetry considerations it can be easily understand that there is no current in the edge CD, and so is can be ignored for the equivalent resistance.
The resistances AD and DB are in series and so equal to $2R$. Similarly resistances AC and CB are in series and so equal to $2R$. Now $2R$, $2R$ and R are in parallel across the terminals A and B. Thus

$$\frac{1}{R_{AB}} = \frac{1}{2R} + \frac{1}{2R} + \frac{1}{R}$$

or $R_{AB} = \dfrac{R}{2}$ **Ans.**

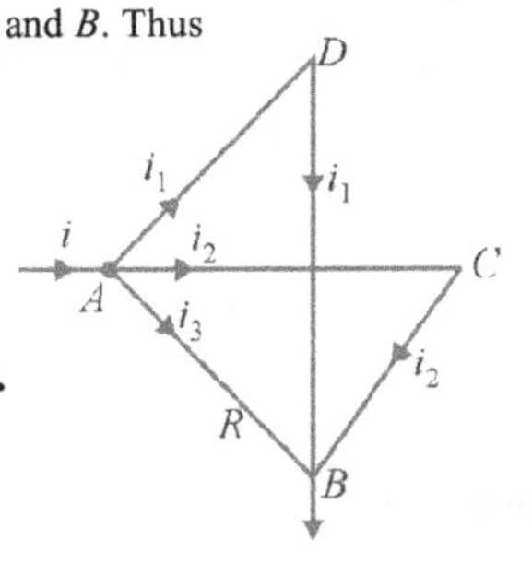

Fig. 3.119

Ex. 29 Determine the resistance R_{AO} between points A and O of the frame formed by eight identical wires of resistance R each (see *fig. 3.120*).

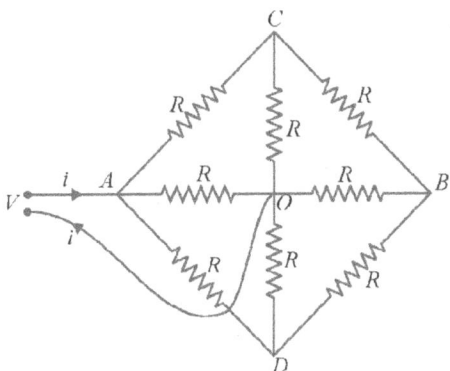

Fig. 3.120

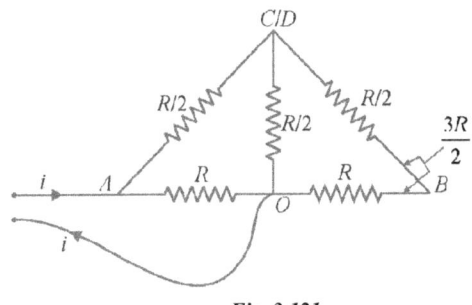

Fig. 3.121

Sol.
From symmetry considerations the potentials of points C and D are equal. Therefore, this circuit can be replaced by joining the junctions C and D.
The equivalent resistance between C and O,

$$R_{CO} = \frac{\frac{R}{2} \times \frac{3R}{2}}{\frac{R}{2} + \frac{3R}{2}} = \frac{3R}{8}$$

Resistance of arm ACO: $= R_{AC} + R_{CO} = \dfrac{R}{2} + \dfrac{3R}{8} = \dfrac{7R}{8}$

Now resistance between A and O

$$R_{AO} = \frac{R\left(\dfrac{7R}{8}\right)}{R + \dfrac{7R}{8}} = \frac{7R}{15}$$

Thus the current $i = \dfrac{V}{R_{AO}} = \dfrac{V}{\dfrac{7R}{15}} = \dfrac{15V}{7R}$ **Ans.**

Ex. 30 Determine the resistance R_{AB} between points A and B of the frame formed by nine identical wires of resistance R each (see *fig. 3.122*).

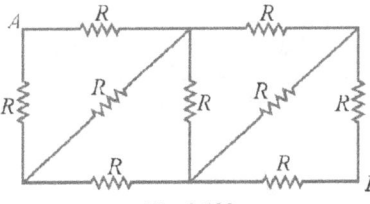

Fig. 3.122

Sol.
This circuit can not be simplified by connecting or disconnecting junction or can not be reduced to series or parallel connection. So it require circuit analysis by Kirchoff's law. Let us apply a p.d. V across the terminals A and B. The current in different resistors are shown in *fig. 3.123*

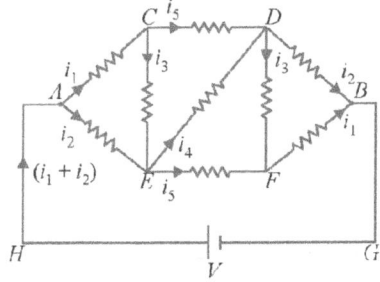

Fig. 3.123

By junction rule,
$$i_2 + i_3 = i_4 + i_5 \quad \ldots(i)$$

Now use Kirchhoff's second law in closed loops $ACEA$, $CDEC$ and $ACDBGHA$, we have

$$-i_1R - i_3R + i_2R = 0 \quad \ldots(ii)$$
$$-i_5R + i_4R + i_3R = 0 \quad \ldots(iii)$$
and $$-i_1R - i_5R - i_2R + V = 0 \quad \ldots(iv)$$

Solving above equations, we get

$$i_2 = \frac{6i_1}{5}, i_3 = \frac{i_1}{5}, i_4 = \frac{3i_1}{5}, i_5 = \frac{4i_1}{5}$$

and $$i_1 = \frac{V}{3R}$$

$$\therefore R_{AB} = \frac{V}{i_1 + i_2} = \frac{V}{i_1 + \frac{6i_1}{5}}$$

$$= \frac{5}{11} \frac{V}{i_1} = \frac{5V}{11 \times \frac{V}{3R}}$$

$$= \frac{15R}{11} \quad \text{Ans.}$$

Ex. 31 The circuit diagram shown in *fig. 3.124* consists of a very large (infinite) number of elements. The resistances of the resistors in each subsequent element differ by a factor k from the resistances of the resistors in the previous elements. Determine the resistance R_{AB} between points A and B if the resistances of the first element are R_1 and R_2.

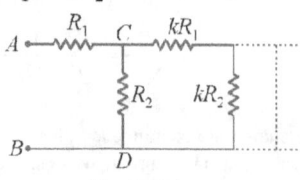

Fig. 3.124

Sol.

From symmetry considerations, we can remove the first element from the circuit; the resistance of the remaining circuit between points C and D will be $R_{CD} = k R_{AB}$. Therefore, the equivalent circuit of the infinite chain will have the form shown in *fig. 3.125*.

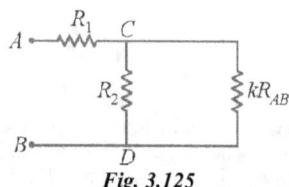

Fig. 3.125

Thus $$R_{AB} = R_1 + \frac{R_2(kR_{AB})}{R_2 + (kR_{AB})}$$

$$R_{AB}[R_2 + (kR_{AB})] = R_1[R_2 + kR_{AB}] + kR_2 R_{AB}$$

$$R_2 R_{AB} + kR_{AB}^2 = R_1 R_2 + kR_1 R_{AB} + kR_2 R_{AB}$$

or $$kR_{AB}^2 + (R_2 - kR_1 - kR_2)R_{AB} - R_1 R_2 = 0$$

$$\therefore R_{AB} = \frac{-(R_2 - kR_1 - kR_2) \pm \sqrt{(R_2 - kR_1 - kR_2)^2 + 4kR_1 R_2}}{2k}$$

As resistance can not be negative, so

$$R_{AB} = \frac{(kR_1 + kR_2 - R_2) + \sqrt{(R_2 - kR_1 - kR_2)^2 + 4kR_1 R_2}}{2k}$$

Ans.

Ex. 32 An electric circuit is shown in *fig. 3.126*. The cells are of negligible internal resistances. Find

(a) the current in $3\,\Omega$ resistance and the cell of 8 volt
(b) the charge on the capacitor.

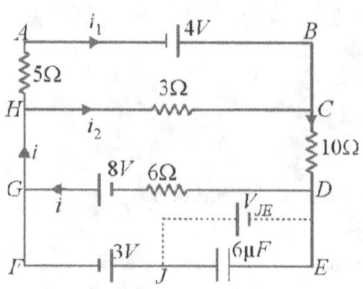

Fig. 3.126

Sol.

At steady state there is no current in the branch of capacitor. The currents in the different branches of the circuit are shown in *fig. 3.126*. At junction H

$$i = i_1 + i_2 \quad \ldots(i)$$

Applying Kirchhoff's loop rule in close loop $A\,B\,C\,H\,A$

$$+4 + 3i_2 - 5i_1 = 0$$

or $$5i_1 - 3i_2 = 4 \quad \ldots(ii)$$

In close loop $H\,C\,D\,G\,H$

$$-3i_2 - 10i - 6i + 8 = 0$$

or $$-3i_2 - 16(i_1 + i_2) + 8 = 0$$

or $$16i_1 + 19i_2 = 8 \quad \ldots(iii)$$

Solving equations (ii) and (iii), we get

$$i_2 = 0.51 \text{ A}$$
and $$i_1 = 1.11 \text{ A}$$

The current in $8V$ cell

$$i = i_1 + i_2$$
$$= 1.11 + 0.51 = 1.61 \text{ A}$$

To get the p.d. across the capacitor, join point J and D by a hypothetical cell V_{JE}, which obviously be the p.d. across the capacitor. In close loop $G\,D\,J\,F\,G$, we have

$$-8 + 6i + V_{JE} - 3 = 0$$

or $$-8 + 6 \times 1.61 + V_{JE} - 3 = 0$$

or $$V_{JE} = 1.33 \text{ V}$$

Thus the charge on the capacitor

$$Q = CV$$
$$= 6 \times 1.33$$
$$= 7.98 \text{ μC} \quad \text{Ans.}$$

Ex. 33 A wire forms a regular hexagon and the angular points are joined to the centre by wires each of which has a resistance $\left(\dfrac{1}{n}\right)$ of the side of the hexagon. Find the current entering at one angular point and leaving it by opposite point if r is the resistance of any one side of hexagon.

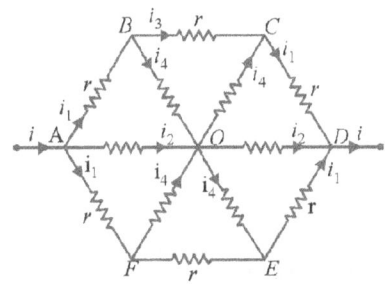

Fig. 3.127

Sol.

Suppose r' is the resistance of each wire connected to centre, where

$$r' = \dfrac{r}{n}.$$

Because of symmetry the currents in upper half and lower half of the circuit are equal. Using Kirchhoff's laws, we have

$$i_1 = i_3 + i_4 \qquad \ldots(i)$$
$$\text{and} \qquad i = 2i_1 + i_2 \qquad \ldots(ii)$$

In close loop $ABOA$, we have

$$-i_1 r - i_4 \dfrac{r}{n} + i_2 \dfrac{r}{n} = 0$$

or $\qquad ni_1 + i_4 = i_2 \qquad \ldots(iii)$

In close loop $BCOB$, we have

$$-i_3 r + i_4 \dfrac{r}{n} + i_4 \dfrac{r}{n} = 0$$

or $\qquad 2i_4 = ni_3 \qquad \ldots(iv)$

From equations (i) and (iv), we get

$$i_3 = \left(\dfrac{2i_2}{n+2}\right) \text{ and } i_4 = \left(\dfrac{ni_1}{n+2}\right)$$

From equation (iii)

$$ni_1 + \dfrac{ni_1}{n+2} = i_2$$

$\therefore \qquad i_1 = \dfrac{n+2}{n(n+3)} i_2$

Putting the value of i_1 in equation (ii), we get

$$i = \dfrac{2(n+2)}{n(n+3)} i_2 + i_2 = \dfrac{(n+4)(n+1)}{n(n+3)} i_2$$

$\therefore \qquad i_2 = \dfrac{n(n+3)}{(n+4)(n+1)} i.$ **Ans.**

Ex. 34 Find the resistance between the terminals A and B in fig. 3.128.

Sol.

The delta FDE may be replaced by its equivalent star as shown in fig. 3.128 (b). In fig. 3.128 (c), two series resistances along CES and CDS have been replaced by a single resistance. The equivalent resistance

$$R_{AB} = 2R \parallel \left(\dfrac{3R}{2}\right) = \dfrac{6R}{7}.$$

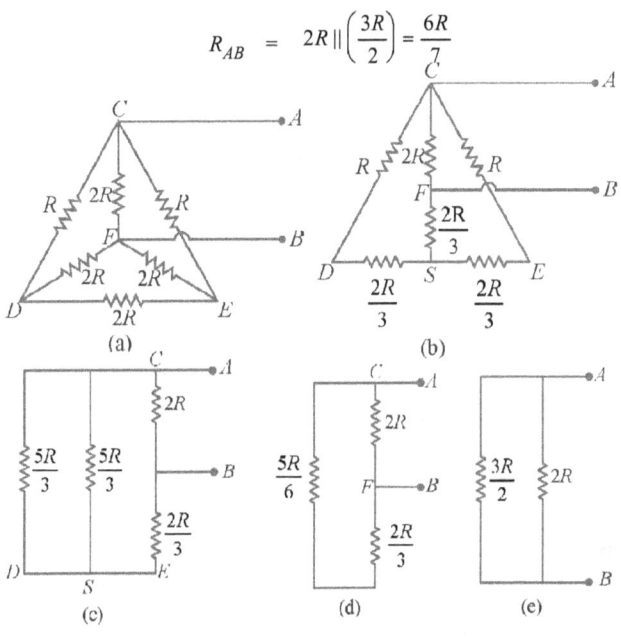

Fig. 3.128

Ex. 35 Using Kirchhoff's law, find the magnitude and polarity of voltage V shown in fig. 3.127. The directions of the two current sources are as shown.

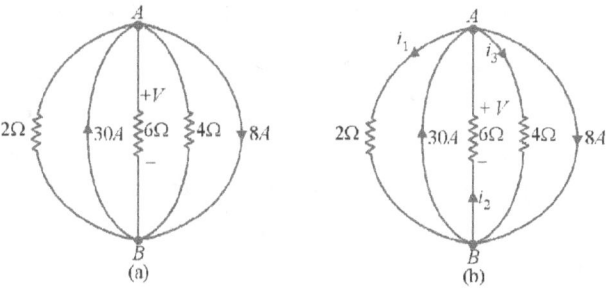

Fig. 3.129

Sol.

Suppose the directions of current in the circuit are as shown in fig. 3.129 (b). At junction A

$$i_1 + i_3 + 8 = i_2 + 30$$
or $\qquad i_1 - i_2 + i_3 = 22 \qquad \ldots(i)$

where $\quad i_1 = \dfrac{V}{2},\ i_2 = \dfrac{-V}{6}\ $ and $\ i_3 = \dfrac{V}{4}$

Substituting these values in equation (i), we get

$$\dfrac{V}{2} - \left(\dfrac{-V}{6}\right) + \dfrac{V}{4} = 22$$

or $\qquad \dfrac{V}{2} + \dfrac{V}{6} + \dfrac{V}{4} = 22$

or $V = 24 V$

$\therefore \quad i_1 = \dfrac{V}{2} = \dfrac{24}{2} = 12 A$

$i_2 = -\dfrac{V}{6} = -\dfrac{24}{6} = -4A$

$i_3 = \dfrac{V}{4} = \dfrac{24}{4} = 6A$ **Ans.**

Ex. 36 In *fig. 3.130*, all the resistors have a resistance of 4.0 Ω and all the batteries are ideal and have an emf of 4.0V each. What is the current through resistor R ?

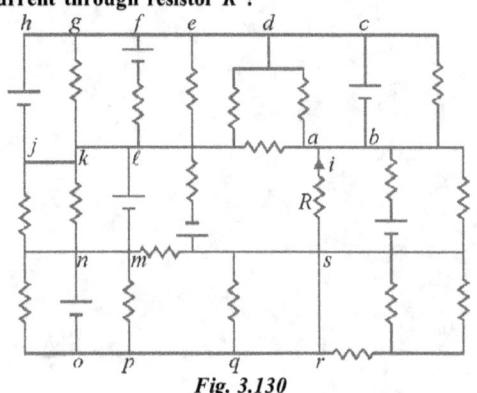

Fig. 3.130

Sol.
Taking a close loop $a\,b\,c\,d\,e\,f\,g\,h\,j\,k\,l\,m\,n\,o\,p\,q\,r\,s\,a$ and assuming current i in the direction of movement of loop, we have

$+4 - 4 - 4 - 4 - i \times 4 = 0$

or $\quad i = 2A.$ **Ans.**

Ex. 37 Determine the resistance R_{AB} between points A and B of the frame made of thin homogeneous wire (*fig. 3.131*), assuming that the number of successively embedded equilateral triangles (wide sides decreasing by half) tends to infinity. Side AB is equal to a, and the resistance of unit length of the wire is ρ.

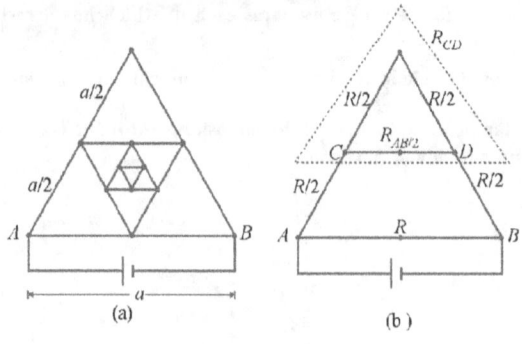

Fig. 3.131

Sol.
The resistance of the network between A and B will not change if we add one more triangle across C and D. As the side $CD = AB/2$, and so its resistance will be $R_{AB}/2$. The equivalent network can be drawn as in *fig. 3.131* (b). Thus

$R_{CD} = \left(\dfrac{R \dfrac{R_{AB}}{2}}{R + \dfrac{R_{AB}}{2}} \right)$. Again $R/2$ and $R/2$ are in series with R_{CD}.

$\therefore$ Net becomes $\left(R + \dfrac{R \dfrac{R_{AB}}{2}}{R + \dfrac{R_{AB}}{2}} \right)$, Finally $= \dfrac{R\left(R + \dfrac{R \dfrac{R_{AB}}{2}}{R + \dfrac{R_{AB}}{2}} \right)}{\left(R + R + \dfrac{R \dfrac{R_{AB}}{2}}{R + \dfrac{R_{AB}}{2}} \right)}$

On solving, we get $\quad R_{AB} = \dfrac{R(\sqrt{7}-1)}{3} = a\rho \dfrac{(\sqrt{7}-1)}{3}$.

3.6 Electrical instruments

Meter bridge

The most simple practical application of Wheatstone bridge is meter bridge. It consist of one meter long straight and uniform wire of manganin or constantan stretched along a meter scale. We know the balanced bridge condition, i.e. $\dfrac{P}{Q} = \dfrac{R}{S}$. After getting balance condition we can measure unknown resistance by $S = \dfrac{Q}{P} R$. Let balance point is at a distance of ℓ from A, then $\dfrac{Q}{P} = \dfrac{1-\ell}{\ell} \quad \therefore \quad S = \left(\dfrac{1-\ell}{\ell} \right) R$

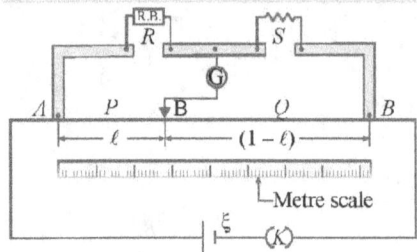

Fig. 3.132

Post office box

It is the compact form of Wheatstone's bridge originally designed to measure the resistances of electric cables and telegraph wires in post offices. It consists of three arms AB, BC and AD of the Wheatstone bridge. The unknown resistance S is connected in the fourth arm CD. Two spring keys K_1 and K_2 are also provided, which when pressed make internal connections with terminals A and B respectively. Key K_1 is known as battery

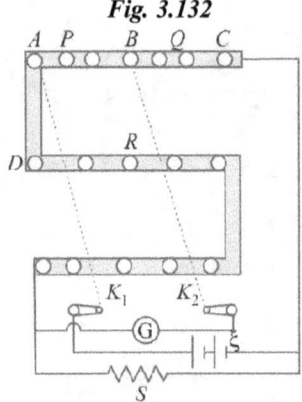

(a) Post office box

key and key K_2 as the galvanometer key. To determine the unknown resistance, the connectors are made as shown in *fig. 3.133*. Unknown resistance can then be calculated by $S = \dfrac{Q}{P} R$.

Potentiometer

It is an ideal device which is used to measure emf of a cell or to compare emf of the cells. It is also used to measure internal resistance of a cell. It consists of a long wire usually 10 m in length and made up of manganin or constantan and a battery of known emf.

Potential gradient across the wire

It is the potential drop per unit length of the potentiometer wire. In the given figure

$$V_{AB} = i R_0 = \dfrac{eR_0}{R_0 + R_h}$$

∴ potential gradient $= \dfrac{V_{AB}}{L} = \dfrac{eR_0}{(R_0 + R_h)L}$ V/m

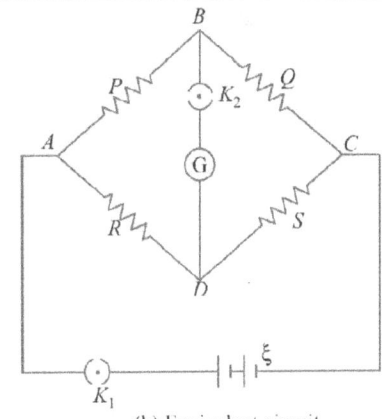

(b) Equivalent circuit

Fig. 3.133

Why long wire used in potentiometer ?

We known that sensitivity of an instrument is inversely proportional to i,

sensitivity $\propto \dfrac{1}{i}$

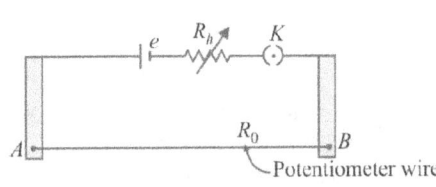

Fig. 3.134

and $i \propto \dfrac{1}{R}$

∴ sensitivity $\propto R$

Since $R \propto \ell$

∴ sensitivity $\propto \ell$.

1. **Emf of the cell :** Connect the cell whose emf, is to be determined and find balancing length with the help of galvanometer. Let it is ℓ from A.

The resistance of ℓ length of wire $R_{AJ} = \dfrac{R_0}{L} \ell$

Potential difference across it $V_{AJ} = i R_{AJ} = \left(\dfrac{e}{R_0 + R_h}\right) \times \dfrac{R_0 \ell}{L}$

The emf of the cell $\xi = V_{AJ}$

$= \dfrac{eR_0 \ell}{(R_0 + R_h)L} = k\ell$

i.e., emf of cell $\xi \propto \ell$

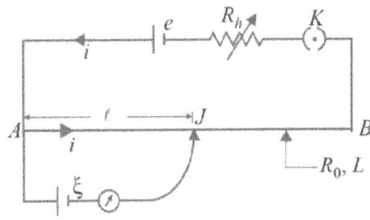

Fig. 3.135

Note: It should be remembered that $\xi < e$.

2. **Comparision of emf's of cells :** The given cells are connected in turn to the galvanometer by means of two-way key and the position of balance point on the potentiometer wire is obtained for each cell. Let ℓ_1 and ℓ_2 be the balancing lengths with the cells ξ_1 and ξ_2 respectively, then

$$\dfrac{\xi_1}{\xi_2} = \dfrac{\ell_1}{\ell_2}$$

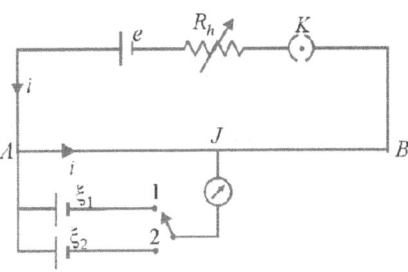

Fig. 3.136

3. **Determine internal resistance of the cell :** Initially key K' remains open and balancing length ℓ_1 is obtained. Which determine the emf of cell i.e.,

$\xi = k\ell_1$ ....(i)

252 ELECTRICITY & MAGNETISM

Now key K' is closed. Again find the new balancing length. Let it is ℓ_2. In close loop 1-2-3-4-1,

$$i' = \left(\frac{\xi}{R+r}\right)$$

The p.d. across resistor $R = iR = \left(\frac{e}{R+r}\right)R$

This p.d. must equal to the p.d. across ℓ_2 length of potentiometer wire.

$$\therefore \quad \frac{\xi R}{R+r} = k\ell_2 \qquad ...(ii)$$

From equations (i) and (ii), we have

$$\frac{(k\ell_1)R}{R+r} = k\ell_2$$

or $\quad \ell_1 R = (R+r)\ell_2$

$$\therefore \quad r = \frac{(\ell_1 - \ell_2)R}{\ell_2}.$$

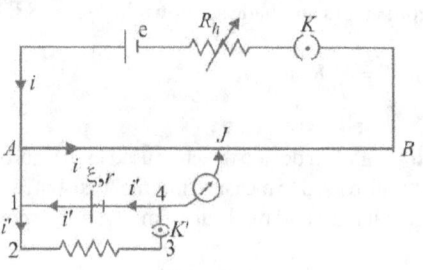

Fig. 3.137

Ex. 38 Consider the potentiometer circuit arranged as in fig. 3.136. The potentiometer wire is 600 cm long. (a) At what distance from A should jockey touch the wire to get zero deflection in the galvanometer? (b) If the jockey touches the wire at a distance of 560 cm from A, what will be the current in the galvanometer?

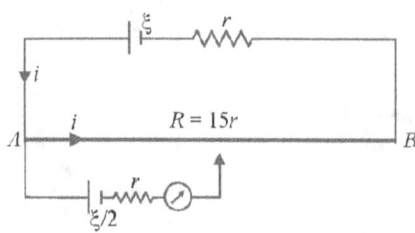

Fig. 3.138

Sol.

(a) Let C is the balancing point and ℓ is the distance of jockey at which deflection is zero in the galvanometer. The p.d., across ℓ length of potential wire

$$= iR_{AC}$$

$$V_{AC} = \frac{\xi}{16r} \times \left(\frac{15r}{600}\right)\ell$$

This p.d. is equal to the emf of cell. That is

$$\xi/2 = \frac{\xi}{16r} \times \frac{15r}{600}\ell$$

which gives $\quad \ell = 320$ cm Ans.

(b) The resistance of 560 cm length of wire

$$= \frac{15r}{600} \times 560 = 14r$$

Let i is the current in the galvanometer

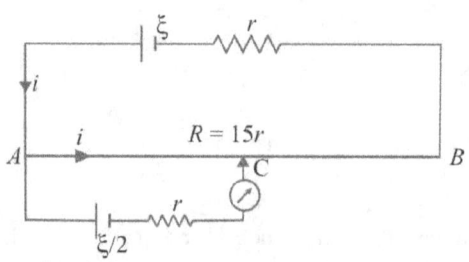

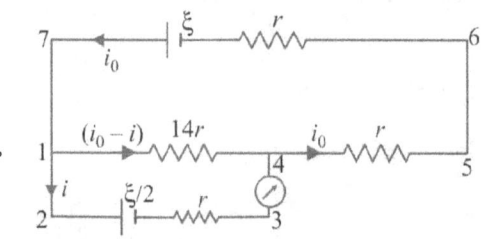

Fig. 3.139

In close loop 1-2-3-4-1

$$-\xi/2 - ir + 14r(i_0 - i) = 0$$

or $\quad 14 i_0 r - 15 ir = \xi/2 \qquad ...(i)$

In close loop 1-4-5-6-7-1

$$-14r(i_0 - i) - i_0 r - i_0 r + \xi = 0$$

$$-16 i_0 r + 14 ir = -\xi \qquad ...(ii)$$

Solving equations (i) and (ii), we get

$$i = \frac{3\xi}{22r}. \qquad \text{Ans.}$$

Galvanometer

Galvanometer usually uses to detect the direction of current. When used for this purpose its resistance becomes immaterial. If it uses to measure current or potential without any modification, its resistance affect the circuit parameters. Therefore to make it a useful instrument, galvanometer is to be modified according to requirement. Let i_g is the full scale deflection current of galvanometer, and G is its resistance then potential difference across it

$$V = i_g G$$

Ammeter

It is used to measure direct current. A galvanometer can be changed into an ammeter by connecting small resistance S, called shunt in parallel with the galvanometer. To measure the current in a circuit, an ammeter must be placed in series in the circuit so that the current to be measured actually passes through the ammeter.

Figure shows an ammeter in which shunt S is connected in parallel with galvanometer
Resistance of ammeter

$$R_A = \left(\frac{SG}{S+G}\right) < S \quad ...(i)$$

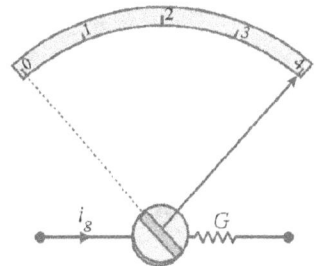

Fig. 3.140 Galvanometer

If i is the current to be measured, then

$$S(i - i_g) = G i_g$$

$$\therefore \quad S = \left(\frac{i_g}{i - i_g}\right) G \quad ...(ii)$$

or

$$i_g = i \frac{S}{S+G} \quad ...(1)$$

Equation (1) is the working equation of an ammeter

Also

$$i_g = \frac{i}{G}\left(\frac{SG}{S+G}\right)$$

or

$$i_g = i \frac{R_A}{G} \quad ...(2)$$

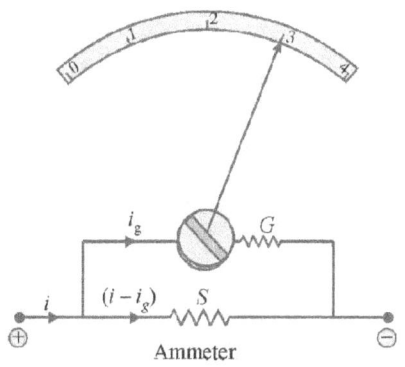

Ammeter

Fig. 3.141

Let us consider a circuit having a source of emf ξ without the aid of ammeter, actual current $i = \xi/R$.

When ammeter is connected to measure the current, its value changed due to resistance of ammeter. Let it is i'.

$$i' = \frac{\xi}{R + R_A} < i$$

$$i' = \frac{\xi}{R} = i, \text{ if } R_A = 0 \text{ (ideal ammeter)}$$

Percentage error in measuring current by ammeter

$$\frac{i - i'}{i} \times 100 = \frac{\frac{\xi}{R} - \frac{\xi}{R + R_A}}{\frac{\xi}{R}} \times 100 = \frac{R_A}{R + R_A} \times 100$$

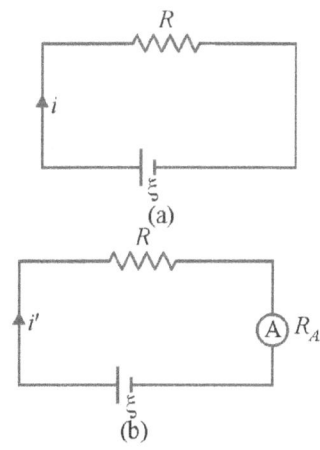

Fig. 3.142

Conversion of an ammeter into other ammeter

It is same as the conversion of galvanometer into ammeter. If i_1 is the initial range of ammeter and i_2 is the final range, then

$$i_1 = i_2\left(\frac{S}{S + R_A}\right)$$

$$i_g = i\left(\frac{S}{S+G}\right) \quad ...(i)$$

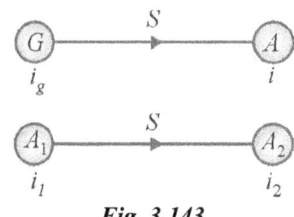

Fig. 3.143

If s_1 and s_2 are the sentivities of ammeters, then

$$\frac{s_1}{s_2} = \frac{i_2}{i_1}$$

The equation (1) now can be written as

$$\therefore \quad \frac{i_1}{i_2} = \frac{s_2}{s_1} = \left(\frac{S}{S+R_A}\right) \quad ...(3)$$

Voltmeter

It is used to measure potential difference between two points of a circuit containing direct current source. A galvanometer can be changed into a voltmeter by connecting a very large resistance (R_0) in series with the galvanometer. The voltmeter is always connected in parallel across the points.

The potential difference across R = potential difference across voltmeter

or $\quad V = i_g R_V = i_g (G + R_0)$

or $\quad R_0 = \dfrac{V}{i_g} - G \quad ...(4)$

The resistance of voltmeter $\quad R_V = G + R_0$

The actual potential difference across resistor R

$$V = iR$$

When it is measured with a voltmeter of resistance R_V, it is

$$V = i \frac{R R_V}{R + R_V}$$

$$= \frac{iR}{1 + \dfrac{R}{R_V}}.$$

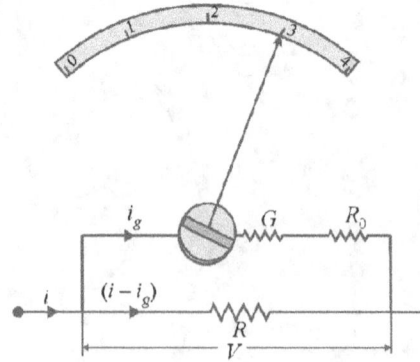

Fig. 3.144

If $R_V \to \infty$, $V' = iR = V$

Thus, the resistance of ideal voltmeter is infinite.

Percentage error in measuring potential difference with a voltmeter

$$\frac{V - V'}{V} \times 100 = \left[\frac{iR - \dfrac{iR}{\left(1 + \dfrac{R}{R_V}\right)}}{iR}\right] \times 100$$

$$= \frac{\left(\dfrac{R}{R_V}\right)}{\left(1 + \dfrac{R}{R_V}\right)} \times 100 = \frac{R}{R_V + R} \times 100$$

$$= \left(\dfrac{1}{1 + \dfrac{R_V}{R}}\right) \times 100.$$

for $R_V \to \infty$, % error = 0

Conversion of one voltmeter into other voltmeter :
It is like to change galvanometer into voltmeter.

$$V = i_g R_V = i_g (G + R_0)$$

$$V_2 = i_g (R_{V_1} + R_0)$$

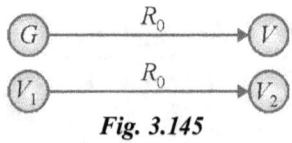

Fig. 3.145

Ex. 39 An electrical circuit is shown in *fig. 3.146*. Calculate the potential difference across the resistor of 400 ohm as will be measured by the voltmeter V of resistance 400 ohm either by applying Kirchhoff's rules or otherwise.

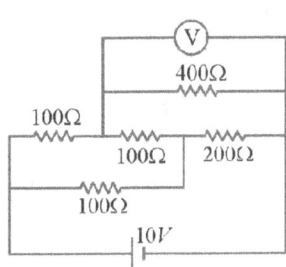

Fig. 3.146

Sol. The given circuit with the voltmeter reduces to a balanced Wheatstone's bridge.

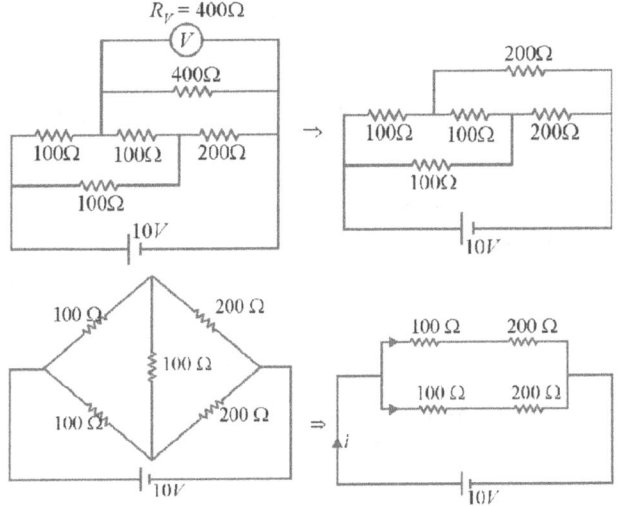

Fig. 3.147

The effective resistance across the source = 150Ω.
Current drawn from the cell

$$i = \frac{10}{150} = \frac{1}{15} A$$

The current is equally divided into both the branches. Therefore current in $200\,\Omega$ is $\frac{1}{30}\,A$

∴ The p.d. across $200\,\Omega = 200 \times \frac{1}{30} = \frac{20}{3}\,V$. **Ans.**

Ex. 40 A galvanometer has a resistance of 30Ω and current of 2 mA is needed to give full scale deflection. What is the resistance needed and how is it to be connected to convert the galvanometer
(a) into an ammeter of 0.3 A range?
(b) into a voltmeter of 0.2 V range?

Sol.
Given $G = 30\,\Omega$, $i_g = 2\,mA = 2 \times 10^{-3}\,A$.
(a) If S is the required shunt connected in parallel with the galvanometer, then

$$i_g = \frac{S}{S+G}i$$

or $\quad 2 \times 10^{-3} = \frac{S}{S+30} \times 0.3$

After solving, we get $S = \frac{30}{149}\Omega$ **Ans.**

(b) To convert galvanometer into voltmeter a high resistance R_0 is connected in series with galvanometer, and so

$$V = i_g(G + R_0)$$

or $\quad 0.2 = 2 \times 10^{-3}(30 + R_0)$

or $\quad R_0 = 70\,\Omega$. **Ans.**

Ex. 41 A galvanometer having 30 divisions has a current sensitivity of 20 μA / division. It has a resistance of 25 ohm. How will you convert it into an ammeter measuring upto 1 A? How will you now convert this ammeter into a voltmeter reading upto 1 V?

Sol.

The full scale deflection current

$$i_g = 30 \times (20 \times 10^{-6})$$
$$= 6 \times 10^{-4}\,A.$$

If S is the required value of the shunt connected in parallel with the galvanometer, then

$$i_g = \frac{S}{S+G}i$$

or $\quad 6 \times 10^{-4} = \frac{S}{S+25} \times 1$

After solving, we get $S = \frac{150}{9994}\Omega = 0.0150\,\Omega$ **Ans.**

The resistance of the ammeter

$$R_A = \frac{SG}{S+G}$$

$$= \frac{0.0150 \times 25}{0.0150 + 25} = 0.0150\,\Omega$$

To convert this ammeter into the voltmeter, we can use

$$V = i_g(R_A + R_0)$$

Here $\quad V = 1V,\ i_g = 1A$

∴ $\quad 1 = 1(0.0150 + R_0)$

or $\quad R_0 = 0.985\,\Omega$. **Ans.**

Review of formulae & Important Points

1. **Electric current :** An electric current i in a conductor is defined by
$$i = \frac{dq}{dt}.$$
By convention, the direction of electric current is taken as the direction in which positive charge carriers would move.

2. **Current density :** Current density is related to the current as
$$i = \int \vec{J} \cdot d\vec{A}$$
where $d\vec{A}$ is a vector perpendicular to a surface element of area dA, and the integral is taken over any surface cutting across the conductor. $\vec{J}$ has the same direction as the velocity of the moving positive charges.

3. **Drift speed :** When an electric field $\vec{E}$ is established in a conductor, the charge carriers (assumed positive) acquire a drift speed v_d in the direction of $\vec{E}$; the velocity is related to current density $\vec{j}$ as
$$\vec{J} = (ne)\vec{v}_d$$

4. **Resistance of a conductor :** If V is the p.d. applied across the conductor and i is the corresponding current, then its resistance is defined as :
$$R = \frac{V}{i}.$$
Similarly we can define resistivity ρ and conductivity σ of a material :
$$\rho = \frac{1}{\sigma} = \frac{E}{J}$$
Also $\vec{E} = \vec{J}\rho$
If n is the number of free electrons per unit volume and τ is the relaxation time, then
$$\rho = \frac{2m}{ne^2 \tau}$$
The resistance R of a conducting wire of length L and uniform cross-section A is
$$R = \frac{\rho L}{A}.$$

5. **Change in ρ or R with temperature :** If R_0 is the resistance of a wire at temperature 0°C, then resistance at any temperature t is
$$R_t \quad ; \quad R_0(1+\alpha t)$$
where α is the temperature coefficient of resistance. It can be defined as
$$\alpha = \frac{1}{R_0}\frac{dR_t}{dt}$$

6. **Ohm's law :** Under given physical conditions the current i produced in the conductor is proportional to the applied potential difference across the conductor.

7. **Combination of resistances :**
   (i) In series : $R = R_1 + R_2 + ...$
   (ii) In parallel : $\frac{1}{R} = \frac{1}{R_1} + \frac{1}{R_2} + ...$

8. **Changing the size of the resistor :**
If the conductor is stretched from length ℓ to ℓ', then its resistance changes from R to R' as
$$R' = R\left(\frac{\ell'}{\ell}\right)^2$$
In terms of radius of cross-section of the conductor
$$R' = R\left(\frac{r}{r'}\right)^4.$$

9. **EMF of the cell :** It is the work done in circulating unit charge in the entire circuit. Thus
$$\xi = \frac{dW}{dq}.$$
Potential difference across the terminals of the cell
$$V = \xi - ir$$
where r is the internal resistance of the cell.
In case when cell is charging, the p.d. across the terminals of the cell
$$V = \xi + ir.$$

10. **Combination of cells :**
   (i) **In series :** If n identical cells each of emf ξ and internal resistance r are connected in series, then current in external resistor R
   $$i = \left[\frac{n\xi}{nr + R}\right]$$
   In case when $nr << R$,
   $$i \simeq n\frac{\xi}{R}$$
   (ii) **In parallel :** $\quad i = \dfrac{\xi}{\left[\dfrac{r}{n} + R\right]}$
   In case $R << nr$,
   $$i \simeq n\frac{\xi}{r}.$$
   (iii) **Series-parallel :** If n cells are connected in series and m cells are in parallel, then
   $$i = \left[\frac{n\xi}{\frac{nr}{m} + R}\right]$$
   For maximum current
   $$\frac{nr}{m} = R.$$

11. In a series of five identical cells each of emf ξ and internal resistance r, if one of the cells is wrongly connected, then net emf
$$\xi_{net} = 3\xi \text{ and } r_{net} = 5r$$

Similarly in a series of n cells if m cells are wrongly connected, then

$$\xi_{net} = (n-2m)\xi \text{ and } r_{net} = nr$$

12. If two cells of emfs ξ_1 and ξ_2 and internal resistances r_1 and r_2 are connected in parallel, then p.d. across the combination

$$\xi = \left[\frac{\xi_1 r_2 + \xi_2 r_1}{r_1 + r_2}\right]$$

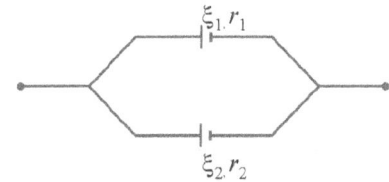

13. **Circuit analysis by Kirchhoff's laws :**
    (i) Junction rule : At any junction, the algebraic sum of currents is equal to zero. i.e.,
    $$\Sigma i = 0$$
    (ii) Loop rule : In a close loop, the algebraic sum of p.d. across all circuit elements is equal to zero, i.e.,
    $$\Sigma V = 0.$$
    For a circuit having resistors and cells
    $$\Sigma \xi + \Sigma iR = 0$$

    Sign conventions :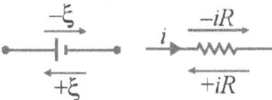

14. **Wheatstone bridge :** It is the combination of four resistances in the form of bridge. For the balanced bridge with the resistors P, Q, R and S

    $$\frac{P}{Q} = \frac{R}{S} \text{ or } \frac{P}{R} = \frac{Q}{S}$$

    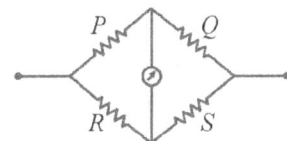

    The equivalent resistance across the terminals of the cell

    $$\frac{1}{R_{eq}} = \frac{1}{P+Q} + \frac{1}{R+S}$$

15. **Delta–star transformation :** A combination of three resistors in the form of delta can be effectively converted into star. A delta of three resistors R_1, R_2 and R_3 is equivalent to a star with three resistors R_{12}, R_{13} and R_{23}, where

    $$R_{12} = \left[\frac{R_1 R_2}{R_1 + R_2 + R_3}\right]$$

    $$R_{13} = \left[\frac{R_1 R_3}{R_1 + R_2 + R_3}\right]$$

    $$R_{23} = \left[\frac{R_2 R_3}{R_1 + R_2 + R_3}\right]$$

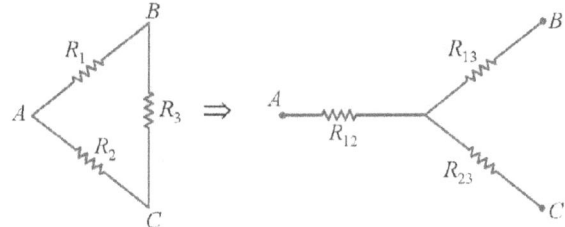

(a) Delta of three resistors   (b) Star of three resistors

For any two junctions R_{AB} in delta is equal to R_{AB} in star, similarly R_{AC} and R_{BC}.

16. **Metre bridge :** It is used to find unknown resistance. If ℓ be the balanced length and R is the known resistance, then unknown resistance

    $$S = R\left(\frac{1-\ell}{\ell}\right).$$

17. **Potentiometer :** It is an ideal device of finding emf of the cells, internal resistance of the cell etc.

    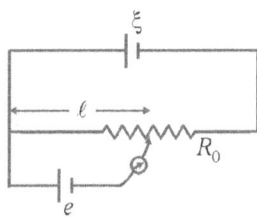

    If R_0 is the resistance of the potentiometer wire, then emf of the cell

    $$e = \xi \frac{\ell}{\ell_0},$$

    where ℓ is the balancing length and ℓ_0 is the length of the potentiometer wire.
    Internal resistance

    $$r = R\left(\frac{\ell_1 - \ell_2}{\ell_2}\right),$$

    where ℓ_1 and ℓ_2 are the balancing lengths without R and with R.

18. **Ammeter :** Galvanometer of resistance G and full scale deflection current i_g can be converted into an ammeter of range i by connecting a shunt of resistance S, such that

    $$i_g = i\frac{S}{S+G}$$

    Resistance of ammeter $\quad R_A = \frac{SG}{S+G}$

19. **Voltmeter :** A galvanometer of resistance G and full scale deflection current i_g can be converted into a voltmeter of range V by connecting a large resistance R_0 in series, such that

    $$V = i_g(G + R_0).$$

★★★

ELECTRICITY — MCQ Type 1

Exercise 3.1

LEVEL - 1

Only one option correct

1. The value of the resistance as measured across terminals A and B in figure would be

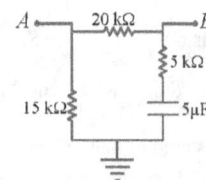

   (a) $5\,k\Omega$ (b) $10\,k\Omega$
   (c) $15\,k\Omega$ (d) $20\,k\Omega$

2. The equivalent resistance between A and B is

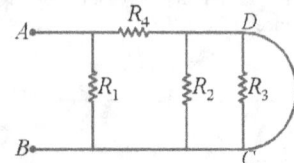

   (a) $R_1 + R_2 + R_3$ (b) R_2
   (c) $\dfrac{R_2 R_4}{R_2 + R_4} + R_1$ (d) $\dfrac{R_1 R_4}{R_1 + R_4}$

3. The time constant of the circuit is :

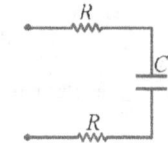

   (a) RC (b) $RC/2$
   (c) $2RC$ (d) ∞

4. In the figure, the resistors are in series or parallel. Select the right trend :

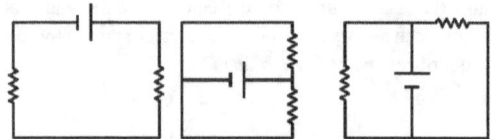

   (a) series, series, series (b) series, series, parallel
   (c) series, parallel, parallel (d) none

5. The figure here shows conduction electrons moving leftward through a wire. Select the quantity/(ies) which have direction rightward :

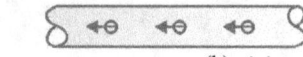

   (a) i, v_d (b) i, j
   (c) j, E, v_d (d) i, j and E.

6. Figure shows four situations in which positive and negative charges move horizontally through a region and gives the rate at which each charge moves. The situations according to the effective current through the region, greatest first :

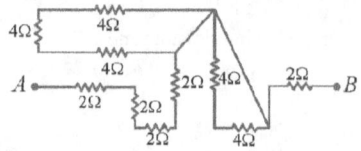

   (a) $A > B > C > D$ (b) $(A = B) > C > D$
   (c) $A < B < C < D$ (d) $(A = C) > D > B$

7. The equivalent resistance between A and B is :

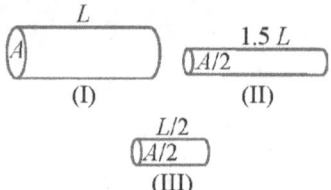

   (a) $10\,\Omega$ (b) $20\,\Omega$
   (c) $15\,\Omega$ (d) none

8. The figure shows three cylindrical copper conductors along with their face areas and lengths. Rank them according to the current through them, greatest first

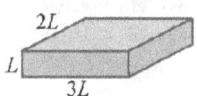

   (a) $i_1 = i_2 = i_3$ (b) $i_1 > i_2 > i_3$
   (c) $i_1 < i_2 < i_3$ (d) $(i_1 = i_3) < i_2$

9. Figure shows a rectangular solid conductor of edge lengths L, $2L$, and $3L$. A certain potential difference V is to be applied between pairs of opposite faces of the conductor as shown in figure : left-right, top-bottom and front-back. In which pair current is maximum :

   (a) left-right (b) top-bottom
   (c) front-back (d) equal in all

Answer Key (Sol. from page 287)

1	(d)	2	(d)	3	(c)	4	(c)	5	(d)
6	(d)	7	(a)	8	(d)	9	(b)		

10. A resistance of 2 Ω is connected across one gap of a metre-bridge (the length of the wire is 100 cm) and an unknown resistance, greater than 2 Ω, is connected across the other gap. Where these resistances are interchanged, the balance point shifts by 20 cm. Neglecting any correction, the unknown resistance is

(a) 3 Ω
(b) 4 Ω
(c) 5 Ω
(d) 6 Ω

11. A wire of resistance 4 Ω is bent to form a circle. The resistance between A and B is

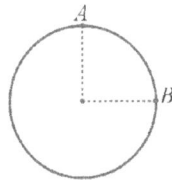

(a) 4 Ω
(b) 3 Ω
(c) $\frac{3}{4}$ Ω
(d) none of these

12. When a piece of aluminium wire of finite length is drawn through a series of dies to reduce its diameter to half its original value, its resistance will become

(a) two times
(b) four times
(c) eight times
(d) sixteen times

13. A steady current flows in a metallic conductor of non-uniform cross-section. The quantity/quantities constant along the length of the conductor is/are

(a) current, electric field and drift speed
(b) drift speed only
(c) current and drift speed
(d) current only

14. A strip of copper and another of germanium are cooled from room temperature to 80 K. The resistance of

(a) each of these increases
(b) each of these decreases
(c) copper strip increases and that of germanium decreases
(d) copper strip decreases and that of germanium increases

15. Express which of the following setups can be used to verify Ohm's law

(a)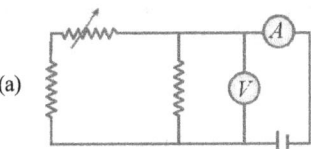

(b)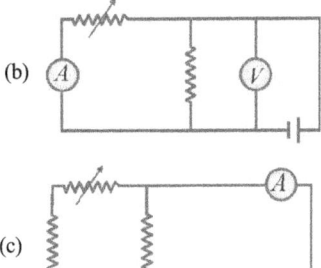

(c)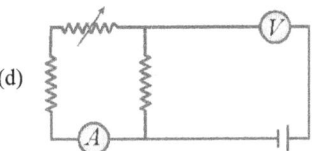

(d)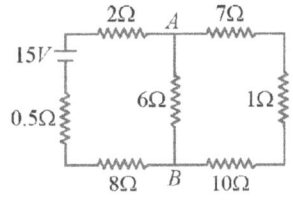

16. The current from the battery in circuit diagram shown is

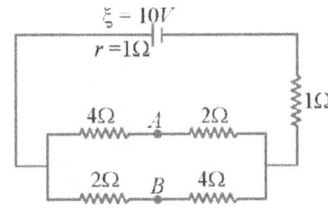

(a) 1 A
(b) 2 A
(c) 1.5 A
(d) 3 A

17. In the circuit shown below, the cell has an e.m.f. of 10 V and internal resistance of 1 ohm. The other resistances are shown in the figure. The potential difference $V_A - V_B$ is

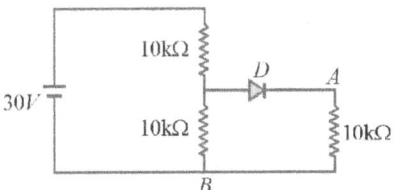

(a) 6 V
(b) 4 V
(c) 2 V
(d) –2 V

18. In the given figure, potential difference between A and B is

(a) 0
(b) 5 volt
(c) 10 volt
(d) 15 volt

Answer Key	10	(a)	11	(c)	12	(d)	13	(a)	14	(d)
Sol. from page 287	15	(a)	16	(a)	17	(d)	18	(c)		

19. If each resistance in the figure is of $9\,\Omega$ then reading of ammeter is

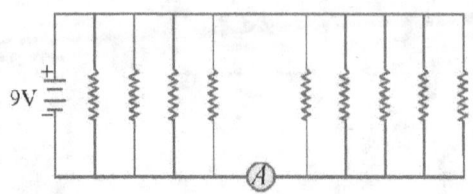

(a) 5 A (b) 8 A
(c) 2 A (d) 9 A

20. Two wires of equal diameters, of resistivities ρ_1 and ρ_2 and lengths ℓ_1 and ℓ_2, respectively, are joined in series. The equivalent resistivity of the combination is

(a) $\dfrac{\rho_1\ell_1 + \rho_2\ell_2}{\ell_1 + \ell_2}$ (b) $\dfrac{\rho_1\ell_2 + \rho_2\ell_1}{\ell_1 - \ell_2}$

(c) $\dfrac{\rho_1\ell_2 + \rho_2\ell_2}{\ell_1 + \ell_2}$ (d) $\dfrac{\rho_1\ell_1 - \rho_2\ell_2}{\ell_1 - \ell_2}$

21. In the arrangement of resistances shown below, the effective resistance between points A and B is

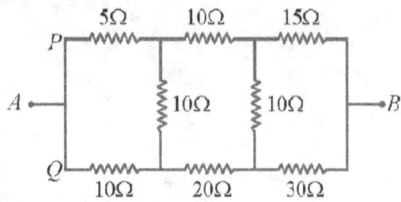

(a) $20\,\Omega$ (b) $30\,\Omega$
(c) $90\,\Omega$ (d) $110\,\Omega$

22. Calculate the equivalent resistance between A and B

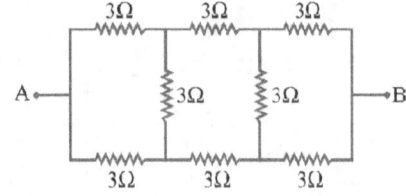

(a) $\dfrac{9}{2}\,\Omega$ (b) $3\,\Omega$
(c) $6\,\Omega$ (d) $\dfrac{5}{3}\,\Omega$

23. Six equal resistances are connected between points P, Q and R as shown in the figure. Then the net resistance will be maximum between

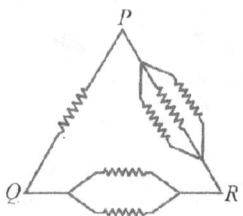

(a) P and Q (b) Q and R
(c) P and R (d) Any two points

24. The total current supplied to the circuit by the battery is

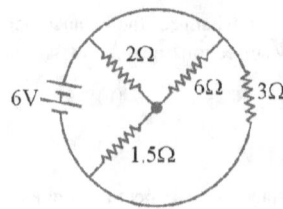

(a) 1 A (b) 2 A
(c) 4 A (d) 6 A

25. A cell of e.m.f. ξ is connected with an external resistance R, then p.d. across cell is V. The internal resistance of cell will be

(a) $\dfrac{(\xi - V)R}{\xi}$ (b) $\dfrac{(\xi - V)R}{V}$

(c) $\dfrac{(V - \xi)R}{V}$ (d) $\dfrac{(V - \xi)R}{\xi}$

26. The potential difference in open circuit for a cell is 2.2 volt. When a 4 ohm resistor is connected between its two electrodes the potential difference becomes 2 volt. The internal resistance of the cell will be

(a) 1 ohm (b) 0.2 ohm
(c) 2.5 ohm (d) 0.4 ohm

27. Eels are able to generate current with biological cells called electroplaques. The electroplaques in an eel are arranged in 100 rows, each row stretching horizontally along the body of the fish containing 5000 electroplaques. The arrangement is suggestively shown below. Each electroplaques has an emf of 0.15 V and internal resistance of $0.25\,\Omega$

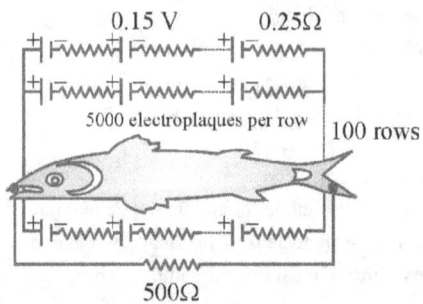

The water surrounding the eel completes a circuit between the head and its tail. If the water surrounding it has a resistance of $500\,\Omega$, the current an eel can produce in water is about

(a) 1.5 A (b) 3.0 A
(c) 15 A (d) 30 A

Answer Key	19	(a)	20	(a)	21	(a)	22	(a)	23	(a)
Sol. from page 287	24	(c)	25	(b)	26	(d)	27	(a)		

28. Find out the value of current through 2 Ω resistance for the given circuit

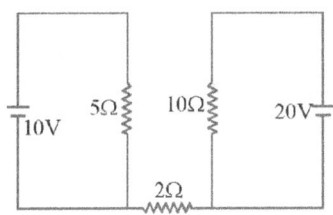

(a) 5 A (b) 2 A
(c) zero (d) 4 A

29. A 2 volt battery, a 15Ω resistor and a potentiometer of 100 cm length, all are connected in series. If the resistance of potentiometer wire is 5Ω, then the potential gradient of the potentiometer wire is
(a) 0.005 V/cm (b) 0.05 V/cm
(c) 0.02 V/cm (d) 0.2 V/cm

30. In the diagram shown, the reading of voltmeter is 20 V and that of ammeter is 4 A. The value of R should be (Consider given ammeter and voltmeter are not ideal)

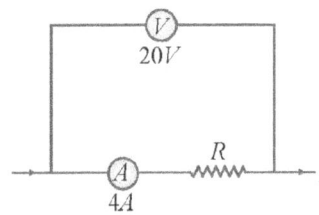

(a) equal to 5Ω
(b) greater than 5Ω
(c) less than 5Ω
(d) greater or less than 5Ω depends on the material of R

31. AB is a wire of uniform resistance. The galvanometer G shows no current when the length AC = 20 cm and CB = 80 cm. The resistance R is equal to

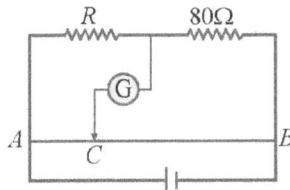

(a) 2 Ω (b) 8 Ω
(c) 20 Ω (d) 40 Ω

32. In the circuit shown $P \neq R$, the reading of the galvanometer is same with switch S open or closed. Then

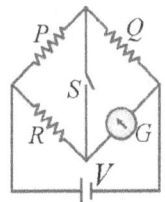

(a) $I_R = I_G$ (b) $I_P = I_G$
(c) $I_Q = I_G$ (d) $I_Q = I_R$

33. For the post office box arrangement to determine the value of unknown resistance, the unknown resistance should be connected between

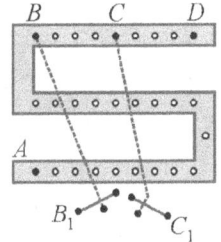

(a) B and C (b) C and D
(c) A and D (d) B_1 and C_1

34. In a metre bridge experiment null point is obtained at 20 cm from one end of the wire when resistance X is balanced against another resistance Y. If X < Y, then where will be the new position of the null point from the same end, if one decides to balance a resistance of 4X against Y
(a) 50 cm (b) 80 cm
(c) 40 cm (d) 70 cm

35. A moving coil galvanometer of resistance 100Ω is used as an ammeter using a resistance 0.1 Ω. The maximum deflection current in the galvanometer is 100µA. Find the minimum current in the circuit so that the ammeter shows maximum deflection
(a) 100.1 mA (b) 1000.1 mA
(c) 10.01 mA (d) 1.01 mA

36. Potentiometer wire of length 1 m is connected in series with 490 Ω resistance and 2V battery. If 0.2 mV/cm is the potential gradient, then resistance of the potentiometer wire is
(a) 4.9 Ω (b) 7.9 Ω
(c) 5.9 Ω (d) 6.9 Ω

Answer Key	28	(c)	29	(a)	30	(c)	31	(c)	32	(a)
Sol. from page 287	33	(c)	34	(a)	35	(a)	36	(a)		

37. Twelve wires of equal length and same cross-section are connected in the form of a cube. If the resistance of each of the wires is R, then the effective resistance between the two diagonal ends would be

(a) 2R
(b) 12R
(c) $\frac{5}{6}R$
(d) 8R

38. The potential difference across 8 ohm resistance is 48 volt as shown in the figure. The value of potential difference across X and Y points will be

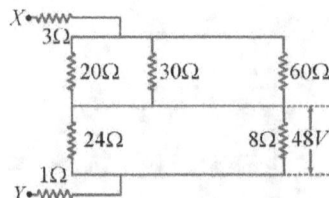

(a) 160 volt
(b) 128 volt
(c) 80 volt
(d) 62 volt

39. In the circuit element given here, if the potential at point B, $V_B = 0$, then the potentials of A and D are given as

(a) $V_A = -1.5V, V_D = +2V$
(b) $V_A = +1.5V, V_D = +2V$
(c) $V_A = +1.5V, V_D = +0.5V$
(d) $V_A = +1.5V, V_D = -0.5V$

40. The current in a conductor varies with time t as $i = 2t + 3t^2$ where i is in ampere and t in seconds. Electric charge flowing through a section of the conductor during $t = 2$ sec to $t = 3$ sec is

(a) 10 C
(b) 24 C
(c) 33 C
(d) 44 C

41. As the switch S is closed in the circuit shown in figure, current passed through it is

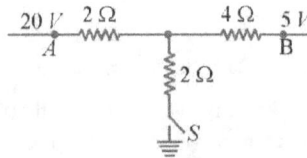

(a) 4.5 A
(b) 6.0 A
(c) 3.0 A
(d) zero

42. What will be the change in the resistance of a circuit consisting of five identical conductors if two similar conductors are added as shown in the figure. If R_1 is the initial resistance and R_2 that after connecting the two identical conductors, then $\frac{R_2}{R_1}$ is :

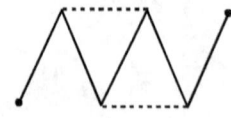

(a) 1.4
(b) 0.4
(c) 0.5
(d) 0.6

43. A voltmeter has a resistance G ohm and range V volt. The value of resistance used in series to convert it into voltmeter of range nV volt is :

(a) nG
(b) $(n-1)G$
(c) $\frac{G}{n}$
(d) $\frac{G}{(n-1)}$

44. In the circuit shown, each resistance is 2. The potential V_1 as indicated in the circuit, is equal to

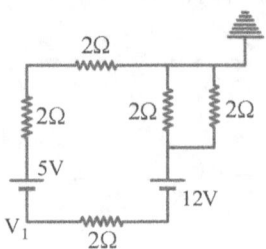

(a) 11 V
(b) – 11V
(c) 9 V
(d) – 9 V

45. The potential difference, in volt, across the resistance R_2 in the circuit shown is :

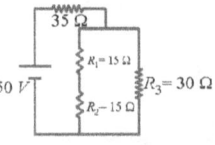

(a) 5
(b) 7.5
(c) 10
(d) 15

46. The length of a wire of a potentiometer is 100 cm, and the emf of its standard cell is ξ volt. It is employed to measure the e.m.f. of a battery whose internal resistance is $0.5\,\Omega$. If the balance point is obtained at $\ell = 30$ cm from the positive end, the emf of the battery is (where i is the current in the potentiometer)

(a) $\frac{30\xi}{100}$
(b) $\frac{30\xi}{100.5}$
(c) $\frac{30\xi}{(100-0.5)}$
(d) $\frac{30(\xi - 0.5i)}{(100)}$

Answer Key	37	(c)	38	(a)	39	(c)	40	(b)	41	(a)
Sol. from page 287	42	(d)	43	(b)	44	(d)	45	(b)	46	(a)

47. In the figure shown, the capacity of the condenser C is $2\mu F$. The current in $2\,\Omega$ resistor is

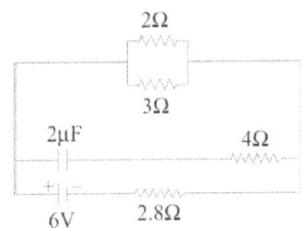

(a) $9\,A$
(b) $0.9\,A$
(c) $\dfrac{1}{9}A$
(d) $\dfrac{1}{0.9}A$

48. In the given circuit, it is observed that the current I is independent of the value of the resistance R_6. Then the resistance values must satisfy

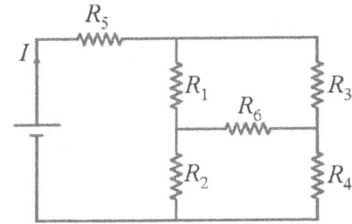

(a) $R_1 R_2 R_5 = R_3 R_4 R_6$
(b) $\dfrac{1}{R_5}+\dfrac{1}{R_6}=\dfrac{1}{R_1+R_2}+\dfrac{1}{R_3+R_4}$
(c) $R_1 R_4 = R_2 R_3$
(d) $R_1 R_3 = R_2 R_4 = R_5 R_6$

49. In the shown arrangement of the experiment of the meter bridge if AC corresponding to null deflection of galvanometer is x, what would be its value if the radius of the wire AB is doubled

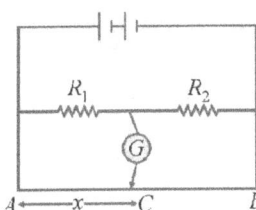

(a) x
(b) $x/4$
(c) $4x$
(d) $2x$

50. Current i as shown in the circuit will be

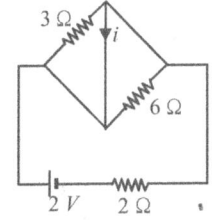

(a) 0.5 A
(b) 1 A
(c) Zero
(d) 0.25 A

51. In the circuit, the values of resistances are such that $\dfrac{R_1}{R_2}=\dfrac{R_3}{R_G}$, where R_G is the internal resistance of the galvanometer. The reading of the galvanometer

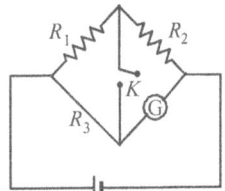

(a) always shows zero value
(b) increases when the switch K is ON
(c) increases when the switch condition is charged from ON to OFF
(d) remains constant whether the switch K is ON or OFF.

52. If $\sigma_1, \sigma_2, \sigma_3$ are the conductances of three conductors, of equal size then their equivalent conductance, when they are joined in series, will be

(a) $\sigma_1+\sigma_2+\sigma_3$
(b) $\dfrac{1}{\sigma_1}+\dfrac{1}{\sigma_2}+\dfrac{1}{\sigma_3}$
(c) $\dfrac{3\sigma_1\sigma_2\sigma_3}{\sigma_1\sigma_2+\sigma_2\sigma_3+\sigma_1\sigma_3}$
(d) none of these

53. In the given diagram the current through the battery and the charge on the capacitor respectively in steady state are

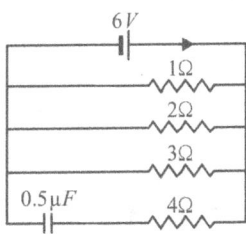

(a) $1\,A$ and $3\,\mu C$
(b) $17\,A$ and $0\,\mu C$
(c) $\dfrac{6}{7}A$ and $\dfrac{12}{7}\mu C$
(d) $11\,A$ and $3\,\mu C$

54. In the circuit shown, the point 'B' is earthed. The potential at the point 'A' is

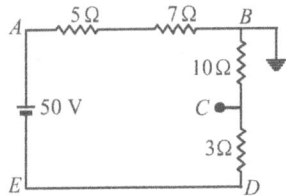

(a) 14 V
(b) 24 V
(c) 26 V
(d) 50 V

Answer Key	47	(b)	48	(c)	49	(a)	50	(b)
Sol. from page 287	51	(d)	52	(c)	53	(d)	54	(b)

264 ELECTRICITY & MAGNETISM

55. The effective resistance across the points A and I is

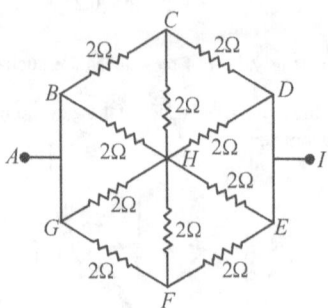

(a) $2\,\Omega$ (b) $1\,\Omega$
(c) $0.5\,\Omega$ (d) $5\,\Omega$

56. Two wires of equal diameters, of resistivities ρ_1 and ρ_2 and lengths l_1 and l_2, respectively, are joined in series. The equivalent resistivity of the combination is

(a) $\dfrac{\rho_1 l_1 + \rho_2 l_2}{l_1 + l_2}$ (b) $\dfrac{\rho_1 l_2 + \rho_2 l_1}{l_1 - l_2}$

(c) $\dfrac{\rho_1 l_2 + \rho_2 l_1}{l_1 + l_2}$ (d) $\dfrac{\rho_1 l_1 + \rho_2 l_2}{l_1 - l_2}$

57. Find the equivalent resistance across AB.

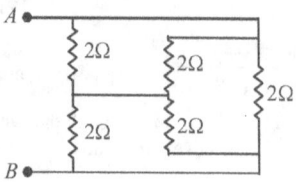

(a) $1\,\Omega$ (b) $2\,\Omega$
(c) $3\,\Omega$ (d) $4\,\Omega$

58. Thirteen resistances each of resistance R ohm are connected in the circuit as shown in the figure below. The effective resistance between A and B is

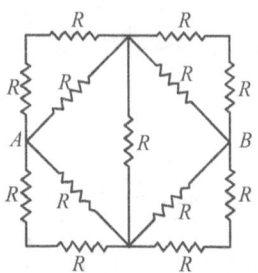

(a) $2R\,\Omega$ (b) $\dfrac{4R}{3}\,\Omega$

(c) $\dfrac{2R}{3}\,\Omega$ (d) $R\,\Omega$

59. See the electrical circuit shown in this figure. Which of the following equations is a correct equation for it?

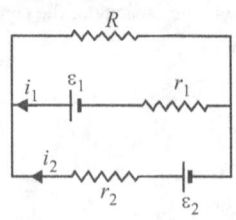

(a) $\varepsilon_1 - (i_1 + i_2)R - i_1 r_1 = 0$ (b) $\varepsilon_2 - i_2 r_2 - \varepsilon_1 - i_1 r_1 = 0$
(c) $-\varepsilon_2 - (i_1 + i_2)R + i_2 r_2 = 0$ (d) $\varepsilon_1 - (i_1 + i_2)R + i_1 r_1 = 0$

60. In the given circuit the current I_1 is

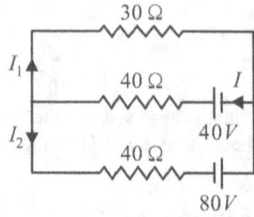

(a) $0.4\,A$ (b) $-0.4\,A$
(c) $0.8\,A$ (d) $-0.8\,A$

61. The batteries, one of emf 18 volt and internal resistance 2Ω and the other of emf 12 volt and internal resistance 1Ω, are connected as shown. The voltmeter V will record a reading of

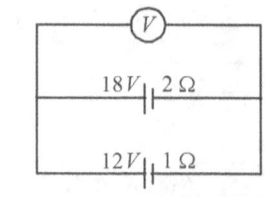

(a) $15\,V$ (b) $30\,V$
(c) $14\,V$ (d) $18\,V$

62. Shown in the figure below is a meter-bridge set up with null deflection in the galvanometer. The value of the unknown resistor R is

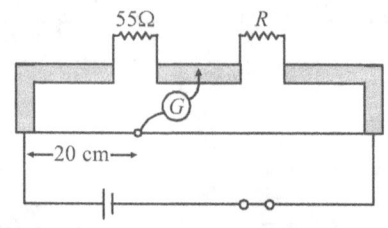

(a) $220\,\Omega$ (b) $110\,\Omega$
(c) $55\,\Omega$ (d) $13.75\,\Omega$

63. The resistance of a galvanometer is $50\,\Omega$ and it shows full scale deflection for a current of 1 mA. To convert it into a voltmeter to measure 1V and as well as 10 V (refer circuit diagram) the resistance R_1 and R_2 respectively are

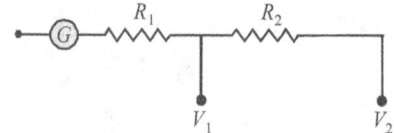

(a) $950\,\Omega$ and $9150\,\Omega$ (b) $900\,\Omega$ and $9950\,\Omega$
(c) $900\,\Omega$ and $9900\,\Omega$ (d) $950\,\Omega$ and $9000\,\Omega$

Answer Key	55	(b)	56	(a)	57	(a)	58	(c)	59	(a)
Sol. from page 287	60	(b)	61	(c)	62	(a)	63	(d)		

DC AND DC CIRCUITS   265

64. A resistance of 4 Ω and a wire of length 5 metres and resistance 5 Ω are joined in series and connected to a cell of e.m.f. 10 V and internal resistance 1 Ω. A parallel combination of two identical cells is balanced across 300 cm of the wire. The e.m.f. E of each cell is

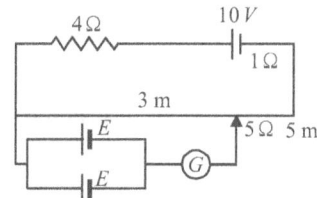

(a) 1.5 V (b) 3.0 V
(c) 0.67 V (d) 1.33 V

65. Two resistance R_1 and R_2 are made of different materials. The temperature coefficient of the material of R_1 is α and of the material of R_2 is −β. The resistance of the series combination of R_1 and R_2 will not change with temperature, if R_1/R_2 equals

(a) $\dfrac{\alpha}{\beta}$
(b) $\dfrac{\alpha+\beta}{\alpha-\beta}$
(c) $\dfrac{\alpha^2+\beta^2}{\alpha\beta}$
(d) $\dfrac{\beta}{\alpha}$

66. A group of N cells whose emf varies directly with the internal resistance as per the equation $E_N = 1.5\, r_N$ are connected as shown in the figure below. The current I in the circuit is

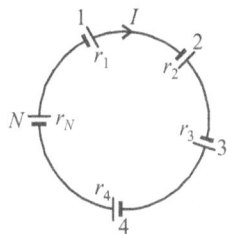

(a) 0.51 A (b) 5.1 A
(c) 0.15 A (d) 1.5 A

Answer Key	64	(b)	65	(d)	66	(d)
Sol. from page 287						

LEVEL - 2

Only one option correct

1. The time constant of the circuit is :

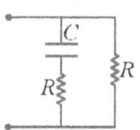

(a) RC/2 (b) RC
(c) 2RC (d) zero

2. The equivalent resistance between A and B is :

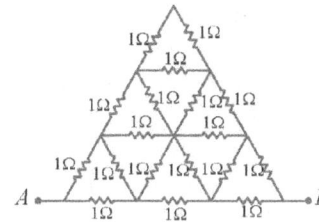

(a) $\dfrac{33}{21}\Omega$ (b) $\dfrac{66}{45}\Omega$
(c) $\dfrac{8}{7}\Omega$ (d) none

3. Consider the following statements regarding the network shown in the figure :

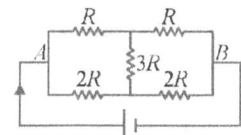

1. The equivalent resistance of the network between points A and B is $\dfrac{4R}{3}$.

2. The current in resistor 3 R is zero.

3. The potential difference across R is equal to the potential difference across 2R.

Which of the above statement (s) is/are correct ?

(a) 1 alone (b) 2 alone
(c) 2 and 3 (d) 1, 2 and 3.

4. What is the effective resistance between the terminals A and B of the mesh shown in figure?

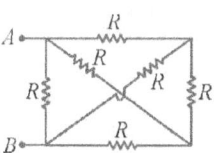

(a) 2R (b) R
(c) R/2 (d) R/3

5. The temperature coefficient of resistance for a wire is 0.00125/°C. At 300K its resistance is 1 ohm. The temperature at which the resistance becomes 2 ohm is

(a) 1154 K (b) 1100 K
(c) 1400 K (d) 1127 K

Answer Key	1	(b)	2	(b)	3	(d)
Sol. from page 290	4	(c)	5	(d)		

266 ELECTRICITY & MAGNETISM

6. In the adjoining circuit, the battery ξ_1 has an e.m.f. of 12 volt and zero internal resistance while the battery ξ has an e.m.f. of 2 volt. If the galvanometer G reads zero, then the value of the resistance X in ohm is

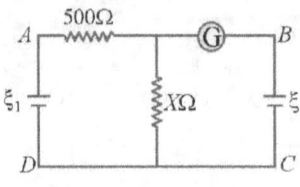

(a) 10 (b) 100
(c) 500 (d) 200

7. Two sources of equal emf are connected to an external resistance R. The internal resistances of the two sources are R_1 and $R_2 (R_2 > R_1)$. If the potential difference across the source having internal resistance R_2 is zero, then

(a) $R = R_1 R_2 / (R_1 + R_2)$

(b) $R = R_1 R_2 / (R_2 - R_1)$

(c) $R = R_2 \times (R_1 + R_2)/(R_2 - R_1)$

(d) $R = R_2 - R_1$

8. In the given figure, battery ξ is balanced on 55 cm length of potentiometer wire but when a resistance of 10 Ω is connected in parallel with the battery then it balances on 50 cm length of the potentiometer wire then internal resistance r of the battery is

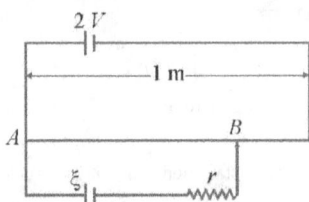

(a) 1 Ω (b) 3 Ω
(c) 10 Ω (d) 5 Ω

9. A voltmeter has a range $0 - V$ with a series resistance R. With a series resistance $2R$, the range is $0 - V'$. The correct relation between V and V' is

(a) $V' = 2V$ (b) $V' > 2V$
(c) $V' \gg 2V$ (d) $V' < 2V$

10. A microammeter has a resistance of 100 Ω and full scale range of 50 μA. It can be used as a voltmeter or as a higher range ammeter provided a resistance is added to it. Pick the correct range and resistance combination

(a) 50 V range with 10 kΩ resistance in series
(b) 10 V range with 200 kΩ resistance in series
(c) 10 mA range with 1 Ω resistance in parallel
(d) 10 mA range with 0.1 Ω resistance in parallel

11. In the given circuit, with steady current, the potential drop across the capacitor must be

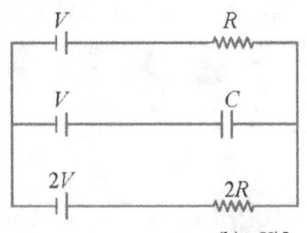

(a) V (b) $V/2$
(c) $V/3$ (d) $2V/3$

12. A wire of length L and 3 identical cells of negligible internal resistances are connected in series. Due to current, the temperature of the wire is raised by ΔT in a time t. A number N of similar cells is now connected in series with a wire of the same material and cross-section but of length $2L$. The temperature of the wire is raised by the same amount ΔT in the same time t. the value of N is

(a) 4 (b) 6
(c) 8 (d) 9

13. The effective resistance between points P and Q of the electrical circuit shown in the figure is

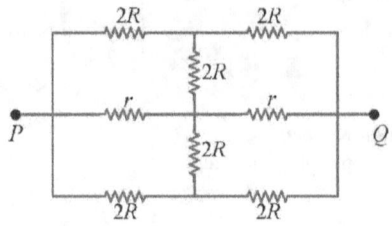

(a) $2Rr/(R+r)$ (b) $8R(R+r)/(3R+r)$
(c) $2r + 4R$ (d) $5R/2 + 2r$

14. The two ends of a uniform conductor are joined to a cell of e.m.f. ξ and some internal resistance. Starting from the midpoint P of the conductor, we move in the direction of current and return to P. The potential V at every point on the path is plotted against the distance covered (x). Which of the following graphs best represents the resulting curve?

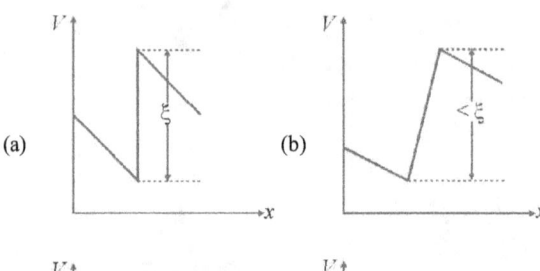

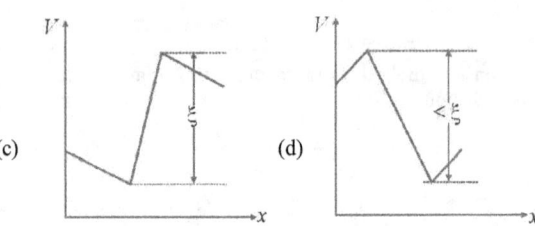

Answer Key	6	(b)	7	(d)	8	(a)	9	(d)	10	(b)
Sol. from page 290	11	(c)	12	(b)	13	(a)	14	(b)		

15. A voltmeter connected to the terminals of a battery reads 6 V. When the lamps are lighted with the battery, the voltmeter reads 4 V. If the resistance of the lamps is 10 Ω, the internal resistance of the battery is :
(a) 0.5 Ω (b) 10 Ω
(c) 3 Ω   (d) 5 Ω

16. Three batteries of negligible internal resistance and three resistors of 4, 8 and 12 Ω are connected as shown in figure here. The current through the 12 Ω resistor is :

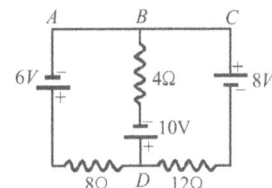

(a) 0.57 A   (b) 1.09 A
(c) 0.04 A   (d) 1.14 A

17. In the given circuit I_a, V_a and the power supplied by the 15 V battery respectively are :

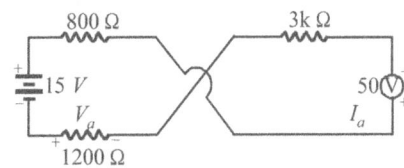

(a) 7 mA, 8.4 V and 58.8 mW
(b) 0.01 mA, 2 V and 0.02 mW
(c) 7 mA, 8.4 V and 105 mW
(d) 0.01 mA, 8.4 V and 105 mW

18. In the given network of four resistances, the equivalent resistance is :

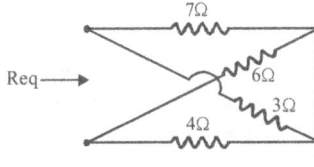

(a) 20 Ω   (b) 5.4 Ω
(c) 12 Ω   (d) 4.5 Ω

19. In the part of a circuit shown in the figure, the potential difference between G and H $(V_G - V_H)$ will be :

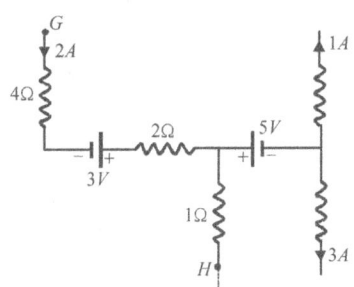

(a) 0 V   (b) 15 V
(c) 7 V   (d) 3 V

20. What is the resistance between P and Q of the following circuit ? Each resistance is of 1 Ω :

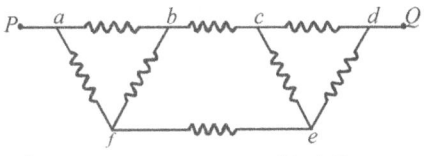

(a) 1 Ω   (b) 2 Ω
(c) 3 Ω   (d) $\frac{3}{2}$ Ω

21. Point a in figure is maintained at a constant potential of 300 V above ground. The reading of a voltmeter of the proper range, and of resistance 3×10^4 Ω, when connected between point b and ground is nearly :
(a) 10 V
(b) 42 V
(c) 50 V
(d) 62 V

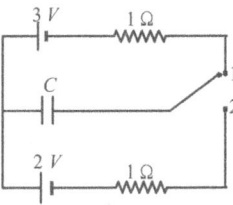

22. If energy stored in the capacitors C_1 and C_2 are same, then what is the value of $\frac{C_1}{C_2}$?

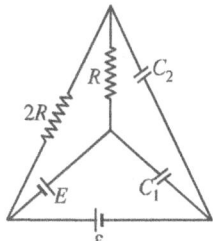

(a) $\frac{25}{36}$ (b) $\frac{1}{36}$
(c) $\frac{4}{9}$ (d) $\frac{9}{4}$

23. The key K is connected in turn to each of the contacts over short identical time intervals so that change in charge on the capacitor over each connection is small. The final charge q_0 on the capacitor is

(a) 2.5 C   (b) 8 C
(c) 5 C   (d) $\frac{C}{2}$

Answer Key	15	(d)	16	(d)	17	(c)	18	(d)	19	(c)
Sol. from page 290	20	(d)	21	(d)	22	(a)	23	(a)		

268 ELECTRICITY & MAGNETISM

24. In the given mesh, each resistor has resistance R. The effective resistance between the terminals A and B is

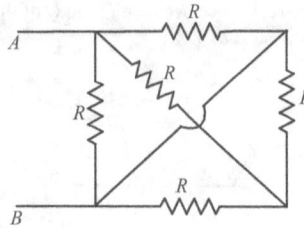

(a) $\dfrac{3R}{8}$ (b) $\dfrac{R}{2}$
(c) R (d) $2R$

25. The total current drawn from the battery is:

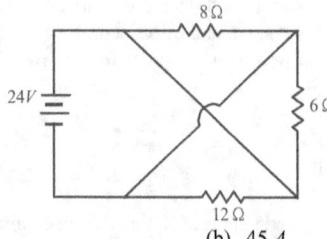

(a) $3 A$ (b) $45 A$
(c) $6 A$ (d) $9 A$

26. Plates of a parallel plate capacitor C have charges CV and $3CV$ on its plates. If switch is closed at $t = 0$. Then initial rate at which heat energy is produced in resistance R is

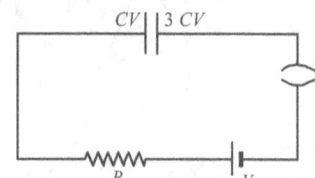

(a) $\dfrac{V^2}{R}$ (b) $\dfrac{4V^2}{R}$
(c) $\dfrac{9V^2}{R}$ (d) $\dfrac{16V^2}{R}$

27. A battery of emf $E_0 = 6$ V is connected across a 2 m long uniform wire having resistance $4\Omega/m$. The cells of small emf $\varepsilon_1 = 2$ V and $\varepsilon_2 = 3$ V having internal resistance $2\ \Omega$ & $1\ \Omega$ respectively are connected as shown in the figure. The null point will be obtained at

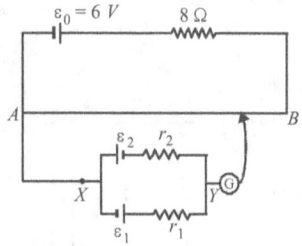

(a) $\dfrac{1}{5\,m}$ (b) $0.25\,m$
(c) $0.50\,m$ (d) none of these

28. Potential of certain points in circuit are maintained as marked. What is reading of voltmeter (If ammeter reads zero)?

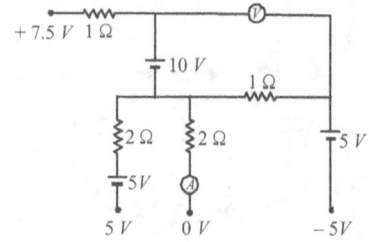

(a) $10\,V$ (b) $2.5\,V$
(c) $5\,V$ (d) $20\,V$

29. The terminal network shown in the figure consists of 6 resistors. The points A, C and E all are at potential 20 V while points B, D and F are at potential -10 volt then potential of junction O will

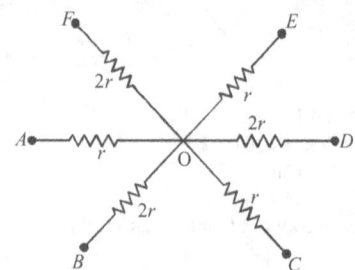

(a) zero   (b) $10\,V$
(c) $15\,V$ (d) $-5\,V$

30. All wires have same resistance and equivalent resistance between A and B is R_0. Now keys are closed, then the equivalent resistance will become

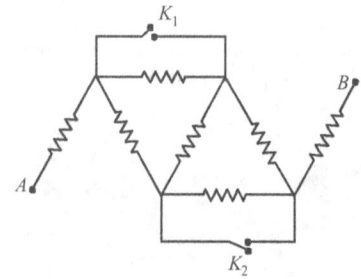

(a) $\dfrac{7R_0}{3}$ (b) $\dfrac{7R_0}{9}$
(c) $7R_0$ (d) $\dfrac{R_0}{3}$

Answer Key	24	(a)	25	(d)	26	(c)	27	(d)
Sol. from page 290	28	(a)	29	(b)	30	(b)		

31. Find equivalent resistance between A & B in the following circuit

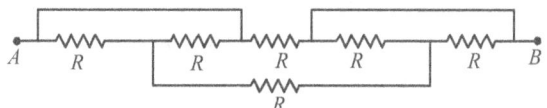

(a) $\dfrac{3R}{2}$ (b) $\dfrac{2R}{3}$
(c) $2R$ (d) $3R$

32. Two wires are of same length and same area of cross-section. If first wire has resistivity ρ_1 and temperature coefficient of resistance α_1 but second wire has resistivity ρ_2 and temperature coefficient of resistance α_2. Their series equivalent resistance is independent of small temperature changes. Then
(a) $\alpha_1 + \alpha_2 = 0$ (b) $\rho_1 \alpha_1 = \rho_2 \alpha_2$
(c) $\rho_1 \alpha_1 + \rho_2 \alpha_2 = 0$ (d) $\rho_1 \alpha_2 + \rho_2 \alpha_1 = 0$

33. A metal wire has coefficient of linear expression α_1 and temperature coefficient of resistivity α_2. Apparent temperature coefficient of resistance will be
(a) α_2 (b) $\alpha_2 - \alpha_1$
(c) $\alpha_2 + \alpha_1$ (d) $\alpha_2 - 2\alpha_1$

34. In the circuit shown the ammeter A reads a current of i_1 amp. If key K_1 is opened and K_2 is closed ammeter reads i_2, then

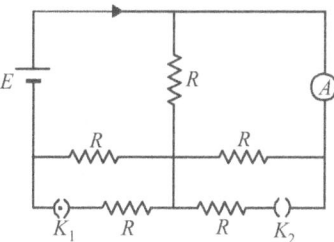

(a) $i_1 > i_2$ (b) $i_1 < i_2$
(c) $i_1 = i_2$ (d) depend on the value of R

35. A capacitor is initially connected to a battery of emf $3V$. At $t = 0$, switch is thrown to B state. Now charge on capacitor at any instant is given by

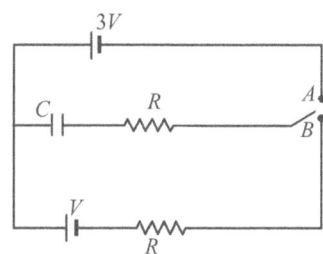

(a) $q = C\left(V + 2V\, e^{\frac{-t}{RC}}\right)$ (b) $q = C\left(V - 2V\, e^{\frac{-t}{RC}}\right)$
(c) $q = C\left(V - 2V\, e^{\frac{-t}{2CR}}\right)$ (d) $q = C\left(V + 2V\, e^{\frac{-2t}{RC}}\right)$

36. In following circuit, key is closed at time $t = 0$, then what will be current through battery at that time?

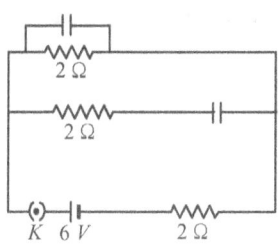

(a) $3A$ (b) $1.5\,A$
(c) $2A$ (d) $6A$

37. A capacitor is charged up to V volts. The space between two plates of capacitor is filled with dielectric medium of constant K and conductivity σ. The time after which charge on capacitor becomes $\dfrac{1}{e}$ times its initial charge is

(a) $\dfrac{K\varepsilon_0}{\sigma}$ (b) $\dfrac{\varepsilon_0}{K\sigma}$
(c) $\dfrac{2k\sigma}{\sigma}$ (d) $\dfrac{k\varepsilon_0 A}{\sigma d^2}$

38. An ammeter and a voltmeter are connected in series to a battery. When a certain resistance is connected in parallel to voltmeter reading of voltmeter becomes half while reading of ammeter becomes double. What is the ratio of voltmeter resistance and ammeter resistance?

(a) $\dfrac{1}{3}$ (b) $\dfrac{3}{2}$
(c) $\dfrac{2}{1}$ (d) $\dfrac{3}{1}$

39. In the shown network charges in capacitors are same, then $\dfrac{C_1}{C_2}$ is

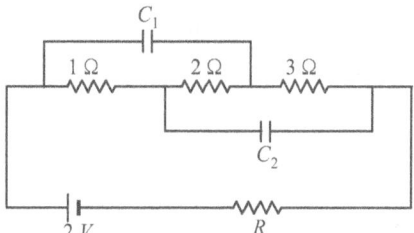

(a) $\dfrac{5}{3}$ (b) $1:1$
(c) $1:3$ (d) $1:5$

Answer Key	31	(b)	32	(c)	33	(b)	34	(c)	35	(c)
Sol. from page 290	36	(a)	37	(a)	38	(c)	39	(a)		

270 ELECTRICITY & MAGNETISM

40. What is potential difference between A and B?

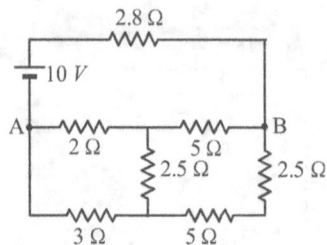

(a) 8.4 V (b) 2.4 V
(c) 4.2 V (d) 7.2 V

41. In following circuit, resistance of potentiometer wire is 10Ω. Power consumption in potentiometer wire is same when jocky is placed at 10 cm from end A or end B. Internal resistance of cell(r) is

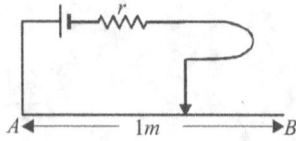

(a) 5 Ω (b) 6 Ω
(c) 2 Ω (d) 3 Ω

42. The effective resistance between the terminals A and B is.

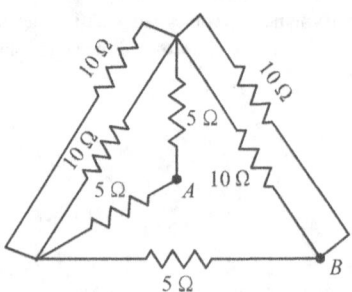

(a) 5 Ω (b) 10 Ω
(c) 15 Ω (d) 20 Ω

43. The reading of ammeters A_1 and A_2 for the circuit shown

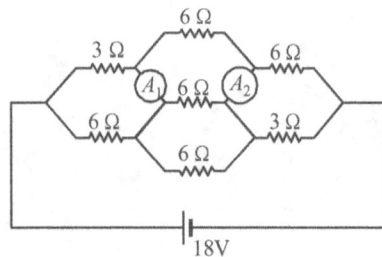

(a) 1 A, 1A (b) 1 A, zero
(c) zero, 1A (d) zero, zero

44. The equivalent resistance of the circuit between A and B is:

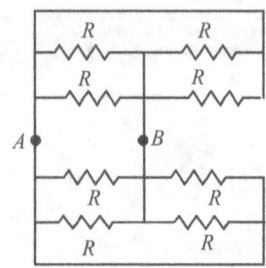

(a) $\frac{R}{8}$ (b) $\frac{R}{4}$
(c) 2 R (d) 4 R

45. If equivalent resistance between points A and X is 5Ω and equivalent resistance between A and B is 10Ω then R_2 is

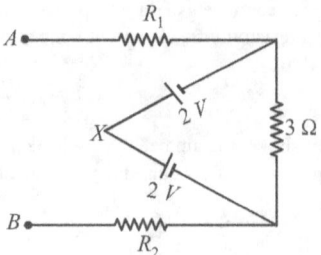

(a) 2 Ω (b) 5 Ω
(c) 3 Ω (d) 10 Ω

46. The current in 2 Ω resistor in the circuit shown is:

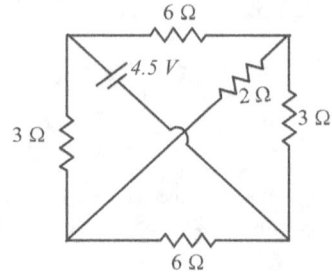

(a) $\frac{1}{4} A$ (b) $\frac{1}{2} A$
(c) $\frac{3}{4} A$ (d) 2 A

47. The resistance between points A and B in the network shown in figure is:

(a) 2.46 Ω

(b) 4.23 Ω

(c) 5.13 Ω

(d) none of these

Answer Key	40	(a)	41	(d)	42	(a)	43	(b)
Sol. from page 290	44	(a)	45	(b)	46	(a)	47	(d)

48. A wire has linear resistance ρ (in Ohm/m). Find the resistance R between points A and B if the side of the larger square is d.
   (a) $\rho d/\sqrt{2}$
   (b) $\sqrt{2}\rho d$
   (c) $2\rho d$
   (d) none of these

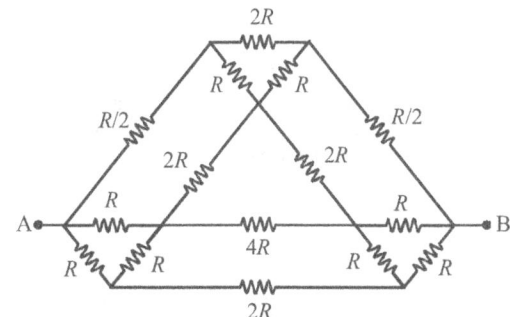

49. For the shown circuit the effective resistance between the points A and B will be

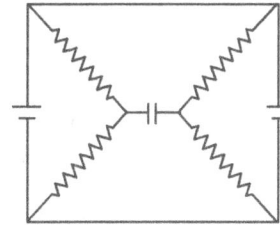

   (a) 2R (b) 4R
   (c) R   (d) R/2

50. What is the voltage across resistor A in the following circuit? Each resistor has a resistance of 2 MΩ and the capacitors have capacitances of 1 μF. The battery voltage is 3V.

   (a) 0 V   (b) 0.5 V
   (c) 0.75 V (d) 1.5 V

51. There is an infinite wire grid with cells in the form of equilateral triangles. The resistance of each wire between neighbouring joint connections is r. The equivalent resistance of a whole grid between the points A and B as shown in figure is:
   (a) $\dfrac{r}{3}$
   (b) $\dfrac{r}{2}$
   (c) $\dfrac{r}{4}$
   (d) r

52. To verify Ohm's law, a student is provided with a test resistor R_T, a high resistance R_1, a small resistance R_2, two identical galvanometers G_1 and G_2, and a variable voltage source V. The correct circuit to carry out the experiment is

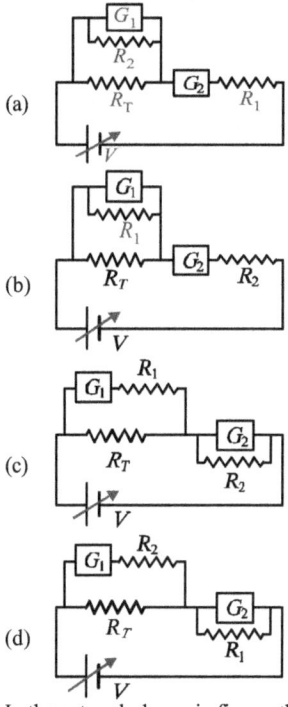

53. In the network shown in figure, the equivalent resistance between the point A and B is :
   (a) 3 Ω
   (b) 2 Ω
   (c) 4 Ω
   (d) 1 Ω

54. A meter bridge is set up as shown, to determine an unknown resistance X using a standard 10 ohm resistor. The galvanometer shows null point when tapping-key is at 52 cm mark. The end-corrections are 1 cm and 2 cm respectively for the ends A and B. The determined value of X is
   (a) 10.2 ohm
   (b) 10.6 ohm
   (c) 10.8 ohm
   (d) 11.1 ohm

Answer Key

| 48 | (a) | 49 | (c) | 50 | (d) | 51 | (a) |
| 52 | (c) | 53 | (d) | 54 | (b) | | |

ELECTRICITY — MCQ Type 2 — Exercise 3.2

Multiple correct options

1. When no current is passed through a conductor:
   (a) the free electrons do not move
   (b) the average speed of a free electron over a large period of time is zero
   (c) the average velocity of a free electron over a large period of time is zero
   (d) the average of the velocities of all the free electrons at an instant is zero.

2. A battery of emf $E_0 = 5V$ and internal resistance 5Ω is connected across a long uniform AB of length 1 m and resistance per unit length $5\,\Omega\,\text{m}^{-1}$. Two cells of $E_1 = 1\,V$ and $E_2 = 2\,V$ are connected as shown in the figure. :

   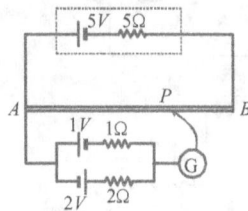

   (a) The null point is at A
   (b) If jockey is touched to point B the current in the galvanometer will be going towards B
   (c) When jockey is connected to point A no current is flowing through 1 V battery.
   (d) The null point is at distance of 8/15 m from A

3. In the circuit shown, the current in

   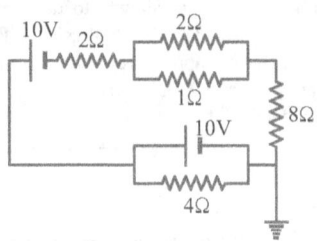

   (a) $4\,\Omega$ resistance is 2.5 A
   (b) $4\,\Omega$ resistance is 0 A
   (c) $8\,\Omega$ resistance is 2.5 A
   (d) $8\,\Omega$ resistance is 0 A

4. Five resistors are connected as shown in the figure. Then :

   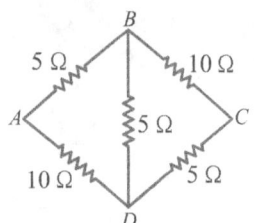

   (a) Equivalent resistance between A and C is $\dfrac{15}{2}\Omega$
   (b) Equivalent resistance between A and C is $7\,\Omega$.
   (c) Equivalent resistance between B and D is $3\,\Omega$.
   (d) Equivalent resistance between B and C is $3\,\Omega$.

5. The resistance of the galvanometer G in the circuit's $25\,\Omega$. The meter deflects full scale for a current of 10 mA. The meter behaves as an ammeter of three different ranges. The range 0–10 A, if the terminals O and P are taken; range 0–1A between O and Q; range is 0–0.1 A between O and R, then :

   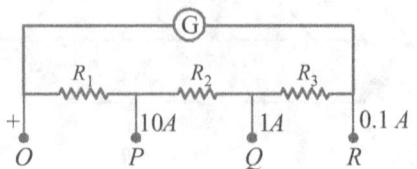

   (a) $R_1 = 0.25\,\Omega$
   (b) $R_2 = 0.25\,\Omega$
   (c) $R_3 = 2.5\,\Omega$
   (d) $R_1 = R_2 + R_3$

6. AB is a part of another large circuit. Also $V_Q - V_B = 12\,V$. Then :

   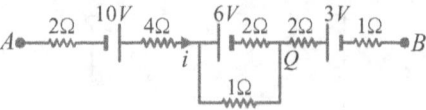

   (a) current, $i = 3\,A$
   (b) current, $i = 5\,A$
   (c) $V_A - V_B = 12\,V$
   (d) $V_A - V_B = 24\,V$

7. In the circuit shown;

   (a) $i_1 = 2\,A$
   (b) $i_2 = 9\,A$
   (c) $i_3 = 5\,A$
   (d) $i = 11\,A$

8. A battery of unknown *emf* is connected across resistances as shown in figure. The voltage drop across $8\,\Omega$ resistor is $20\,V$. Then :

   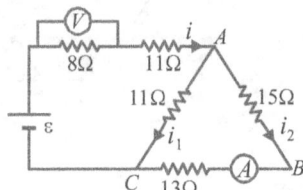

   (a) The reading of ammeter is $2.5\,A$.
   (b) The reading of ammeter is $0.7\,A$.
   (c) The *emf* of the battery is $48\,V$.
   (d) The *emf* of the battery is $67.3\,V$.

Answer Key (Sol. from page 296)

1	(c, d)	2	(a, b)	3	(a, d)	4	(b, c)
5	(b, c)	6	(a, d)	7	(b, d)	8	(b, d)

ELECTRICITY — Statement Questions — Exercise 3.3

DC AND DC CIRCUITS

Read the two statements carefully to mark the correct option out of the options given below:
(a) If both the statements are true and the *statement - 2* is the correct explanation of *statement - 1*.
(b) If both the statements are true but *statement - 2* is not the correct explanation of the *statement - 1*.
(c) If *statement - 1* true but *statement - 2* is false.
(d) If *statement - 1* is false but *statement - 2* is true.

1. **Statement - 1**
   There is no current in the metals in the absence of electric field.
   Statement - 2
   Motion of free electrons are random.

2. **Statement - 1**
   A stream of positively charged particle produces an electric field E at a centrain distance from it.
   Statement - 2
   A current currying conductor produces an electric field 2E at the same distance.

3. **Statement - 1**
   The electric bulb glows immediately when switch is on.
   Statement - 2
   The drift velocity of electrons in a metallic wire is very high.

4. **Statement - 1**
   The connecting wires are made of copper.
   Statement - 2
   The electrical conductivity of copper is high.

5. **Statement - 1**
   Electric field outside the conducting wire which carries a constant current is zero.
   Statement - 2
   Net charge on conducting wire is zero.

6. **Statement - 1**
   Kirchoff's junction rule follows from conservation of charge.
   Statement - 2
   Kirchoff's loop rule follows from conservation of momentum.

7. **Statement - 1**
   Two non-ideal batteries are connected in series. The equivalent emf is larger than either of the two.
   Statement - 2
   The equivalent emf of the batteries will be average of the two.

8. **Statement - 1**
   Two non ideal batteries are connected in parallel. The equivalent emf is smaller than either of the two emfs.
   Statement - 2
   The equivalent internal resistance is smaller than either of the two internal resistances.

9. **Statement - 1**
   The resistivity of a semiconductor increases with temperature.
   Statement - 2
   The atoms of a semiconductor vibrate with smaller amplitude at higher temperature.

10. **Statement - 1**
    In the following circuit emf is $2V$ and internal resistance of the cell is 1Ω and $R = 1\Omega$, then reading of the voltmeter is $1V$.
    Statement - 2

    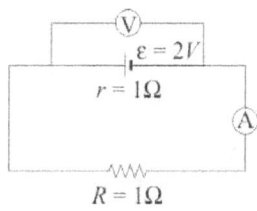

    $V = \xi - ir$ where $\xi = 2V, i = \dfrac{2}{2} = 1A$ and $R = 1\Omega$.

11. **Statement - 1**
    Drift speed v_d is the average speed between two successive collisions.
    Statement - 2
    If $\Delta \ell$ is the average distance moved between two collision and Δt is the corresponding time, then $v_d = \lim\limits_{\Delta t \to 0} \dfrac{\Delta \ell}{\Delta t}$.

12. **Statement - 1**
    When a current is established in a wire, the free electrons drift in the direction opposite to the current and so the number of free electrons in the wire continuously decrease.
    Statement - 2
    Charge is a conserved quantity.

13. **Statement - 1**
    A moving coil ammeter can not measure AC.
    Statement - 2
    AC does not show thermal effect.

Answer Key (Sol. from page 297)

1	2	3	4	5	6	7
(a)	(c)	(c)	(a)	(a)	(c)	(c)

8	9	10	11	12	13
(d)	(d)	(a)	(c)	(d)	(c)

274 ELECTRICITY & MAGNETISM

14. *Statement - 1*
In the figure the resistors are in parallel because they are along parallel lines.
Statement - 2
The resistors are in series because current is not divided between then.

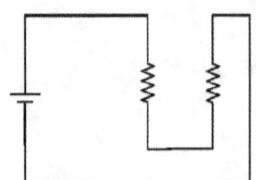

15. *Statement - 1*
In a meter bridge experiment, null point for an unknown resistance is measured. Now, the unknown resistance is put inside an enclosure maintained at a higher temperature. The null point can be obtained at the same point as before by decreasing the value of the standard resistance.
Statement - 2
Resistance of a metal increases with increase in temperature.

Answer Key | 14 | (d) | 15 | (d)
Sol. from page 297

ELECTRICITY — Passage & Matrix — Exercise 3.4

PASSAGES

Passage for Q.1 to Q.3
Two large parallel plates are located in vacuum. One of them serves as a cathode, a source of electrons whose initial velocity is negligible. An electron flow directed toward the opposite plate produces a space charge causing the potential in the gap between the plates to vary as $V = a x^{4/3}$, where a is a positive constant, and x is the distance from the cathode.

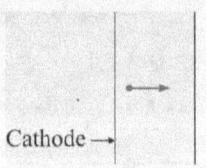

Cathode →

1. The electric field between the plate at a function of x is :
(a) $E = a x^{1/3}$
(b) $E = -a x^{2/3}$
(c) $E = -\dfrac{4a}{3} x^{1/3}$
(d) none of these

2. The volume density of space charge as a functions of x
(a) $a \epsilon_0 x^{1/3}$
(b) $\dfrac{4}{9} a x^{1/3}$
(c) $-\dfrac{4}{9} a \epsilon_0 x^{2/3}$
(d) $\dfrac{4}{9} a \epsilon_0 x^{4/3}$

3. The current density
(a) $-\dfrac{2}{3} \epsilon_0 a^{3/2} \sqrt{\dfrac{2e}{m}}$
(b) $-\dfrac{4}{9} \epsilon_0 a^{3/2} \sqrt{\dfrac{2e}{m}}$
(c) $-\dfrac{2}{3} \epsilon_0 a^{3/2} \sqrt{\dfrac{e}{m}}$
(d) none of these

Passage for Q. 4 to Q.6
The gap between the plates of a parallel plate capacitor is filled up with two dielectric layers 1 and 2 with thicknesses d_1 and d_2, permittivities ϵ_1 and ϵ_2, and resistivities ρ_1 and ρ_2. A DC voltage V is applied to the capacitor, with electric field directed from layer 1 to layer 2.

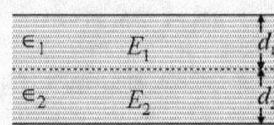

4. The electric field E_1 in dielectric layer 1 is :
(a) $E_1 = \dfrac{V}{d_1}$
(b) $E_1 = \dfrac{d_1 V}{(d_1 + d_2)}$
(c) $E_1 = \dfrac{\rho_1 V}{\rho_1 d_1 + \rho_2 d_2}$
(d) $E_1 = \dfrac{\rho_1 V}{d_1 \rho_2}$

Answer Key | 1 | (c) | 2 | (c) | 3 | (b)
Sol. from page 297 | 4 | (c)

DC AND DC CIRCUITS

5. The electric field E_2 in dielectric layer 2 is :
   (a) $E_2 = \dfrac{V}{d_2}$
   (b) $E_2 = \dfrac{d_2 V}{(d_1 + d_2)}$
   (c) $E_2 = \dfrac{\rho_2}{\rho_1} \dfrac{V}{d_2}$
   (d) $E_2 = \dfrac{\rho_2 V}{\rho_1 d_1 + \rho_2 d_2}$

6. The surface density of extraneous charge at the boundary between the dielectric layers to be zero, the condition is :
   (a) $\epsilon_1 \rho_1 = \epsilon_2 \rho_2$
   (b) $\epsilon_1 \rho_2 = \epsilon_2 \rho_1$
   (c) $\epsilon_1 = \epsilon_2$
   (d) $\epsilon_1 = \dfrac{\rho_1 \epsilon_2}{\rho_1 + \rho_2}$

Passage for Q. 7 to Q. 9
A capacitor C is uncharged and capacitor C_0 has a charge Q_0. These are connected in series with a source of emf ξ in the circuit shown in figure. The switch S is closed at $t = 0$.

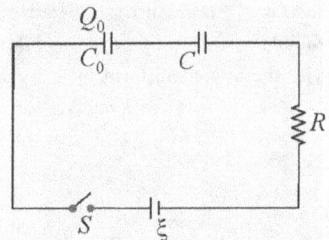

7. If i_0 is the current in resistor R at $t = 0$, then
   (a) $i_0 = \dfrac{\xi}{R}$
   (b) $i_0 = \dfrac{\left(\xi - \dfrac{Q_0}{C}\right)}{R}$
   (c) $i_0 = \dfrac{\left(\xi - \dfrac{Q_0}{C_0}\right)}{R}$
   (d) zero

8. If i is the instantaneous current, then
   (a) $i\left[\dfrac{1}{C} + \dfrac{1}{C_0}\right] + R\dfrac{di}{dt} = 0$
   (b) $i\dfrac{(C + C_0)}{C} + iR = 0$
   (c) $i\left[\dfrac{1}{C} + \dfrac{1}{C_0}\right] - \dfrac{Ri}{2} = 0$
   (d) none of these

9. The instantaneous current i in the resistor R is :
   (a) $i = i_0 e^{-\dfrac{t}{RC}}$
   (b) $i = i_0 e^{-\dfrac{t}{RC_0}}$
   (c) $i = i_0 e^{\dfrac{-t}{R(C+C_0)}}$
   (d) $i = i_0 e^{-\left[\dfrac{t(C+C_0)}{RCC_0}\right]}$

Passage for Q. 10 to Q. 12
In the circuit shown in figure E, F, G and H are cells of emf 2, 1, 3 and 1 volt and their internal resistances are 2, 1, 3 and 1 ohm respectively.

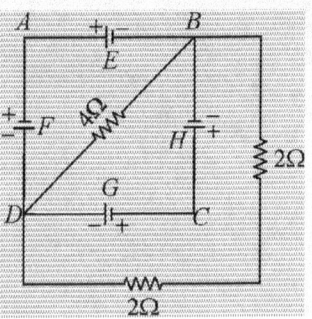

10. If i is the current in the $2\,\Omega$ resistor, then
    (a) $i = \dfrac{5}{13} A$
    (b) $i = \dfrac{6}{13} A$
    (c) $i = \dfrac{1}{13} A$
    (d) $i = \dfrac{1}{26} A$

11. The potential difference across $4\,\Omega$ resistor is :
    (a) $\dfrac{1}{13}V$
    (b) $\dfrac{2}{13}V$
    (c) $\dfrac{5}{13}V$
    (d) $\dfrac{3}{26}V$

12. The potential difference across the cell G is :
    (a) 1.61 V
    (b) 1.46 V
    (c) 1.02 V
    (d) zero.

Paragraph for question Q. 13 & Q. 14
Electrical resistance of certain materials, known as superconductors, changes abruptly from a nonzero value to zero as their temperature is lowered below a critical temperature $T_C(0)$. An interesting property of superconductors is that their critical temperature becomes smaller than $T_C(0)$ if they are placed in a magnetic field, i.e., the critical temperature $T_C(B)$ is a function of the magnetic field strength B. The dependence of $T_C(B)$ on B is shown in the figure.

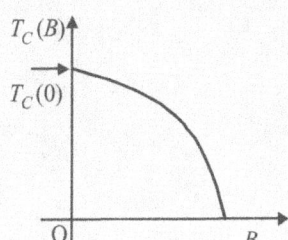

Answer Key	5	(d)	6	(s)	7	(c)	8	(a)
Sol. from page 297	9	(d)	10	(d)	11	(b)	12	(a)

13. In the graphs below, the resistance R of a superconductor is shown as a function of its temperature T for two different magnetic fields B_1 (solid line) and B_2 (dashed line). If B_2 is larger than B_1 which of the following graphs shows the correct variation of R with T in these fields?

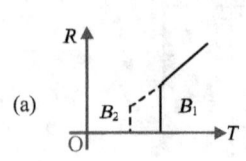
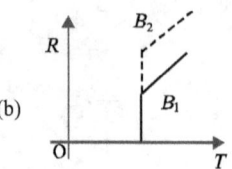

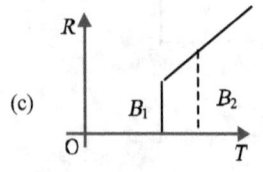
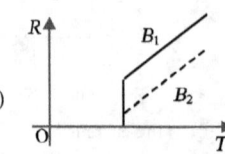

14. A superconductor has $T_C(0) = 100$ K. When a magnetic field of 7.5 Tesla is applied, its T_C decreases to 75 K. For this material one can definitely say that when
   (a) $B = 5$ Tesla, $T_C(B) = 80$ K
   (b) $B = 5$ Tesla, 75 K $< T_C(B) < 100$ K
   (c) $B = 10$ Tesla, 75K $< T_C(B) < 100$ K
   (d) $B = 10$ Tesla, $T_C(B) = 70$K

Paragraph for question Q. 15 & Q. 16
Consider a block of conducting material of resistivity ρ shown in the figure. Current I enters at A and leaves from D. We apply superposition principle to find voltage ΔV developed between B and C. The calculation is done in the following steps:
(i) Take current I entering from A and assume it to spread over a hemispherical surface in the block.
(ii) Calculate field $E(r)$ at distance r from A by using Ohm's law $E = \rho j$, where j is the current per unit area at r.
(iii) From the r dependence of $E(r)$, obtain the potential $V(r)$ at r.
(iv) Repeat (i), (ii) and (iii) for current I leaving D and superpose results for A and D.

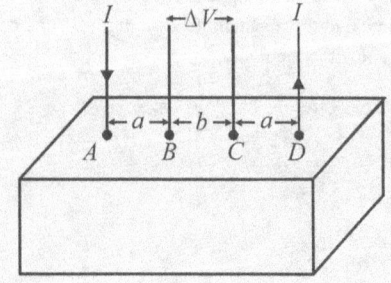

15. ΔV measured between B and C is
   (a) $\dfrac{\rho I}{\pi a} - \dfrac{\rho I}{\pi(a+b)}$
   (b) $\dfrac{\rho I}{a} - \dfrac{\rho I}{(a+b)}$
   (c) $\dfrac{\rho I}{2\pi a} - \dfrac{\rho I}{2\pi(a+b)}$
   (d) $\dfrac{\rho I}{2\pi(a-b)}$

16. For current entering at A, the electric field at a distance 'r' from A is
   (a) $\dfrac{\rho I}{8\pi r^2}$
   (b) $\dfrac{\rho I}{r^2}$
   (c) $\dfrac{\rho I}{2\pi r^2}$
   (d) $\dfrac{\rho I}{4\pi r^2}$

Passage for Q. 17 to Q. 19
In the circuit shown AB is a 10 Ω uniform slide wire 50 cm long. ε_1 is 2 V accumulator of negligible internal resistance. R_1 and R_2 are 15 Ω and 5 Ω respectively. When K_1 and K_2 are both open, the galvanometer shows no deflection when $AJ = 31.25$ cm when K_1 and K_2 are both closed the balance length $AJ = 5$ cm.

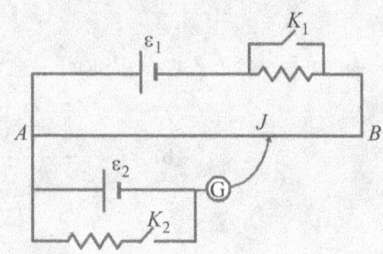

17. The emf of the cell ε_2 is
   (a) 0.5 V (b) 1 V
   (c) 1.5 V (d) 2 V

18. The internal resistance of the cell ε_2.
   (a) 7.5 Ω (b) 8 Ω
   (c) 10 Ω (d) 2 Ω

19. The balance length AJ when K_2 is open and K_1 is closed
   (a) 12.5 cm (b) 13.5 cm
   (c) 14.5 cm (d) 15.5 cm

Answer Key Sol. from page 297	13	(a)	14	(b)	15	(a)	16	(c)
	17	(a)	18	(a)	19	(a)		

MATRIX MATCHING

20. Column I gives certain situations in which a straight metallic wire of resistance R is used and Column II gives some resulting effects.

Column I
A. A charged capacitor is connected to the ends of the wire
B. The wire is moved perpendicular to its length with a constant velocity in a uniform magnetic field perpendicular to the plane of motion
C. The wire is placed in a constant electric field that has a direction along the length of the wire
D. A battery of constant emf is connected to the the ends of the wire

Column II
(p) A constant current flows through the wire
(q) Thermal energy is generated in the wire
(r) A constant potential difference develops between the ends of the wire
(s) charges of constant magnitude appear at ends of the wire.

21. A galvanometer of resistance 99Ω is converted into an ammeter using a shunt of 1Ω and connected as shown in figure. The ammeter reads 3A. The same galvanometer is converted into a voltmeter by connecting a resistance of 101Ω in series. If reading is fond to be 4/5 of the full scale reading.

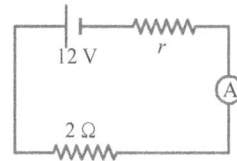
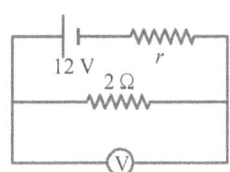

Column I
A. Internal resistance of the cell (r) in ohm is
B. Range of ammeter in ampere is
C. Range of voltmeter in volts is
D. Full scale deflection current of the galvanometer is

Column II
(p) 10
(q) 0.05
(r) 1.01
(s) 5
(t) 11.1

22. Consider a network of resistances each of value of R as shown in figure.

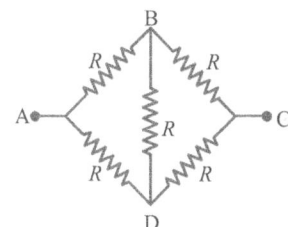

Column I
A. Equivalent of net work between A and C is
B. Equivalent resistance between A an B
C. Potential of B and D when voltage source is applied across A and C is
D. Potential of B and D when voltage source is applied across A and B is

Column II
(p) same
(q) 5/8 R
(r) R
(s) 2 R
(t) different

Answer Key Sol. from page 297	20	A-q ; B-r ; C-s ; D-p, q, r	21	A-r ; B- q ; C - p ; D -q
	22	A-r ; B -(q) ; C - (p) ; D-(t)		

278 ELECTRICITY & MAGNETISM

23. Match the following

	Column I		Column II
A.	Electric conductivity of a conductor depends on	(p)	Dimensions (length and area of cross-section)
B.	Conductance of a conductor depend on	(q)	Temperature
C.	For a given conductor and at a given temperature, current density depends on	(r)	Nature of conductor
D.	For a given potential difference a applied across a conductor, current in it will depend on	(s)	Electric field strength
		(t)	None of the above

24. Column I gives some electrical circuits, with points A and B indicated in the circuit. Column II gives possible values of potential difference between the points $V_A - V_B$ and $V_B - V_C$. Match appropriately.

Column I

A. Current I in branch BD does not change, even if key K is closed

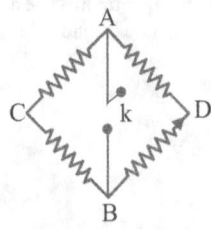

Column II

(p) $V_A - V_B = 0$

B. The circuit is in transient state

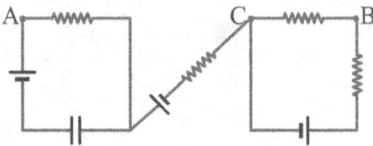

(q) $V_A - V_B =$ positive

C. Dielectric constant of dielectric is varying with y

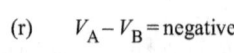

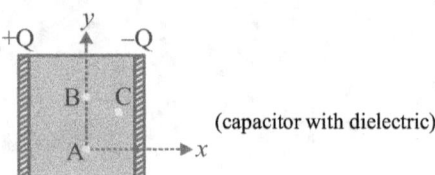
(capacitor with dielectric)

(r) $V_A - V_B =$ negative

D. Space between capacitor plates is filled with three dielectric slabs of different dielectric constants ($k_1 \neq k_2 \neq k_3$)

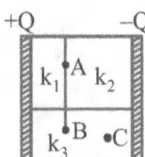

(s) $V_B - V_C = 0$

(t) $V_B - V_C =$ positive

Answer Key (Sol. from page 297)

| 23 | A-q, r ; B-p, q, r ; C-s ; D-p, q, r | 24 | A-p ; B- p, q, r, t ; C - p, t ; D -p, q, r, t |

25. Column I gives some electrical circuits in steady state. Column II gives some statements regarding the circuits. Match appropriately.

Column I

A.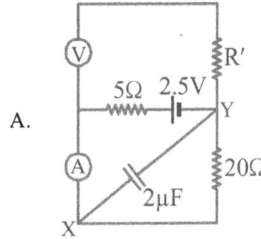

B.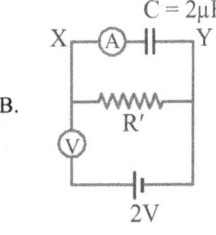

C.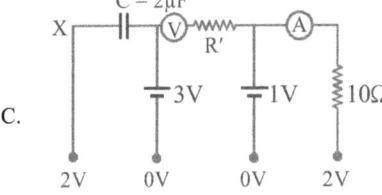

D.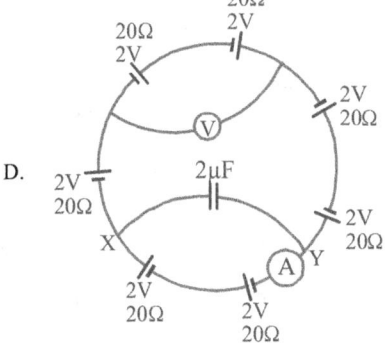

Column II

(p) Reading of voltmeter is 2 V

(q) Reading of ammeter is 0.1 A

(r) Current through R' is zero

(s) Charge on capacitor is 2 μC

(t) Point marked Y is at lower potential relative to point marked X

Answer Key — 25   A-p, q, r, t ; B-p, r, t ; C-p, q, r, s ; D-q, t

Sol. from page 297

Electricity — Subjective Integer Type — Exercise 3.5

Solution from page 299

1. The current through a wire depends on time as $i = (20 + 4t)$. Find the charge crossed through a section of the wire in 10 second.
   Ans. 400 C

2. The switch S shown in figure is kept closed for a long time and is then opened at $t = 0$. Find the current in the middle 10 Ω resistor at $t = 1.0$ ms.

   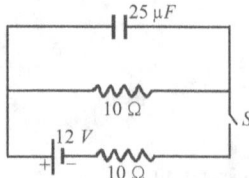

   Ans. 11 mA.

3. In the circuit shown in figure, find the value of unknown resistor R.

   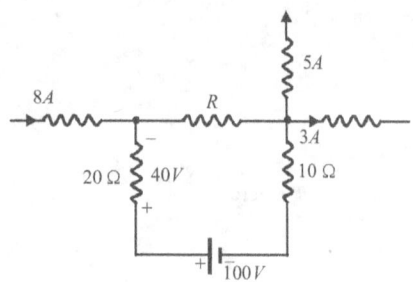

   Ans. 4 Ω.

4. What are the values of V_1 and V_2 in the circuit shown in figure?

   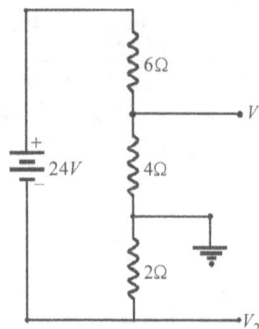

   Ans. $V_1 = 8V$, $V_2 = -4V$.

5. Compute the value of battery current in the circuit shown in figure. All the resistances are in ohm.

   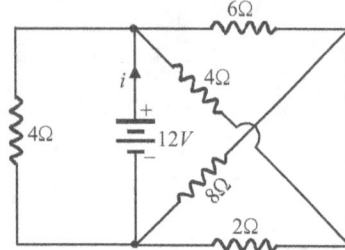

   Ans. 6A.

6. Find the current supplied by the battery in the circuit shown in figure.

   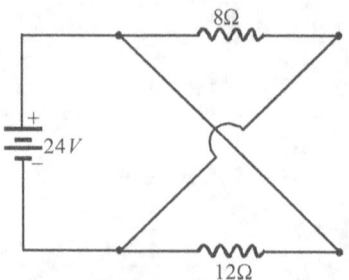

   Ans. 5 A.

7. Find the effective resistance between the points A and B in figure.

   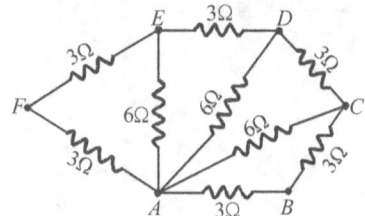

   Ans. 2 Ω

8. The ammeter current in the circuit shown in figure is $\dfrac{1}{x}$. Find the value of x.

   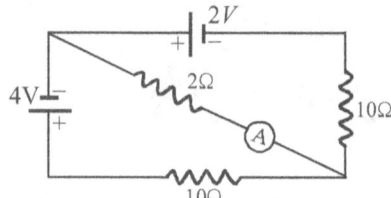

   Ans. $x = 7$

9. Find the potential difference $V_1 - V_2$ between points 1 and 2 of the circuit shown in figure if $R_1 = 10\Omega$, $R_2 = 20\Omega$, $\xi_1 = 5.0$ V and $\xi_2 = 2.0$ V. The internal resistances of the current sources are negligible.

   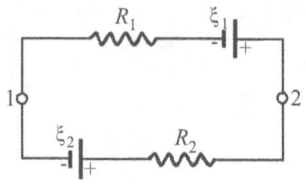

   Ans. $V_1 - V_2 = \dfrac{(\xi_1 - \xi_2)R_1}{(R_1 + R_2)} - \xi_1 = -4V$.

10. When two identical batteries of internal resistance 1Ω each are connected in series across a resistor R, the rate of heat produced in R is J_1. When the same batteries are connected in parallel across R, the rate is J_2. If $J_1 = 2.25\, J_2$ then the value of R in Ω is
    Ans. 4 Ω

Electricity — Subjective — Exercise 3.6

Solution from page 301

1. The current in a conductor and the potential difference across its ends are measured by an ammeter and a voltmeter. The meters draw negligible currents. The ammeter is accurate but the voltmeter has a zero error (that is, it does not read zero when no potential difference is applied). Caculate the zero error if the readings for two different conditions are 1.75 A, 14.4 V and 2.75 A, 22.4 V.

   Ans. 0.4 V.

2. Determine the values of currents i_1 and i_2 in the circuit shown in figure.

   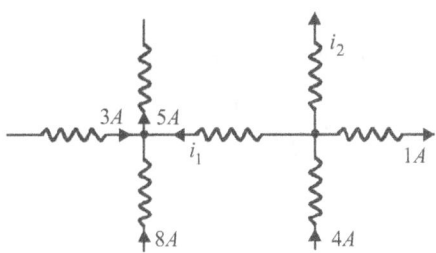

   Ans. $i_1 = -6A$, $i_2 = 9A$.

3. Figure shows an arrangement to measure the emf ξ and internal resistance r of a battery. The voltmeter has a very heigh resistance and the ammeter also has some resistance. The voltmeter reads 1.52 V when the switch S is open. When the switch is closed the voltmeter reading drops to 1.45 V and the ammeter reads 1.0 A. Find the emf and the internal resistance of the battery.

   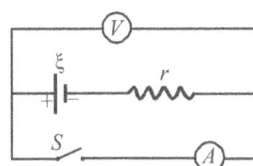

   Ans. 1.52 V, 0.07 Ω.

4. The resistance of the rheostat shown in figure is 30 Ω. Neglecting the meter resistance, find the minimum and maximum currents through the ammeter as the rheostat is varied.

   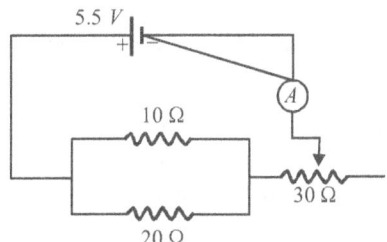

   Ans. 0.15 A, 0.83 A.

5. Find the currents through the three resistors shown in figure.

   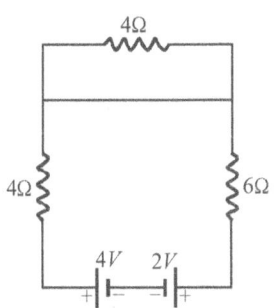

   Ans. Zero in the upper 4 Ω resistor and 0.2 A in the rest two.

6. Find the current measured by the ammeter in the circuit shown in figure.

   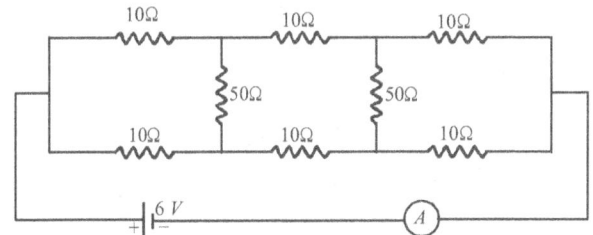

   Ans. 0.4 A.

7. Find the current in each branch of the circuit shown in figure.

   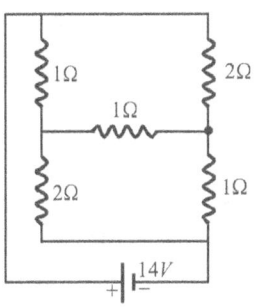

   Ans. 6A, 4A, 2A, 4A, 6A (top to bottom).

8. Find potential difference V_{xy} in the circuit shown in figure.

   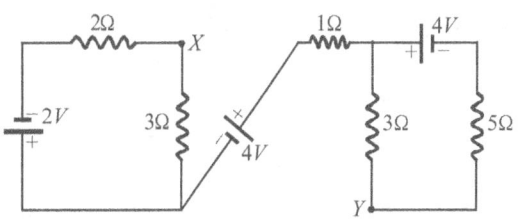

   Ans. 3.7 V.

9. Two capacitors are charged in series by a 12 V battery (see figure).
   (a) What is the time constant of the charging circuit?
   (b) After being closed for the length of the time determined in (a) the switch S is opened. What is the voltage across the 6 μF capacitor?

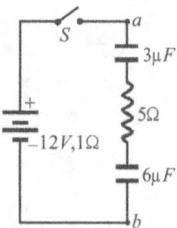

Ans. (a) 12 μs (b) 2.53 V.

10. Calculate the equivalent resistance between A and B of the circuit shown in figure. The value of resistances is in ohm.

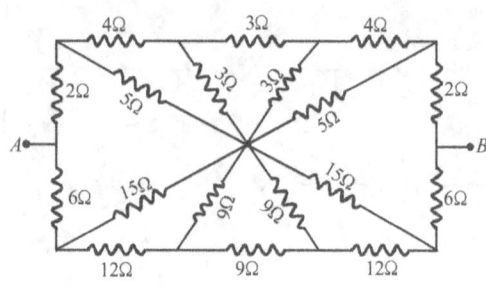

Ans. 6.75 Ω.

11. At what value of the resistance R_x in the circuit shown in figure will the total resistance between points A and B be independent of the number of cells?

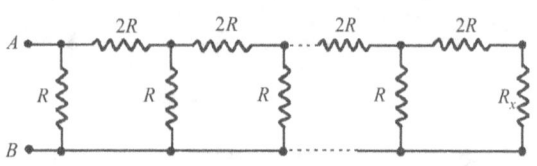

Ans. $R_x = R(\sqrt{3} - 1)$.

12. Figure shows an infinite circuit formed by the repetition of the same link, consisting of resistance $R_1 = 4.0\, \Omega$ and $R_2 = 3.0\, \Omega$. Find the resistance of this circuit between points A and B.

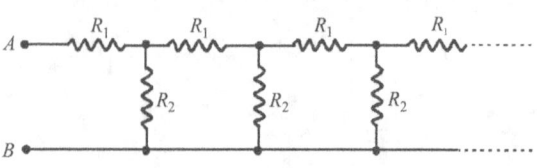

Ans. $R = \left(1 + \sqrt{1 + \dfrac{4R_2}{R_1}}\right) \dfrac{R_1}{2} = 6\,\Omega$.

13. Find the equivalent resistance of the resistors network across points A and B.

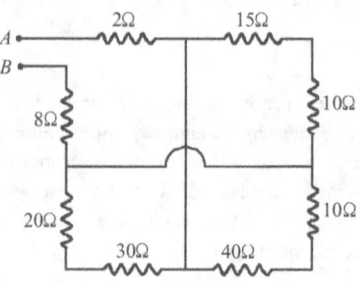

Ans. 22.5 Ω.

14. Consider an infinite ladder network shown in figure. A voltage is applied between points A and B. If the voltage is halved after each section, find the ratio R_1/R_2. Suggest a method to terminate it after a few sections without introducing much error with attention.

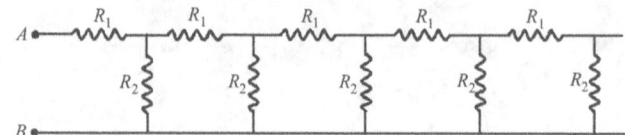

Ans. 1/2.

15. Determine the current through the battery in the circuit shown in figure:
   (a) Immediately after the key K is closed and
   (b) in a long time interval, assuming that the parameters of the circuit are known.

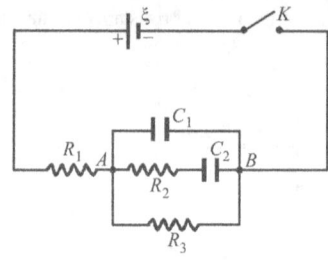

Ans. (a) $\dfrac{\xi}{R_1}$ (b) $\dfrac{\xi}{(R_1 + R_3)}$.

16. A 5.0 μF capacitor having a charge of 20 μC is discharged through a wire of resistance 5.0 Ω. Find the heat dissipated in the wire between 25 to 50 μs after the connections are made.

Ans. 4.7 μJ.

17. A capacitor of capacitance 8.0 μF is connected to a battery of emf 6.0 V through a resistance of 24 Ω. Find the current in the circuit.
   (a) just after the connections are made and
   (b) one time constant after the connections are made.

Ans. (a) 0.25 A (b) 0.09 A.

18. How many time constants will elapse before the power delivered by the battery drops to half of its maximum value in an RC circuit?

Ans. 0.69.

DC AND DC CIRCUITS

19. The circuit shown in figure is made of a homogeneous wire of constant cross section. Find the ratio Q_{12}/Q_{34} of the amounts of heat liberated per unit time in conductors 1-2 and 3-4.

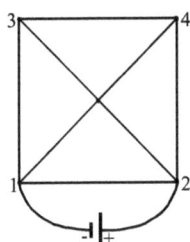

Ans. $\dfrac{Q_{12}}{Q_{34}} = 11 + 6\sqrt{2}$.

20. In figure circuit section AB absorbs energy at a rate of 50 W when a current $i = 1.0$ A passes through it in the indicated direction.

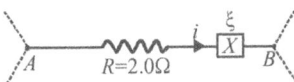

(a) What is the potential difference between A and B?
(b) Emf device X does not have internal resistance. What is its emf?
(c) What is its polarity (the orientation of its positive and negative terminal)?

Ans. (a) 50 V, (b) 48 V, (c) B is connected to negative terminal.

21. In the given circuit $\xi_1 = 3\,\xi_2 = 2\,\xi_3 = 6V$
$R_1 = 2\,R_4 = 6\Omega$, $R_3 = 2\,R_2 = 4\,\Omega$ and $C = 5\,\mu F$
Find the current in R_3 and energy stored in C.

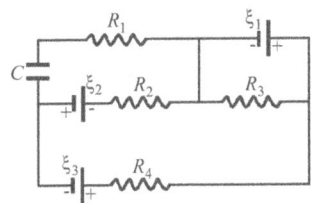

Ans. 1.5 A, 4.0 J.

22. Find the currents i_1, i_2 and i_3 in the circuit shown in figure.

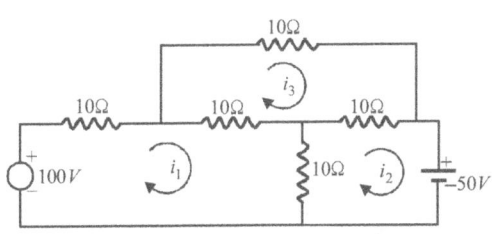

Ans. $i_1 = 3.75\,A$, $i_2 = 0$, $i_3 = 1.25$ A.

23. Find the current in the 2 Ω resistor shown in figure.

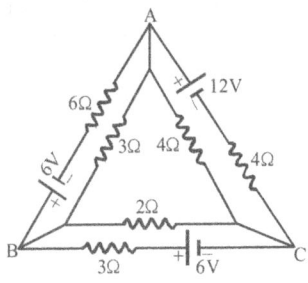

Ans. 1.85 A.

32. When the circuit of figure is in steady state, what would be the p.d. across the capacitor? Also find the discharge current at the instant S is opened.

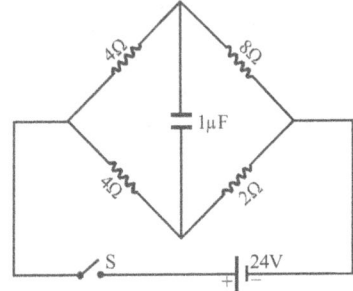

Ans. 8V, 1.8 A.

24. A varying voltage is applied to the clamps AB such that the voltage across the capacitor plates varies as shown in figure.

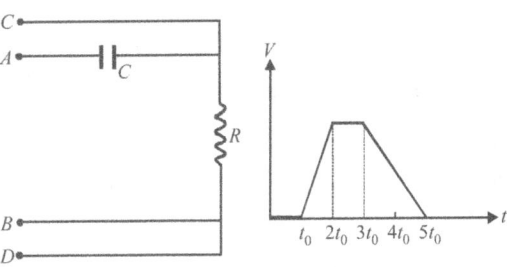

Plot the time dependence of voltage across the terminals C and D.

Ans.

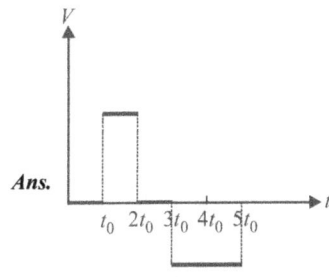

25. A thin uniform wire AB of length $1\ m$, an unknown resistance x and a resistance of $12\ \Omega$ are connected by thick conducting strips, as shown in figure. A battery and a galvanometer (with a sliding jockey connected to it) are also available. Connections are to be made to measure the unknown resistance x using the principle of Wheatstone bridge. Answering the following questions :

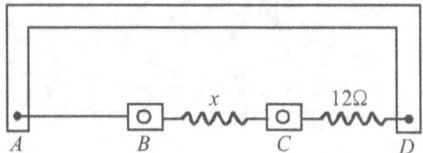

(a) Are there positive and negative terminals on the galvanometer ?
(b) Copy the figure in your answer book and show the battery and the galvanometer (with jockey) connected at appropriate points.
(c) After appropriate connections are made, it is found that no deflection takes place in the galvanometer when the sliding jockey touches the wire at a distance of $60\ cm$ from A. Obtain the value of the resistance of x.

Ans. (a) There are no positive and negative terminals on the galvanometer because only zero deflection is needed in it.
(b) The battery and galvanometer with jockey connections are shown in figure.

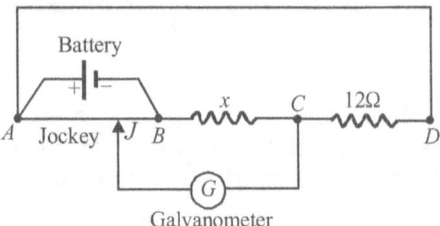

(c) $8\ \Omega$.

26. A long cylinder with uniformly charged surface and cross-sectional radius $a = 1.0\ cm$ moves with a constant velocity $v = 10\ m/s$ along its axis. An electric field strength at the surface of the cylinder is equal to $E = 0.9\ kV/cm$. Find the resulting convection current, that is, the current caused by mechanical transfer of a charge.
Ans. $I = 2\ \pi\varepsilon_0 aEv = 0.5\ \mu A$.

27. The gap between the plates of a parallel plate capacitor is filled with glass of resistivity $\rho = 100\ G\Omega.m$. The capacitance of the capacitor equals $C = 4.0\ nF$. Find the leakage current of the capacitor when a voltage $V = 2.0\ kV$ is applied to it.

Ans. $I = \dfrac{VC}{\rho\varepsilon_0} = 1.5\ \mu A$.

28. Two sources of current of equal emf are connected in series and have different internal resistances R_1 and R_2 ($R_2 > R_1$). Find the external resistance R at which the potential difference across the terminals of one of the sources (which one in particular?) becomes equal to zero.
Ans. $R = R_2 - R_1$, $\Delta V = 0$ in the source of current with internal resistance R_2.

29. In the circuit shown in figure the emf of the source is equal to $\xi = 5.0\ V$ and the resistances are equal to $R_1 = 4.0\ \Omega$ and $R_2 = 6.0\ \Omega$. The internal resistance of the source equals $R = 0.10\ \Omega$. Find the currents flowing through the resistances R_1 and R_2.

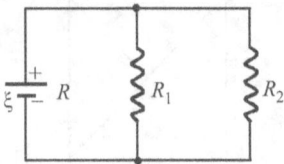

Ans. $I_1 = \dfrac{\xi R_2}{(RR_1 + R_1R_2 + R_2R)} = 1.2 A, I_2 = \dfrac{I_1 R_1}{R_2} = 0.8 A$.

30. In the circuit shown in figure the sources have emf's $\xi_1 = 1.0\ V$ and $\xi_2 = 2.5\ V$ and the resistances have the values $R_1 = 10\ \Omega$ and $R_2 = 20\ \Omega$. The internal resistances of the sources are negligible. Find a potential difference $V_A - V_B$ between the plates A and B of the capacitor C.

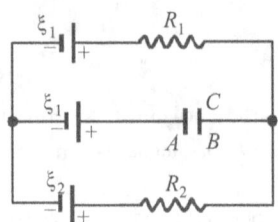

Ans. $V_A - V_B = \dfrac{(\xi_1 - \xi_2)R_1}{(R_1 + R_2)} = -0.5 V$.

31. N sources of current with different emf's are connected as shown in figure. The emf's of the sources are proportional to their internal resistances, i.e. $\xi = \alpha R$, where α is an assigned constant. The lead wire resistance is negligible. Find
(a) the current in the circuit;
(b) the potential difference between points A and B dividing the circuit in n and $N - n$ links.

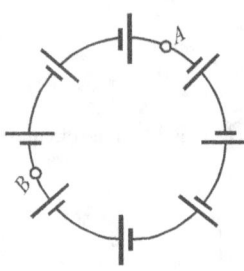

Ans. (a) $I = \alpha$; (b) $V_A - V_B = 0$.

32. Figure illustrates a potentiometric circuit by means of which we can vary a voltage V applied to a certain device possessing a resistance R. The potentiometer has a length l and a resistance R_0, and voltage V_0 is applied to its terminals find the voltage V fed to the device as a function of distance x. Analyse separately the case $R >> R_0$.

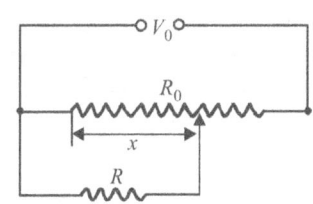

Ans. $V = \dfrac{V_0 R x}{Rl + R_0(l-x)\dfrac{x}{l}}$; for $R \gg R_0$, $V \approx \dfrac{V_0 x}{l}$.

33. A 6 volt battery of negligible internal resistance is connected across a uniform wire AB of length 100 cm. The positive terminal of another battery of emf 4 V and internal resistance 1 Ω is joined to the point A as shown in figure. Take the potential at B to be zero.
    (a) What are the potentials at the points A and C ?
    (b) At which point D of the wire AB, the potential is equal to the potential at C ?
    (c) If the points C and D are connected by a wire,

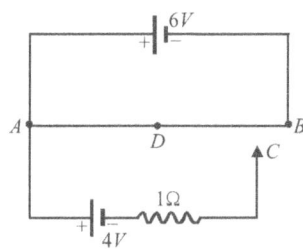

what will be the current through it ?
    (d) If the 4 V battery is replaced by 7.5 V battery, what would be the answers of parts (a) and (b) ?

Ans. (a) 6 V, 2 V (b) $AD = 66.7$ cm (c) zero (d) 6V, –1.5 V, no such point D exists

34. Find the magnitude and direction of the current flowing through the resistance R in the circuit shown in figure, if the emf's of the sources are equal to $\xi_1 = 1.5\,V$ and $\xi_2 = 3.7\,V$ and the resistances are equal to $R_1 = 10\,\Omega$, $R_2 = 20\,\Omega$, $R = 5.0\,\Omega$. The internal resistances of the sources are negligible.

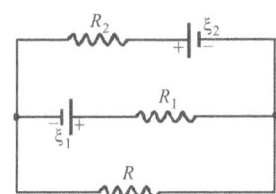

Ans. $I = \dfrac{(R_1 \xi_2 - R_2 \xi_1)}{(RR_1 + R_1 R_2 + R_2 R)} = 0.02A$, the current is directed from the left to the right.

35. Find the emf and the internal resistance of a source which is equivalent to two batteries connected in parallel whose emf's are equal to ξ_1 and ξ_2 and internal resistances to R_1 and R_2.

Ans. $\xi = \dfrac{(\xi_1 R_2 + \xi_2 R_1)}{(R_1 + R_2)}$, $R_1 = \dfrac{R_1 R_2}{(R_1 + R_2)}$.

36. Find the current flowing through the resistance R in the circuit shown in figure. The internal resistances of the batteries are negligible.

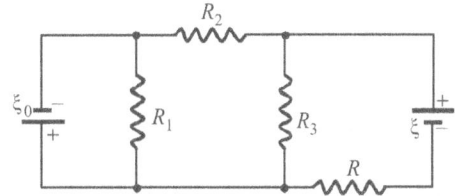

Ans. $I = \dfrac{[\xi(R_2 + R_3) + \xi_0 R_3]}{[R(R_2 + R_3) + R_2 R_3]}$

37. In the circuit shown in figure the sources have emf's $\xi_1 = 1.5\,V$, $\xi_2 = 2.0\,V$, $\xi_3 = 2.5\,V$, and the resistances are equal to $R_1 = 10\Omega$, $R_2 = 20\,\Omega$, $R_3 = 30\,\Omega$. The internal resistances of the sources are negligible. Find :
    (a) The current flowing through the resistance R_1;
    (b) A potential difference $V_A - V_B$ between the points A and B.

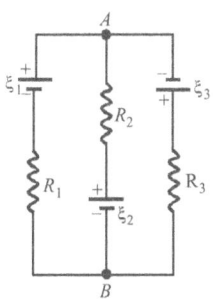

Ans. (a) $I_1 = \dfrac{[R_3(\xi_1 - \xi_2) + R_2(\xi_1 + \xi_3)]}{(R_1 R_2 + R_2 R_3 + R_3 R_1)} = 0.06 A$,

(b) $V_A - V_B = \xi_1 - I_1 R_1 = 0.9$ V.

38. Find how the voltage across the capacitor C varies with time t in figure, after the shorting of the switch S_w at the moment $t = 0$.

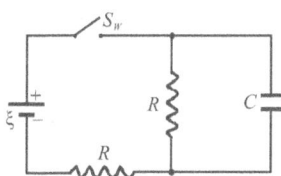

Ans. $V = \dfrac{1}{2}\xi\left(1 - e^{-2t/RC}\right)$.

39. Find a potential difference $V_A - V_B$ between the plates of a capacitor C in the circuit shown in figure, if the sources have emf's $\xi_1 = 4.0$ V and $\xi_2 = 1.0$ V and the resistances are equal to $R_1 = 10\,\Omega$, $R_2 = 20\,\Omega$ and $R_3 = 30\,\Omega$. The internal resistances of the sources are negligible.

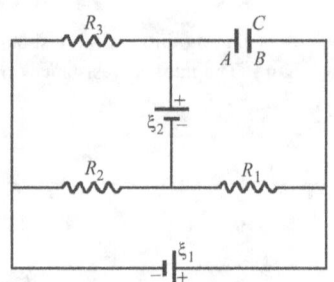

Ans. $V_A - V_B = \dfrac{\xi_2 R_3(R_1 + R_2) - \xi_1 R_1(R_2 + R_3)]}{(R_1 R_2 + R_2 R_3 + R_3 R_1)} = -1.0\,V$.

40. A constant voltage $V = 25\,V$ is maintained between points A and B of the circuit. Find the magnitude and direction of the current flowing through the segment CD if the resistances are equal to $R_1 = 1.0\,\Omega$, $R_2 = 2.0\,\Omega$, $R_3 = 3.0\,\Omega$ and $R_4 = 4.0\,\Omega$.

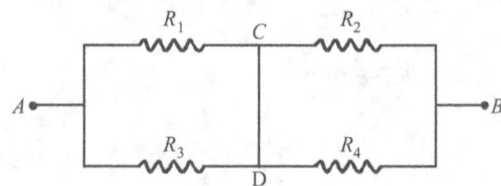

Ans. $I = \dfrac{V}{R_2}\left(\dfrac{R_1 + R_2}{R_1 \dfrac{1 + R_2 R_4(R_1 + R_3)}{R_1 R_3(R_2 + R_4)}} - 1\right) = 1.0\,A$. The current flows from point C to point D.

★★★

DC AND DC CIRCUITS

Hints & Solutions

Solutions Exercise 3.1 Level-1

1. (d) Capacitor offers infinite resistance to dc and so,
$$\frac{1}{R_{AB}} = \frac{1}{20} + \frac{1}{\infty}$$
or $R_{AB} = 20\ k\Omega$

2. (d) The effective circuit is shown in figure
$$R_{AB} = \left(\frac{R_1 R_4}{R_1 + R_4}\right)$$

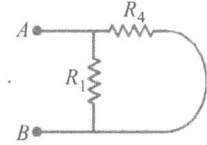

3. (c) Time constant, $\tau = C(2R) = 2\ CR$

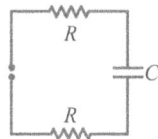

4. (c)

5. (d) The direction of $\vec{i}$ and $\vec{j}$ are opposite of the direction of motion of electron, and the direction of electrons are opposite to that of $\vec{E}$.

6. (d) (A) $i = 7$ C/s (B) $i = 4 - 3 = 1$ C/s
   (C) $i = -2 - 5 = -7$ C/s (D) $i = -3 + 1 = -2$ C/s
   It shows, (A = C) > D > B.

7. (a) $R_{AB} = 2 + 2 + 2 + 2 + 2 = 10\ \Omega$.

8. (d) $i_1 = \frac{\rho L}{A}$; $i_2 = \frac{\rho(1.5L)}{A/2} = \frac{3\rho L}{A}$; $i_3 = \frac{\rho(L/2)}{A/2} = \frac{\rho L}{A}$.

9. (b) As $R = \frac{\rho L}{A}$, and so it is least along top-bottom. Current will be maximum.

10. (a) $\frac{R}{2} = \frac{100 - \ell}{\ell}$ .... (i)

    and $\frac{R}{2} = \frac{(\ell + 20)}{(80 - \ell)}$ .... (ii)

    On solving above equations, we get
    $R = 3\ \Omega$.

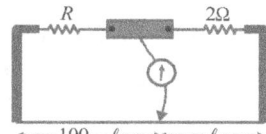

11. (c) $R_{AB} = \frac{1 \times 3}{1 + 3} = \frac{3}{4}\ \Omega$.

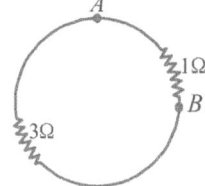

12. (d) $R' = R\left(\frac{r}{r'}\right)^4 = R \times (2)^4 = 16R$.

13. (a)

14. (d) The resistance of semiconductors increases with decrease in temperature while that of metals increase.

15. (a) Effective circuit for Ohm's law is shown in figure.

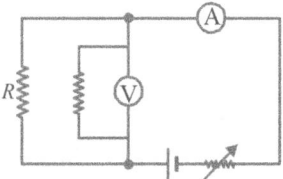

16. (a) The equivalent resistance of the circuit across the cell is
$$R = 0.5 + 8 + 2 + \frac{6 \times 18}{6 + 18} = 15\ \Omega$$

Now current, $i = \frac{V}{R} = \frac{15}{15} = 1\ A$.

17. (d) $V_A - V_B = (V_0 - V_B) - (V_0 - V_A)$
    $= 1 \times 2 - 1 \times 4$
    $= -2\ V$.

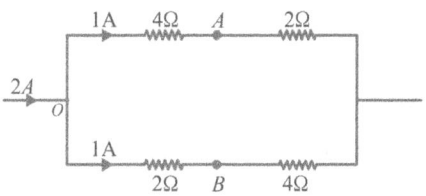

18. (c) Diode in forward bias offers zero resistance.
    $\therefore\ R = 10 + \frac{10 \times 10}{10 + 10} = 15\ k\Omega$.

    Total current $i = \frac{30}{15} = 2$ mA. The current in $10\ k\Omega$ resistance is 1 mA. Thus $V_A - V_B = (1 \times 10^{-3}) \times 10 \times 10^3 = 10$ V.

19. (a) The current through ammeter
    $i = 5$ A.

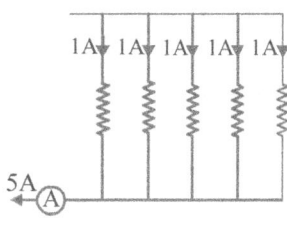

20. (a) $R = R_1 + R_2$

    or $\frac{\rho(\ell_1 + \ell_2)}{A} = \frac{\rho_1 \ell_1}{A} + \frac{\rho_2 \ell_2}{A}$

    $\therefore\ \rho = \left(\frac{\rho_1 \ell_1 + \rho_2 \ell_2}{\ell_1 + \ell_2}\right)$

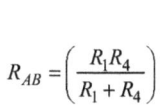

21. (a) The effective circuit is shown in figure.

$$R_{AB} = \left(\frac{30 \times 60}{30 + 60}\right) = 20\ \Omega.$$

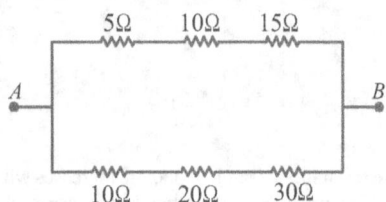

22. (a) The effective circuit is shown in figure.

$$R_{AB} = \frac{9 \times 9}{9 + 9} = \frac{9}{2}\ \Omega.$$

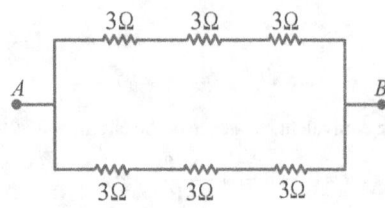

23. (a) The least value of two resistance in series is $\frac{5R}{6}$.

$$R_{PQ} = \frac{R \times \frac{5R}{6}}{R + \frac{5R}{6}} = \frac{5R}{11}.$$

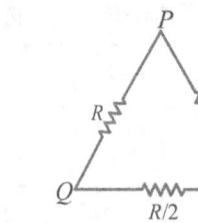

24. (c) The equivalent resistance across the cell is, $R = 1.5\ \Omega$.

Current, $i = \frac{6}{1.5} = 4\ \text{A}$.

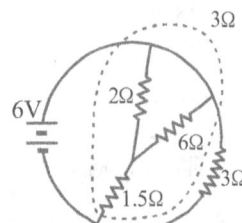

25. (b) As $V = \varepsilon - ir$

$$\therefore\ r = \left(\frac{\varepsilon - V}{i}\right) = \frac{\varepsilon - V}{(V/R)} = \frac{R(\varepsilon - V)}{V}.$$

26. (d) $\varepsilon = 2.2\ V$. Also $i = \frac{V}{R} = \frac{2}{4} = 0.5\ \Omega.$

Using, $V = \varepsilon - ir$
or $\quad 2 = 2.2 - 0.5\ r$
$\therefore\ r = 0.4\ \Omega$

27. (a) The equivalent circuit is shown in figure.

$\varepsilon = 5000 \times 0.15 = 750\ V$, $R = \dfrac{5000 \times 0.25}{100} + 500 = 512.5\ \Omega.$

Now, $i = \dfrac{\varepsilon}{R} = \dfrac{750}{512.50} \approx 1.5\ \text{A}.$

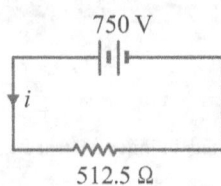

28. (c) $2\ \Omega$ is in open circuit, so there is no current in it.

29. (a) Current, $i = \dfrac{2}{5 + 15} = 0.1\ \text{A}.$

P.d. across potentiometer wire, $V = iR = 0.1 \times 5 = 0.5\ V.$

Now, potential gradient $= \dfrac{0.5}{100} = 0.005\ V/\text{cm}.$

30. (c) If R' is the resistance of ammeter, then
$4(R + R') = 20$
$\therefore\ R = 5 - R'.$

31. (c) $\dfrac{R}{80} = \dfrac{20}{80} \Rightarrow R = 20\ \Omega.$

32. (a) In balanced bridge, $I_P = I_Q$ and $I_R = I_G$.

33. (c) See theory of the chapter.

34. (a) $\dfrac{x}{y} = \dfrac{20}{80} \Rightarrow y = 4x.$

If ℓ be the distance of new balance point, then

$$\dfrac{4x}{y} = \dfrac{\ell}{(100 - \ell)}$$

$\therefore\ \ell = 50\ \text{cm}.$

35. (a) $i_g = i\dfrac{SG}{S + G}$

or $\quad 100 \times 10^{-6} = i\left(\dfrac{0.1 \times 100}{100 + 0.1}\right)$

or $\quad i = 100.1 \times 10^{-3}\ \text{A}.$

36. (a) The p.d. across the potentiometer wire
$V = 0.2 \times 10^{-3} \times 100 = 0.02\ V.$
So, we can write,

$$\dfrac{2}{490 + R} = \dfrac{0.02}{R}$$

$\therefore\ R = 4.9\ \Omega$

37. (c) $R_{eq} = \dfrac{5R}{6}.$

38. (a) Current in $8\ \Omega$ resistor, $i_1 = \dfrac{48}{8} = 6\ \Omega$, and the current in $24\ \Omega$ resistor, $i_2 = \dfrac{48}{24} = 2\ A$. So, total current $= 8\ A$.

Now, $V_{xy} = iR_{xy} = 8 \times (3 + 6 + 10 + 1) = 160\ V.$

39. (c) $V_A - V_B = 1 \times 1.5 = 1.5,\ \therefore\ V_A = 1.5\ V$
Also $V_B - V_D = -1 \times 2.5 + 2$
$\therefore\ V_D = 0.5\ V.$

40. (b) $q = \int_{t_1}^{t_2} i\, dt = \int_{2}^{3} (2t + 3t^2)\, dt$

$$= \left|2\dfrac{t^2}{2} + 3\dfrac{t^3}{3}\right|_{2}^{3} = (3^2 + 3^3) - (2^2 + 2^3)$$

$= 24\ C$

DC AND DC CIRCUITS

41. (a) $i = i_1 + i_2$

    or $\dfrac{V_o - 0}{2} = \dfrac{20 - V_o}{2} + \dfrac{5 - V_o}{4}$

    or $V_o = 9\ V$

    Thus, $i = \dfrac{9}{2} = 4.5\ A$

    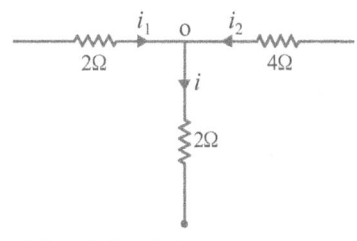

42. (d) $R_1 = 5R$ and $R_2 = 3R$

    $\therefore\ \dfrac{R_2}{R_1} = \dfrac{3R}{5R} = 0.6$

43. (b) $\dfrac{nV}{G + R_0} = \dfrac{V}{G},\ \therefore R_0 = (n-1)G.$

44. (d) $i = \left(\dfrac{12 - 5}{7}\right) = 1\ A$

    $V_1 = -5 - 2 \times 1 - 2 \times 1 = -9\ V$

    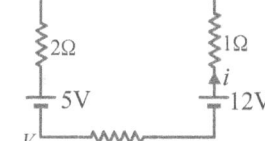

45. (b) $V = iR_2 = 0.5 \times 15 = 7.5\ V$

    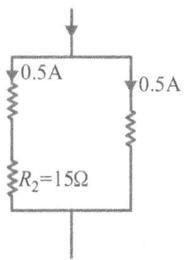

46. (a) emf of the cell, $e = \dfrac{\varepsilon l}{L} = \dfrac{30\varepsilon}{100}$.

47. (b) $i = \dfrac{6}{\left(\dfrac{2 \times 3}{2 + 3} + 2.8\right)} = 1.5\ A.$

    Current in 2Ω resistor.
    $i_1 = 0.9\ A$ and $i_2 = 0.6\ A$.

    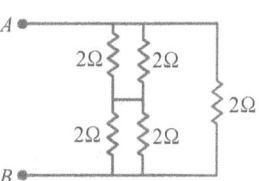

48. (c) $\dfrac{R_1}{R_2} = \dfrac{R_3}{R_4}$ or $R_1 R_4 = R_2 R_3$

49. (a) As $\dfrac{R_1}{R_2} = \dfrac{\rho l_1/\pi r^2}{\rho l_2/\pi r^2} = \dfrac{l_1}{l_2}$, so, balanced distance does not depend on radius of the wire.

50. (b)

51. (d) In balance bridge there is no current in galvanometer arm (here k arm), and so reading of G remains same.

52. (c) In series
    $R = R_1 + R_2 + R_3$

    or $\dfrac{3\ell}{\sigma A} = \dfrac{\ell}{\sigma_1 A} + \dfrac{\ell}{\sigma_2 A} + \dfrac{\ell}{\sigma_3 A}$

    $\therefore\ \dfrac{3}{\sigma} = \dfrac{1}{\sigma_1} + \dfrac{1}{\sigma_2} + \dfrac{1}{\sigma_3}$

    or $\sigma = \left[\dfrac{3\sigma_1 \sigma_2 \sigma_3}{\sigma_1 \sigma_2 + \sigma_2 \sigma_3 + \sigma_1 \sigma_3}\right]$

53. (d) At steady state, there is no current in capacitor arm. So equivalent resistance through battery

    $\dfrac{1}{R} = \dfrac{1}{1} + \dfrac{1}{2} + \dfrac{1}{3};\ \therefore R = \dfrac{C}{11}\Omega$

    Current $i = \dfrac{V}{R} = \dfrac{6}{6/11} = 11\ A$.

    p. d. across capacitor $= 6V$

    $\therefore$ Charge on capacitor $= CV = 0.5 \times 6 = 3\ \mu C.$

54. (b) Current $i = \dfrac{50}{25} = 2\ A$

    Now $V_A - V_B = i \times 12 = 2 \times 12 = 24\ V$

    As $V_B = 0,\ \therefore V_A = 24\ V$.

55. (b) The effective circuit is shown in figure.
    $R_{AB} = 1\Omega$.

    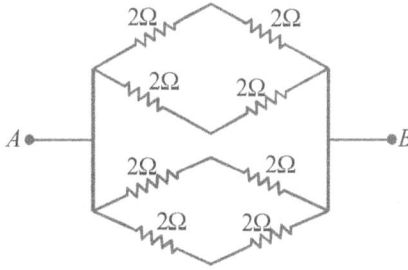

56. (a) $R = R_1 + R_2$

    or $\dfrac{\rho(\ell_1 + \ell_2)}{A} = \dfrac{\rho_1 \ell_1}{A} + \dfrac{\rho_2 \ell_2}{A}$

    $\therefore\ \rho = \left[\dfrac{\rho_1 \ell_1 + \rho_2 \ell_2}{\ell_1 + \ell_2}\right].$

57. (a) The equivalent circuit is shown in figure. So $R_{AB} = 1\Omega$

290 ELECTRICITY & MAGNETISM

58. (c) The equivalent circuit is shown in figure. So

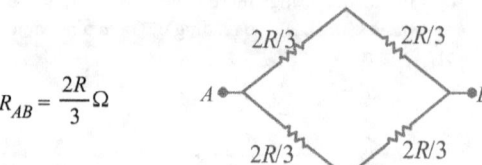

$R_{AB} = \dfrac{2R}{3}\,\Omega$

59. (a) In upper close loop, we can write
$\varepsilon - (i_1 + i_2)R - i_1 r_1 = 0$.

60. (b) Using Kirchoff's loop rule, we have
$-30 I_1 + 40 - 40 (I_1 + I_2) = 0$ ... (i)
and $40(I_1 + I_2) - 40 - 80 + 40 I_2 = 0$ ... (ii)
After solving, we get, $I_1 = -0.9$ A.

61. (c) $V = \dfrac{V_1 r_2 + V_2 r_1}{r_1 + r_2} = \dfrac{18 \times 1 + 12 \times 2}{1 + 2} = 14\,V$

62. (a) We have $\dfrac{R}{55} = \dfrac{80}{20}$
$\therefore R = 220\,\Omega$.

63. (d) $i_g (G + R_1) = 1$
or $10^{-3}(50 + R_1) = 1$
$\therefore R_1 = 950\,\Omega$
Now $i_g (G + R_1 + R_2) = 10$

or $R_1 + R_2 = 10000$
$\therefore R_2 = 9000\,\Omega$

64. (b) $E = \left(\dfrac{e}{R + R_h + r}\right) \times \dfrac{R}{L} \times \ell$

$= \left(\dfrac{10}{5 + 4 + 1}\right) \times \dfrac{5}{5} \times 3 = 3V$.

65. (d) At any temperature,
or $R = R_1(1 + \alpha t) + R_2(1 - \beta t)$

For R to be constant, $\dfrac{dR}{dt} = 0$

or $R_1 \alpha = R_2 \beta$

$\therefore \dfrac{R_1}{R_2} = \dfrac{\beta}{\alpha}$.

66. (d) $E_1 = 1.5 \times 1\,V$, $E_2 = 1.5 \times 2V, \ldots$

Now current $I = \dfrac{E_1 + E_2 + \ldots + E_n}{r_1 + r_2 + \ldots + r_n}$

$= \dfrac{1.5(1 + 2 + \ldots + N)}{(1 + 2 + \ldots + N)}$

$= 1.5$ A

Solutions EXERCISE 3.1 LEVEL -2

1. (b) Time constant $\tau = CR$.

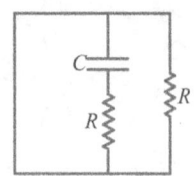

2. (b) The equivalent circuit is shown in figure.
Thus, $R_{AB} = \dfrac{66}{45}\,\Omega$.

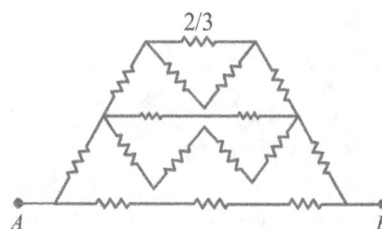

3. (d) It is the balance bridge and so, $3R$ resistor in the circuit is ineffective. So, current in this resistance is zero.

$R_{AB} = \dfrac{2R \times 4R}{2R + 4R} = \dfrac{4}{3}R$.

4. (c) The effective circuit is shown in figure. Thus

$R_{AB} = \dfrac{R}{2}$.

5. (d) We know that, $R_t = R_0(1 + \alpha t)$.
or $1 = R_0(1 + 0.00125 \times 300)$
and $2 = R_0(1 + 0.00125 \times t)$
After simplifying, we get $t = 1127$ K.

6. (b) By Kirchoff's law, we have
$+12 - 500\,i + X i = 0$
Also $-2 + X i = 0$
After simplifying above equations, we get
$X = 100\,\Omega$.

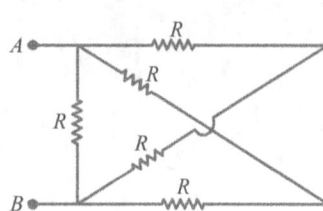

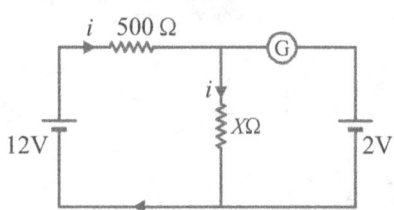

7. (d) The current in the circuit, $i = \left(\dfrac{2\varepsilon}{R_1 + R_2 + R}\right)$

DC AND DC CIRCUITS

P.d. across source of internal resistance R_2,
$V = \varepsilon - iR_2$

or $\quad 0 = \varepsilon - \left(\dfrac{2\varepsilon}{R_1 + R_2 + R}\right) R_2$

or $\quad R = (R_2 - R_1)$.

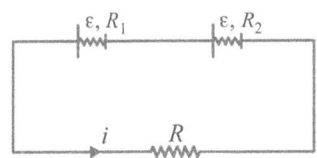

8. (a) Internal resistance, $r = \left(\dfrac{\ell_1 - \ell_2}{\ell_2}\right) R$

$= \left(\dfrac{55 - 50}{50}\right) \times 10 = 1\,\Omega$

9. (d) $V = i_g(G + R)$
and $V' = i_g(G + 2R)$
It shows, $V < V' < 2V$

10. (b) $i_g = i\left(\dfrac{SG}{S+G}\right)$

or $\quad 50 \times 10^{-6} = i\left(\dfrac{S}{S+100}\right)$ .... (i)

Also $\quad V = i_g(G + R_0)$
or $\quad V = 50 \times 10^{-6}(100 + R_0)$ .... (ii)
On simplifying above equations, we get
$V = 10\,V$, $R_0 = 200 \times 10^{-3}\,\Omega$

11. (c) Current, $i = \dfrac{2V - V}{2R + R} = \dfrac{V}{3R}$

Thus p.d. across capacitor,
$V_C = iR = \dfrac{V}{3R} \times R = \dfrac{V}{3}$.

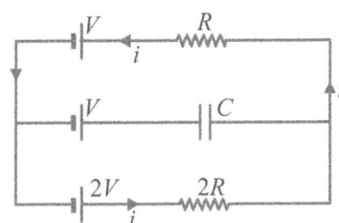

12. (b) $\dfrac{V^2}{R} t = mC\Delta T$

or $\quad \dfrac{(3\varepsilon)^2}{R} t = mC\Delta T$ .... (i)

and $\quad \dfrac{(N\varepsilon)^2}{2R} t = 2mC\Delta T$ .... (ii)

On solving above equations, we get
$N = 6$

13. (a) The effective circuit is shown in figure.
$\therefore\quad R_{PQ} = \left(\dfrac{2Rr}{R+r}\right)$

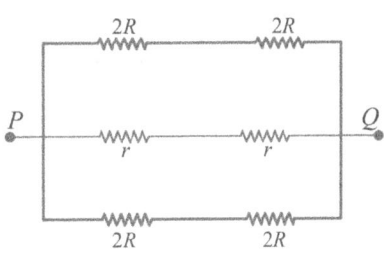

14. (b)
15. (d) $\varepsilon = 6\,V$,

Current, $i = \dfrac{V}{R} = \dfrac{4}{10} = 0.4\,A$

Now, $\quad V = \varepsilon - ir$
or $\quad 4 = 6 - 0.4\,r$
or $\quad r = 5\,\Omega$.

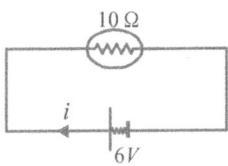

16. (d) In close loop $BCEDB$,
$-4(i - i') + 10 - 12\,i + 8 = 0$
and in close loop $ABDFA$,
$-4(i - i') + 10 + 8(i) - 6 = 0$
On solving above equations, we get
$i = 1.14\,A$.

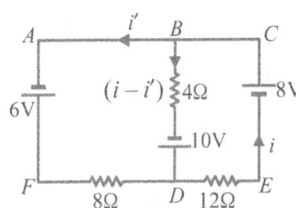

17. (c) $i = \left(\dfrac{50 - 15}{5000}\right) = 7 \times 10^{-3}\,A$

$V_a = iR = 7 \times 10^{-3} \times 1200 = 8.4\,V$

$P = Vi = 15 \times 7 \times 10^{-3} = 105\,mW$.

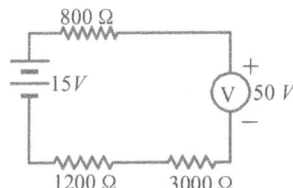

18. (d) The equivalent circuit is shown in figure.

$R = \dfrac{6 \times 4}{6 + 4} + \dfrac{7 \times 3}{7 + 3} = 4.5\,\Omega$

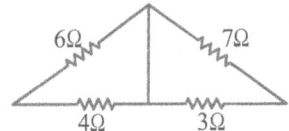

19. (c) $-4 \times 2 + 3 - 2 \times 2 + 1 \times 2 + (V_G - V_H) = 0$
or $V_G - V_H = 7 V.$

20. (d) The effective circuit is shown in figure
$R_{PQ} = \dfrac{3}{2} \Omega.$

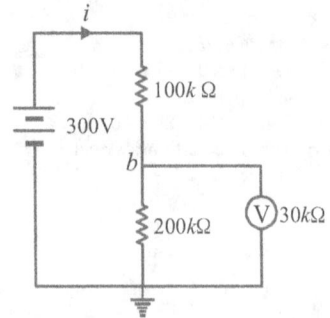

21. (d) The effective resistance of the circuit,
$R = \left(\dfrac{200 \times 30}{200 + 30} + 100\right)$
$= 126 \, k\Omega$
Thus, $i = \dfrac{300}{126} = 2.38 \, mA.$
Now, reading of voltmeter,
$V = 2.38 \times 10^{-3} \times (26 \times 10^3) = 61.88 \, V$

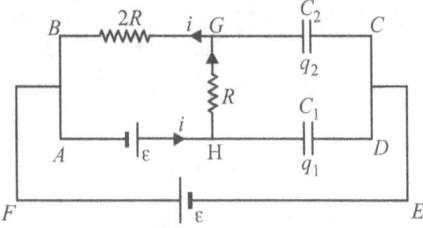

22. (a)

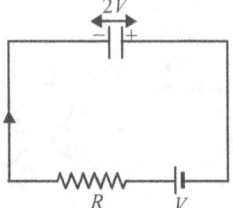

At steady state the current,
$i = \dfrac{\varepsilon}{3R}$
In close loop A H D E F A,
$\varepsilon - \dfrac{q_1}{C_1} + \varepsilon = 0$
or $q_1 = 2C_1\varepsilon$
Now in close loop BGCEFB
$2R \times i - \dfrac{q_2}{C_2} + \varepsilon = 0$
or $2R \times \dfrac{\varepsilon}{3R} - \dfrac{q_2}{C_2} + \varepsilon = 0$
$\therefore q_2 = \dfrac{5C_2\varepsilon}{3}$

Given, $\dfrac{q_1^2}{2C_1} = \dfrac{q_2^2}{2C_2}$

$\therefore \dfrac{C_1}{C_2} = \dfrac{q_1^2}{q_2^2}$

$= \left[\dfrac{2C_1\varepsilon}{5/3C_2\varepsilon}\right]^2$

or $\dfrac{C_1}{C_2} = \dfrac{25}{36}$

23. (a) The final charge
$q_0 = V_{av} \times C$
$= \left(\dfrac{3+2}{2}\right)C$
$= 2.5 \, C.$

24. (a) The effective circuit is shown in figure.
$R_{AB} = \dfrac{3R}{8}$

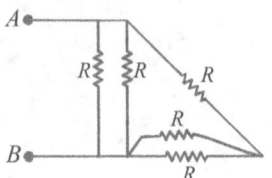

25. (d) The equivalent resistance,
$R = \dfrac{24}{9} \Omega.$
Thus current, $i = \dfrac{24}{24/9} = 9A.$

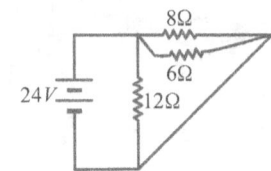

26. (c)

The initial potential difference between plates of capacitor
$= 3V - V = 2V$

The current, $i = \left[\dfrac{2V + V}{R}\right]$
$= \dfrac{3V}{R}$
The rate of heat energy produced
$= i^2 R = \left(\dfrac{3V}{R}\right)^2 \times R = \dfrac{9V^2}{R}$

DC AND DC CIRCUITS

27. (d) Effective emf of two cells in parallel

$$\varepsilon = \frac{\varepsilon_2 r_1 - \varepsilon_1 r_2}{r_1 + r_2} = \frac{3 \times 2 - 2 \times 1}{2 + 1} = \frac{4}{3} V$$

X terminal of the connection is positive. For neutral point, positive terminal of ε_0 must be connected to X.

28. (a) The equivalent circuit is shown in figure.

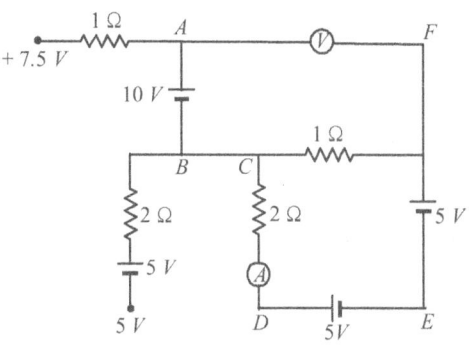

In close loop ABCDEFA,
$-10 - 5 + 5 + V = 0$
or $V = 10$ volt

29. (b) The effective circuit is shown in figure.

$$\frac{20 - V_0}{\frac{r}{3}} = \frac{V_0 + 10}{\frac{2r}{3}}$$

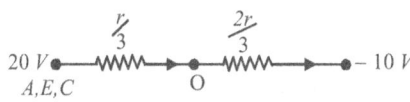

∴ $V_0 = 10$ Volt

30. (b) If each resistor is r, then

$$R_0 = 3r \text{ or } r = \frac{R_0}{3}$$

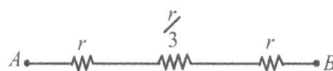

When keys are closed, then

$$R_{eq} = 7\frac{r}{3}$$

$$= \frac{7R_0}{9}$$

31. (b) The equivalent circuit is shown in figure.

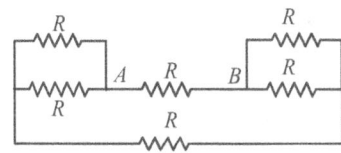

⇩

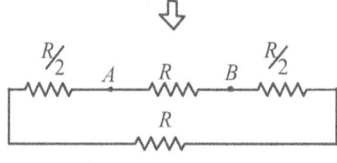

$$R_{eq} = \frac{2R}{3}$$

32. (c) $R = R_1 + R_2$

$$= \frac{l}{A}\left[\rho_1(1 + \alpha_1 t) + \rho_2(1 + \alpha_2 t)\right]$$

For, $\frac{dR}{dt} = 0$

or $\rho_1 \alpha_1 + \rho_2 \alpha_2 = 0$

33. (b) $R = \frac{\rho l}{A} = \frac{\rho_0 (1 + \alpha_2 t) \times l_0 (1 + \alpha_1 t)}{(1 + 2\alpha_1 t)}$

$= R_0 (1 + \alpha_2 t)(1 + \alpha_1 t)(1 - 2\alpha_1 t)$

Now $\frac{1}{R_0}\frac{dR}{dt} = (\alpha_2 - \alpha_1)$

[Neglecting product and higher powers of α_1 and α_2]

34. (c)

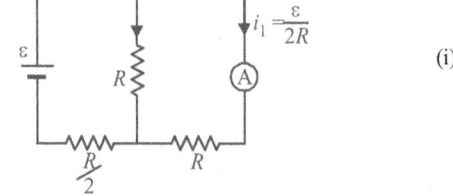 (i)

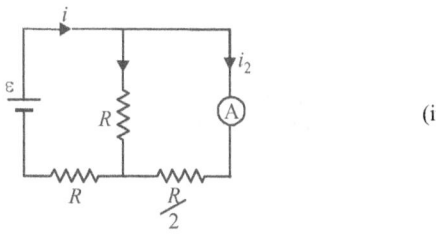 (ii)

In first case, $i_1 = \frac{\varepsilon}{2R}$

In second case, $i = \frac{3\varepsilon}{4R}$

∴ $i_2 = \frac{\varepsilon}{2R}$

35. (c) Initial charge on the capacitor $Q_0 = C \times 3V = 3CV$

$-\frac{q}{C} + i \times 2R + V = 0$

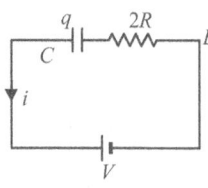

or $2Ri = \left(\frac{q}{C} - V\right)$

or $2R\frac{dq}{dt} = \left(\frac{q}{C} - V\right)$

or $\int_{Q_0}^{q} \frac{dq}{\left(\frac{q}{C} - V\right)} = \int_0^t \frac{dt}{2R}$

$$\frac{\left|\ln\left(\frac{q}{C} - V\right)\right|_{Q_0}^{q}}{\left(\frac{1}{C}\right)} = \frac{t}{2R}$$

$$\left|\ell n\left(\frac{q}{C}-V\right)\right|_{Q_0}^{q}=\frac{t}{2CR}$$

or $\quad \ell n\left(\frac{q}{C}-V\right)-\ell n\left(\frac{Q_0}{C}-V\right)=\frac{t}{2CR}$

or $\quad \ell n\left(\frac{q}{C}-V\right)-\ell n 2V=\frac{t}{2CR}$

or $\quad \ell n 2V-\ell n\left(\frac{q}{C}-V\right)=-\frac{t}{2CR}$

$$\ell n\left[\frac{2V}{\left(\frac{q}{C}-V\right)}\right]=\frac{t}{2CR}$$

or $\quad \dfrac{2V}{\left(\dfrac{q}{C}-V\right)}=e^{-\frac{t}{2CR}}$

or $\quad 2V=\left(\dfrac{q}{C}-V\right)e^{-\frac{t}{2CR}}$

or $\quad q=CV-2CVe^{-\frac{t}{2CR}}$

36. (a) At $t = 0$, capacitors offer zero resistance for dc and so effective resistance of the circuit is $R = 2\,\Omega$

$\therefore i = \dfrac{6}{2} = 3A.$

37. (a) The charge of the capacitor becomes $\dfrac{1}{e}$ of initial charge in time, τ.
$\tau = CR$
$= \dfrac{K\varepsilon_0 A}{d} \times \dfrac{1}{\sigma}\dfrac{d}{A}$
$= \dfrac{K\varepsilon_0}{\sigma}$

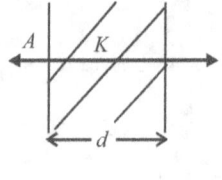

38. (c) In first case,

$i = \dfrac{\varepsilon}{R_A + R_V}$

and $V = iR_V$
In second case,

$2i = \left[\dfrac{\varepsilon}{R_A + \dfrac{R_V R}{R_V + R}}\right]$

and $\dfrac{V}{2} = 2i \times \left[\dfrac{RR_V}{R + R_V}\right]$

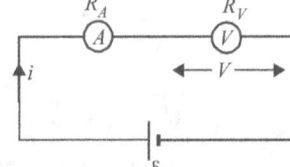

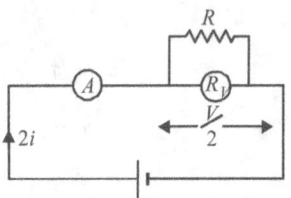

After simplifying above equations, we get

$\dfrac{R_V}{R_A} = \dfrac{2}{1}$

39. (a) $C_1 V_1 = C_2 V_2$

$\therefore \dfrac{C_1}{C_2} = \dfrac{V_2}{V_1}$

$= \dfrac{5i}{3i} = \dfrac{5}{3}$

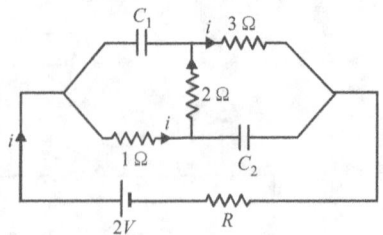

40. (a) The effective circuit is shown in figure.

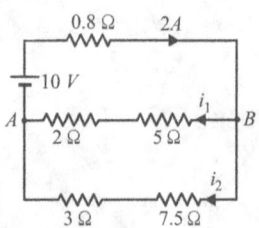

$R = 0.8 + R_{AB}$
$= 0.8 + 4.2 = 5\,\Omega$
$i_1 = 1.2A,\ i_2 = 0.8A$
Now, $V_{AB} = i_1 \times 7$
$= 1.2 \times 7 = 8.4\ V$

41. (d) $\left(\dfrac{\varepsilon}{r+1}\right)^2 \times 1 = \left(\dfrac{\varepsilon}{r+9}\right)^2 \times 9$

$\therefore \quad r = 3\,\Omega$

42. (a) The effective circuit is shown in figure. Thus, $R_{AB} = 5\,\Omega$.

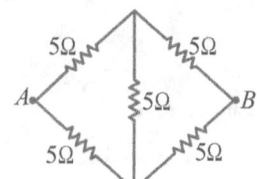

43. (b) Total resistance of the circuit

$R = \dfrac{6 \times 3}{6+3} + 2 + \dfrac{6 \times 3}{6+3} = 6\,\Omega$

$\therefore I = \dfrac{V}{R} = \dfrac{18}{6} = 3A$

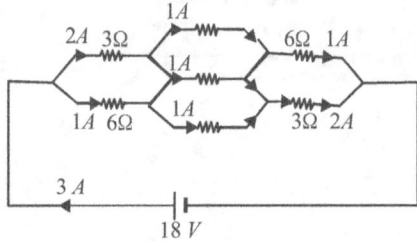

44. (a) All the eight resistors are in parallel, and so

$R_{AB} = \dfrac{R}{8}.$

DC AND DC CIRCUITS

45. (b) As $V_P = V_Q$, so current in 3Ω resistor. The effective circuit is shown in figure.

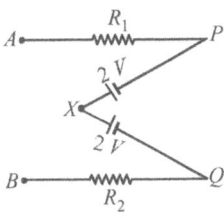

$R_{AB} = R_{AX} + R_{BX}$
∴ $R_{BX} = R_{AB} - R_{AX}$
or $R_2 = 10\Omega - 5\Omega = 5\Omega$

46. (a) The equivalent circuit is shown in figure.
Thus current $i = \dfrac{1}{4} A$

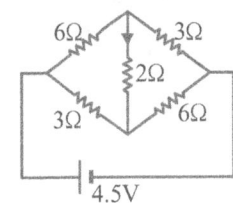

47. (d) $R_{AB} = 3.88\Omega$

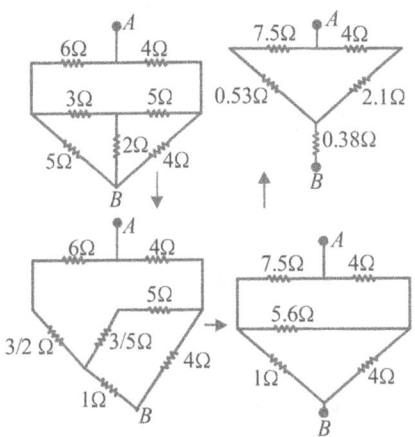

48. (a) Let each half side has resistance $r (= \rho d/2)$

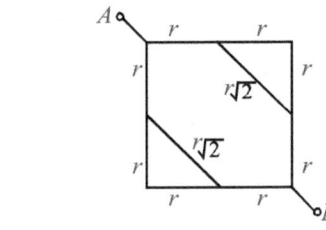

∴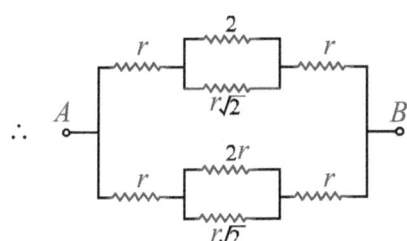

49. (c)

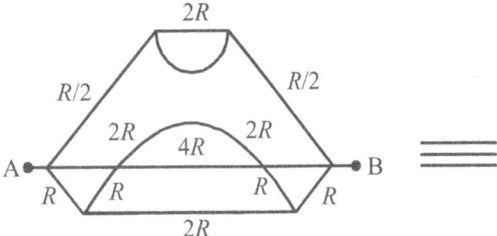

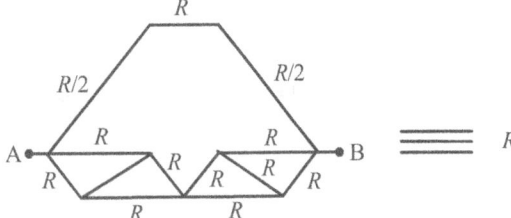

$\therefore R = \dfrac{1}{2}\left[2r + \dfrac{(2r)(r\sqrt{2})}{(2+\sqrt{2})r}\right] = r\sqrt{2}$ (on solving)

$\therefore R = \rho d/\sqrt{2}$

50. (d) 1.5 V

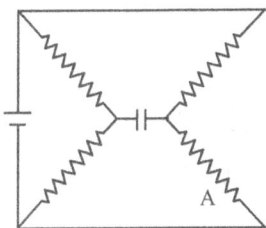

This is a DC circuit because the battery is the only source of voltage. Hence, the capacitors behave like open circuits. An equivalent circuit is then two parallel sets of two identical series resistors, see figure. The voltage drop across each parallel branch must be the battery voltage of 3V. Since the resistors are identical there is an equal voltage drop of 1.5 V across each resistor. In particular there is a drop of 1.5 V across resistor A.

51. (a) When i current enters into the terminal A, by the symmetry $\dfrac{i}{6}$ current will flow from A to B. Similarly when i current leaves the terminal B, current $\dfrac{i}{6}$ also flows from A to B. So net current in the resister between A and B becomes $\dfrac{i}{3}$.

Now $V_{AB} = \left(\dfrac{i}{3}\right)r$

or $i R_{AB} = \dfrac{ir}{3}$

∴ $R_{AB} = \dfrac{r}{3}$

296 ELECTRICITY & MAGNETISM

52. (c) The following points should be considered while making the circuit :

(i) An ammeter is made by connecting a low resistance R_2 in parallel with the galvanometer G_2.

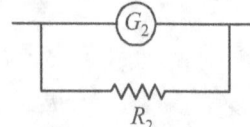

(ii) A voltmeter is made by connecting a high resistance R_1 in series with the galvanometer G_1.

(iii) Voltmeter is connected in parallel with the test resistor R_T.
(iv) Ammeter is connected in series with the test resistor R_T.
(v) A variable voltage source V is connected in series with the test resistor R_T.

53. (d) The equivalent circuit is shown in figure.
$R_{AB} = 1\ \Omega$.

54. (b) At null point

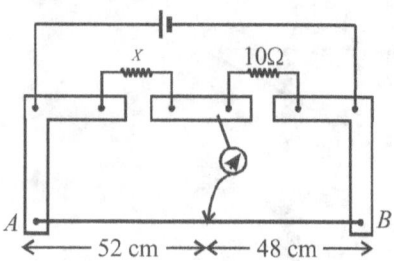

$$\frac{X}{\ell_1} = \frac{10}{\ell_2}$$

Here $\ell_1 = 52 + $ end correction $= 52 + 1 = 53$ cm

$\ell_2 = 48 + $ end correction $= 48 + 2 = 50$ cm

$$\therefore \frac{X}{53} = \frac{10}{50}$$

$$\therefore X = \frac{53}{5} = 10.6\ \Omega$$

Solutions EXERCISE 3.2

1. (c,d) See theory of the chapter.
2. (a,b) The effective emf the two cells in parallel is
$$e = \frac{1 \times 2 - 2 \times 1}{1 + 2} = 0.$$
So null point will be at zero distance from A. When jockey is touched to B, the current flows through 2 V cell towards B.
3. (a,d) In close loop through cells, the net emf of the close loop is zero and so current in 8 Ω resistor will be zero. In 4 Ω resistor,
$$i = \frac{10}{4} = 2.5\ A.$$

4. (b, c)

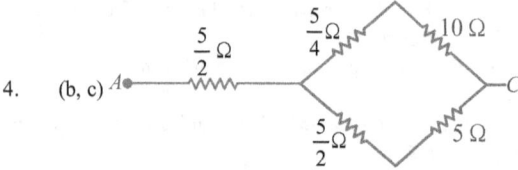

$\Rightarrow R_{AC} = 7\ \Omega$.

Also $\dfrac{1}{R_{BD}} = \dfrac{1}{15} + \dfrac{1}{5} + \dfrac{1}{15} \Rightarrow R_{BD} = 3\ \Omega.$

5. (b, c) For 10 A range : $R_1 + R_2 + R_3 = \dfrac{25}{9}\ \Omega$

$$i_g = i\left(\frac{R_1}{R_1 + R_2 + R_3 + G}\right)$$

or $10 \times 10^{-3} = 10\left(\dfrac{R_1}{\dfrac{25}{9} + 25}\right)$

$\therefore R_1 = \dfrac{1}{36}\ \Omega.$

For 1 A range :
$$i_g = i\left(\frac{R_1 + R_2}{R_1 + R_2 + R_3 + G}\right)$$

or $10 \times 10^{-3} = 1 \times \left(\dfrac{R_1 + R_2}{\dfrac{25}{9} + 25}\right)$

$\therefore R_2 = 0.25\ \Omega.$

For range 0.1 A :
$$10 \times 10^{-3} = 0.1\left(\frac{R_1 + R_2 + R_3}{R_1 + R_2 + R_3 + G}\right)$$

On solving, $R_3 = 2.5\ \Omega$.

6. (a, d) Going from B to Q,
$V_Q - V_B = 12 = 1i + 3 + 2i$
$\therefore\ i = 3\ A$

7. (b,d)

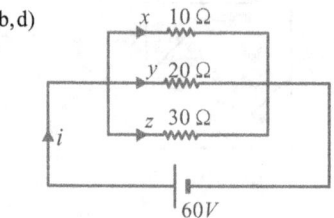

$x = \dfrac{60}{10} = 6\ A,$

$y = \dfrac{60}{20} = 3\ A,$

and $z = \dfrac{60}{30} = 2\ A,$

Thus, $i_1 = y + z = 5\ A, i_2 = x + y = 9\ A.$

DC AND DC CIRCUITS

8. (b,d) Current in 8 Ω resistor, $i = \dfrac{20}{8} = 2.5\,A$.

    Thus, $i_2 = 2.5 \times \dfrac{11}{11+28} = 0.7\,A$.

    Resistance between A and C = $\dfrac{28 \times 11}{39} = \dfrac{308}{39}\,\Omega$.

Total circuit resistance, $R = 8 + 11 + \dfrac{308}{39} = \dfrac{1049}{39}\,\Omega$

$\varepsilon = iR$

$= 2.5 \times \dfrac{1049}{39} = 67.3\,V$.

Solutions EXERCISE-3.3

1. (a) Free electrons in metals more randomly. So net flow of charge through any section of the metal is zero.
2. (c) The net charge on current carrying conductor is zero, and so its electric field is also zero.
3. (c) The drift velocity of electrons in metals is order of 10^{-4} m/s.
4. (a)
5. (a) Statement-2 is the explanation of statement-1.
6. (c) Kirchoff's loop rule follows from conservation of energy.
7. (c) The equivalent emf of two batteries in series,

    $e = e_1 + e_2$.
8. (d) The equivalent emf of the two batteries in parallel,

    $e = \left(\dfrac{e_1 r_2 + r_2 r_1}{r_1 + r_2}\right)$. e may be; $e_1 \le e \le e_2$.

    Internal resistance, $r = \left(\dfrac{r_1 r_2}{r_1 + r_2}\right)$. This value is smaller than either of r_1 and r_2.

9. (d) The resistivity of semiconductor decreases with increase in temperature.
10. (a) $i = \dfrac{V}{r+R} = \dfrac{2}{1+1} = 1\,A$, and $V = ir = 1 \times 1 = 1\,V$.
11. (c) Drift speed is the average speed between two successive collision.
12. (d) The free electron density in any part of the conductor remains constant.
13. (d)
14. (d)
15. (d) With increase in temperature, resistance of metal wire increases, but balance conduction will not change.

Solutions EXERCISE-3.4

Passage for Q.1 to Q.3

1. (c) $E = -\dfrac{dV}{dx} = -\dfrac{4ax^{1/3}}{3}$ ...(i)

2. (c) If σ is the surface charge density, then

    $E = \dfrac{\sigma}{\epsilon_0}$ ... (ii)

    On comparing (i) and (ii), we get

    $\sigma = -\dfrac{4a}{3}\epsilon_0 x^{1/3}$

    Volume charge density,

    $\rho = \dfrac{d\sigma}{dx} = -\dfrac{4}{9} a \epsilon_0 x^{2/3}$

3. (b) Current density, $j = \rho v$

    where $v = \sqrt{\dfrac{2eV}{m}}$

Passage for Q.4 to Q.6

4. (c)
5. (d) $V = E_1 d_1 + E_2 d_2$ ...(i)

    By equation of continuity

    $j_1 = j_2$ or $\dfrac{E_1}{\rho_1} = \dfrac{E_2}{\rho_2}$ ...(ii)

    On solving (i) and (ii), we can get E_1 and E_2.

6. (a). At the boundary between dielectrics, the surface density of extraneous charge

    $0 = \sigma = \sigma_2 - \sigma_1 = \epsilon_0 \epsilon_2 E_2 - \epsilon_0 \epsilon_1 E_1$.]

Passage for Q.7 to Q.9,

7. (c) If V is the potential of the capacitor, then

    $V = \dfrac{Q_0}{C_0}$.

    The current in the resistor, $i = \dfrac{\xi - V}{R} = \dfrac{\xi - Q_0/C_0}{R}$.

8. (a) If q is the charge on each capacitor, then

    $\dfrac{q}{C} + \dfrac{q}{C_0} + iR = 0$

    or $\dfrac{dq}{dt}\left(\dfrac{1}{C} + \dfrac{1}{C_0}\right) + \dfrac{di}{dt} R = 0$

    or $i\left(\dfrac{1}{C} + \dfrac{1}{C_0}\right) + \dfrac{di}{dt} R = 0$

9. (d) After simplifying above equation, we get

    $i = i_0 e^{-\left[\dfrac{t(C+C_0)}{RCC_0}\right]}$.

Electricity & Magnetism

Passage for Q.10 to Q.12,
The equivalent circuit is shown in figure. See examples.

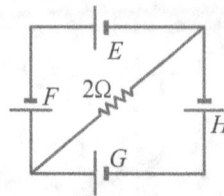

Passage for Q.13 & Q.14,

13. (a) From the given graph it is clear that with increase of the magnitude of magnetic field (B), the critical temperature T_C (B) decreases.
Given $B_2 > B_1$. Therefore for B_2, the temperature at which the resistance becomes zero should be less. The above statement is true for graph (a).

14. (b) We know that as B increases, T_C decreases but the exact dependence is not known.
Given at $B = 0$, $T_C = 100$ K
and at $B = 7.5T$, $T_C = 75$ K
∴ At $B = 5T$, T_C should be between 75 K and 100 K.

Passage for Q.15 & Q.16,

15. (a) Let j be the current density.
Then $j \times 2\pi r^2 = I \Rightarrow j = \dfrac{I}{2\pi r^2}$

∴ $E = \rho j = \dfrac{\rho I}{2\pi r^2}$

Now, $\Delta V'_{BC} = -\displaystyle\int_{a+b}^{a} \vec{E} \cdot \vec{dr} = -\int_{a+b}^{a} \dfrac{\rho I}{2\pi r^2} dr$

$= -\dfrac{\rho I}{2\pi} \left[-\dfrac{1}{r}\right]_{a+b}^{a} = \dfrac{\rho I}{2\pi a} - \dfrac{\rho I}{2\pi (a+b)}$

On applying superposition as mentioned we get

$\Delta V_{BC} = 2 \times \Delta V'_{BC} = \dfrac{\rho I}{\pi a} - \dfrac{\rho I}{\pi(a+b)}$

16. (c) As shown in Answer. $E = \dfrac{\rho I}{2\pi r^2}$

Passage for Q.17 & Q.19,

17. (a) $\varepsilon_2 = iR_{AJ} = \left(\dfrac{2}{10+15}\right) \times \left(\dfrac{10}{50} \times 31.25\right) = 0.5 V.$

18. (a) The effective circuit is shown in figure.
The current in potentiometer wire,

$i = \dfrac{2}{10} = 0.2\ A,$

and current in R_2, $i' = \left(\dfrac{0.5}{5+r}\right).$

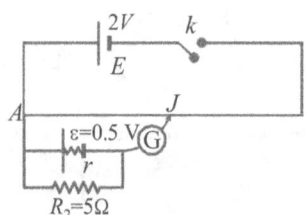

Now $V_{AJ} = i'R_2$
or $iR_{AJ} = i'R_2$
or $0.2 \times \dfrac{10}{50} \times 5 = \left(\dfrac{0.5}{5+r}\right) \times 5$
∴ $r = 7.5\ \Omega.$

19. (a) $\xi_2 = iR_{AJ}$
or $0.5 = \left(\dfrac{2}{10}\right) \times \dfrac{10}{50} (AJ)$
∴ $AJ = 12.5$ cm.

20. A-q : Energy stored in capacitor will convert into thermal energy.
B-r : Induced emf, $e = B\ v\ell$.
C-s : Because of electric force ends of wire will have opposite charges.
D-p, q, r : When battery is connected to wire a constant current flows in the wire which produces heating effect.

21. A-r : Resistance of ammeter, $R_A = \dfrac{SG}{S+G} = \dfrac{1 \times 99}{1+99} = 0.99\ \Omega$

Current $i = \dfrac{V}{R}$

or $3 = \dfrac{12}{2+0.99+\Omega}$; ∴ $r = 1.01\ \Omega.$

B - q : Using kirchoff's loop rule, we have
$12 - 1.01(i_1 + i_2) - 2i_1 = 0$
and $2i_1 - 200\ i_2 = 0$
After solving above equations, we get
$i_2 \approx 0.04 A$
∴ $i_g = \dfrac{5}{4} i_2 = 0.05 A.$

C-p Now $i_g = i\left(\dfrac{S}{S+G}\right)$
or $0.05 = i\left(\dfrac{1}{100}\right)$; ∴ $i = 5A$

D-q Also $V = i_g(G+R) = 0.05(99+101) = 10\ V$

22. A-r : $R_{AC} = R$

B-q : $R_{AB} = \dfrac{5R}{8}$

C-p : It is the balance bridge and so $V_B = V_D$.

D-t : $V_B \neq V_D$.

DC AND DC CIRCUITS

23. See theory of the chapter.
24. A-p : If current in branch BD is not charge even K is closed, this is the condition of balanced bridge and so $V_A = V_B$.

    B-p, q, r, t : p.d. depends on emfs of the cells.

    C- p, t : In this case p.d. occurs along x-axis, and no p.d. along y-axis.

    D- p, q, r, t : p.d. depends on the values of k_1, k_2 and k_3.
25. For ideal voltmeter, its resistance is infinite and so there is no current in the branch in which it connected.

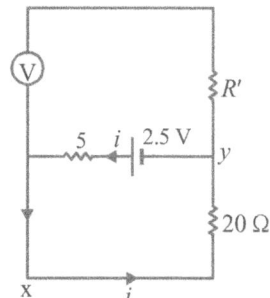

A - p, q, r, t :

$$i = \frac{2.5}{25} = 0.1\ A$$

and $V = 2.5 - 0.1 \times 5 = 2\ V$

or $V_x - V_y = 2V$.

B-p, r, t There is no current in R' and capacitor.

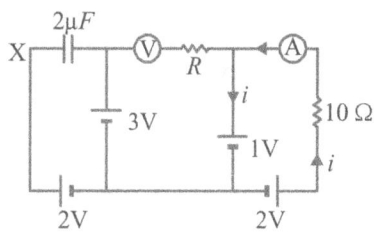

C-p, q, r, s : $i = \frac{2-1}{10} = 0.1\ A$

P.d. across capacitor is

$V = 3 - 2 = 1\ V$

Charge on capacitor

$q = CV = 2 \times i$
$= 2\mu F.$

D-q, t : $i = \frac{7 \times 2}{7 \times 20} = 0.1\ A.$

Solutions EXERCISE-3.5

1. We know that, charge

   $$q = \int_0^t i\,dt$$

   $$= \int_0^{10} (20 + 4t)\,dt$$

   $$= \left|20t + \frac{4t^2}{2}\right|_0^{10}$$

   $$= 400\ C \quad \text{Ans.}$$

2. At steady state, the p.d. across the capacitor, $V_0 = 6$ V. When switch with S is opened the current starts flowing from capacitor towards resistor. The initial current

   $$i_0 = \frac{V_0}{R} = \frac{6}{10} = 0.6\ A$$

   The time constant, $\tau = CR = 25 \times 10^{-6} \times 10$

   $= 25 \times 10^{-5}$ s

   We know that, $i = i_0 e^{-t/\tau}$

   $= 0.6\,e^{-[10^{-3}/25 \times 10^{-5}]}$

   $= 0.6\,e^{-4}$

   $= 11 \times 10^{-3}$ A Ans.

3. The current in 20Ω resistor, i_1

   $= \frac{40}{20} = 2$ A.

   Thus current in R will be, $i_2 = 8 + 2 = 10$ A

   In close loop, we have

   $-i_2 R - i_1 \times 10 + 100 - 40 = 0$

   or $-10R - 2 \times 10 + 100 - 40 = 0$

   $\therefore R = 4\Omega$

4. The current in the circuit $i = \frac{24}{12} = 2A$

   The p.d. across 4Ω resistor. $V_1 - V_0 = 4 \times 2$

   As, $V_0 = 0$,

   $\therefore V_1 = 8V$

   Similarly p.d. across 2Ω resistor

   $V_0 - V_2 = 2 \times 2$

   $\therefore V_2 = -4V$ Ans.

5. The effective circuit is shown in figure.

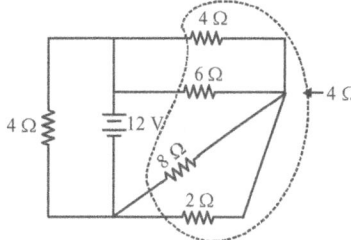

   The equivalent resistance, $R = 2\Omega$

   $\therefore$ Current $i = \frac{12}{2} = 6A$

6. The equivalent resistance $R = \frac{12 \times 8}{12 + 8} = \frac{96}{20}\ \Omega$

The current, $i = \dfrac{24}{96/20} = 5A$ **Ans.**

7. The successive reduction of the circuit is as :
Clearly equivalent resistance,
$$R = 2\Omega$$

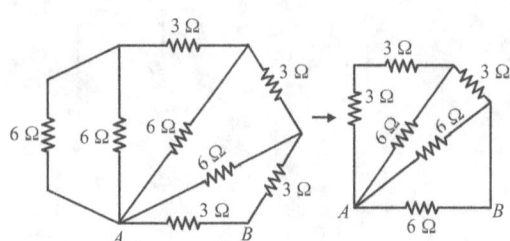

8. In close loop (1), we have $4 - 10i - 2i_1 = 0$, and in close loop (2), we have
$$-10(i - i_1) + 2 + 2i_1 = 0$$

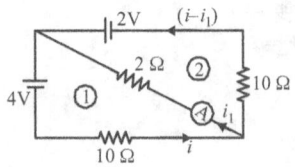

After solving above equations, we have
$$i_1 = \dfrac{1}{7}A \quad \text{Ans.}$$

9. The current in the circuit,
$$i = \left[\dfrac{\xi_1 + \xi_2}{R_1 + R_2}\right] = \dfrac{5-2}{10+20} = \dfrac{1}{10}A$$

Thus $V_1 - V_2 = -(\xi_2 + iR_2)$
$$= -\left(2 + \dfrac{1}{10} \times 20\right) = -4V. \text{ Ans.}$$

10.
Cells connected in series

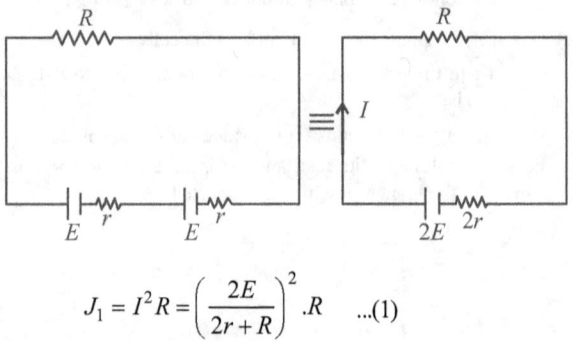

$$J_1 = I^2 R = \left(\dfrac{2E}{2r + R}\right)^2 .R \quad ...(1)$$

Cells connected in parallel

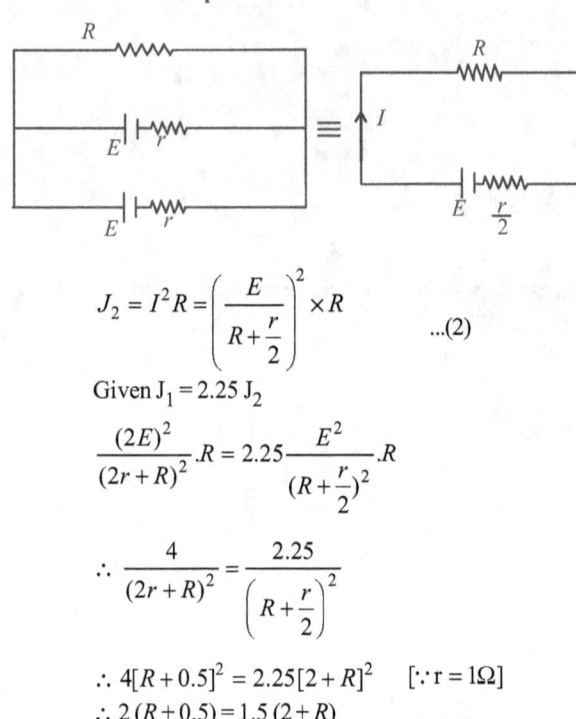

$$J_2 = I^2 R = \left(\dfrac{E}{R + \dfrac{r}{2}}\right)^2 \times R \quad ...(2)$$

Given $J_1 = 2.25 J_2$

$$\dfrac{(2E)^2}{(2r + R)^2} .R = 2.25 \dfrac{E^2}{(R + \dfrac{r}{2})^2} .R$$

$$\therefore \dfrac{4}{(2r + R)^2} = \dfrac{2.25}{\left(R + \dfrac{r}{2}\right)^2}$$

$\therefore 4[R + 0.5]^2 = 2.25[2 + R]^2 \quad [\because r = 1\Omega]$
$\therefore 2(R + 0.5) = 1.5(2 + R)$
$\therefore R = 4\Omega$

DC AND DC CIRCUITS

Solutions EXERCISE-2.6

1. If V_0 is the zero error in the voltmeter, then we can write
    $V = V_0 + ir$
    or $14.4 = V_0 + 1.75 \times r$
    and $22.4 = V_0 + 2.75 \times r$
    After simplifying, we get
    $V_0 = 0.4$ V **Ans.**

2. At the left junction,
    $3 + 5 + 8 + i_1 = 0$
    $\therefore \quad i_1 = -6$A.
    Similarly $i_2 = 9$A.

3. We know that
    $V = \xi - ir$
    or $1.52 = \xi - 0$
    $\therefore \quad \xi = 1.52$ V.
    In second case
    $V = \xi - ir$
    or $1.45 = 1.52 - 1 \times r$
    $\therefore \quad r = 0.07 \, \Omega$ **Ans.**

4. For maximum current,
    $R = \dfrac{20 \times 10}{20 + 10} + 0 = \dfrac{20}{3} \, \Omega$
    The current, $i_{max} = \dfrac{V}{R} = \dfrac{5.5}{\frac{20}{3}} = 0.83$ A.
    For minimum current
    $R = \dfrac{20 \times 10}{20 + 10} + 30 = \dfrac{110}{3} \, \Omega$
    $\therefore \quad i_{min} = \dfrac{V}{R} = \dfrac{5.5}{\frac{110}{3}} = 0.15$ A **Ans.**

5. Upper $4 \, \Omega$ resistor is shorted, so current in it is zero. Then other two resistors are in series, so
    $i = \left(\dfrac{4-2}{4+6}\right) = 0.2$ A **Ans.**

6. The effective circuit is shown in figure.

    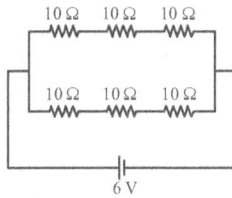

    The equivalent resistance, $R = 15 \, \Omega$
    $\therefore$ Current, $i = \dfrac{V}{R} = \dfrac{6}{15} = 0.4$ A **Ans.**

7. The currents in different resistors are as shown in figure :
    In close loops, we have

    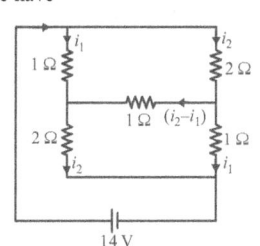

    $-2i_2 - 1(i_2 - i_1) + 1i_1 = 0$
    and $-1i_1 + 2i_2 + 1(i_2 - i_1) = 0$
    After simplifying, we get $i_1 = 6A, i_2 = 4A$. **Ans.**

8. $i_1 = \dfrac{2}{5} = 0.4 A$

    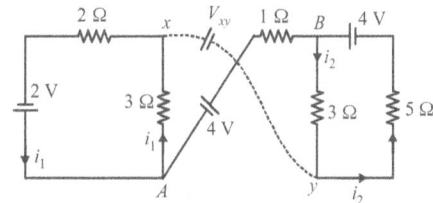

    and $i_2 = \dfrac{4}{8} = 0.5 A$
    In close loop $x - A - B - y - x$, we have
    $3i_1 + 4 - 3i_2 + V_{xy} = 0$
    $\therefore \quad V_{xy} = 3.7$ V **Ans.**

9. (a) The equivalent resistance of the circuit
    $R = 1 + 5 = 6 \, \Omega$
    and $C = \dfrac{3 \times 6}{3 + 6} = 2 \, \mu F$
    The time constant, $\tau = CR = 2 \times 6 = 12 \, \mu s$.
    (b) P.d. across both the capacitors together
    $V = V_0(1 - e^{-t/\tau})$
    $= 12(1 - e^{-\tau/\tau}) = 12\left(1 - \dfrac{1}{e}\right)$
    $= 7.6$ V
    If V_1 and V_2 one the p.d. across $3\mu F$ and $6\mu F$ capacitors, then
    $V_1 + V_2 = 7.6$
    and $3V_1 = 6V_2$
    $\therefore \quad V_2 = 2.53$ V **Ans.**

10. The effective circuit may be drawn as :

    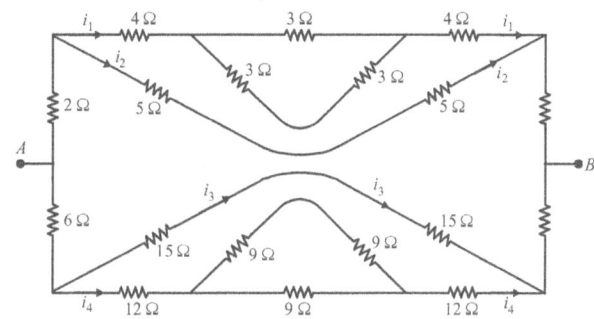

    Clearly the effective resistance $R = 6.75 \, \Omega$ **Ans.**

11. One unit cell consists of

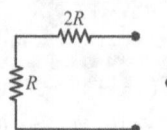

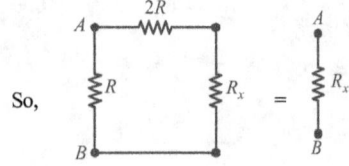

or $\dfrac{(2R+R_x)R}{(2R+R_x)+R} = R_x$

After simplifying, we get $R_x = (\sqrt{3}-1)R$.   **Ans.**

12. If R is the resistance between A and B, then
$$R_{AB} = R_{A'B'}$$
or $$R = \dfrac{R_2 R}{R_2 + R} + R_1$$

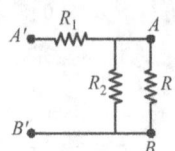

After substituting the values and simplifying, we get $R = 6\,\Omega$.   **Ans.**

13. The effective circuit is shown in figure

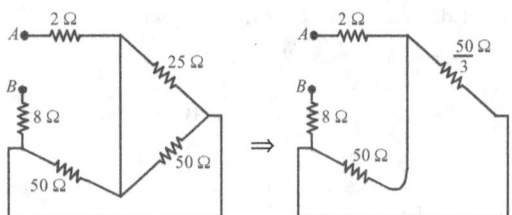

Thus equivalent resistance,
$$R = 2 + \dfrac{50 \times 50/3}{50 + 50/3} + 8$$
$$= 22.5\,\Omega.\quad \text{Ans.}$$

14. The currents in two successive restores are as :

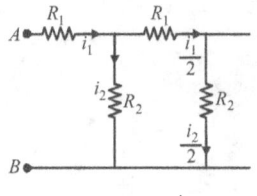

Clearly $\quad i_2 = \dfrac{i_1}{2}$

or $\quad \dfrac{i_1}{i_2} = 2$

∴ $\quad \dfrac{R_1}{R_2} = \dfrac{1}{2}$.   **Ans.**

15. (a) Immediately after the key is closed, the capacitor offers zero resistance. The circuit will be completed through least resistance branch, which is shown in figure.

The current, $\quad i = \dfrac{\xi}{R_1}$.

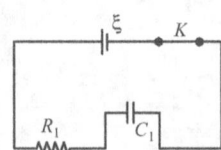

(b) After a long time capacitors will offer infinite resistance and so effective circuit is as :

The current $\quad i = \dfrac{\xi}{R_1 + R_3}$.

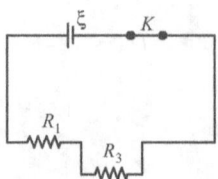

16. The p.d. across the capacitor
$$V_0 = \dfrac{Q}{C} = \dfrac{20}{5} = 4\,\text{V}$$

The initial current, $\quad i_0 = \dfrac{V}{R} = \dfrac{4}{5} = 0.8\,\text{A}$.

$\quad \tau = CR = 20 \times 5 = 100\,\mu\text{s}$.

The current in the resistor at any time t
$$i = i_0 e^{-t/\tau}$$

The heat dissipated, $\quad H = \displaystyle\int_{t_1}^{t_2} i^2 R\,dt$

$$= \int_{t_1}^{t_2} \left[i_0 e^{-t/\tau}\right]^2 R\,dt$$

$$= i_0^2 R \left|\dfrac{e^{-2t/\tau}}{(-2/\tau)}\right|_{t_1}^{t_2}$$

$$= \dfrac{i_0^2 R\tau}{2}\left[\dfrac{1}{e^{2t_1/\tau}} - \dfrac{1}{e^{2t_2/\tau}}\right]$$

After substituting and simplifying, we get
$$H = 4.7\,\mu\text{J}.\quad \text{Ans.}$$

17. (a) The current in the circuit just after connection,
$$i_0 = \dfrac{V_0}{R} = \dfrac{6}{24} = 0.25\,\text{A}.$$

(b) Current in the circuit, one time constant after connection are mate,
$$i = i_0 e^{-t/\tau}$$
$$= 0.25\, e^{-1}$$
$$= 0.09\,\text{A}.\quad \text{Ans.}$$

18. Power delivered by the battery
$$P = \xi i$$
or $\quad P = \xi i_0 e^{-t/\tau}$
or $\quad P = P_0 e^{-t/\tau}$

For, $\quad P = \dfrac{P_0}{2}$, we have

DC and DC Circuits

$$\frac{P_0}{2} = P_0 e^{-t/\tau}$$

or $\quad e^{t/\tau} = 2$

∴ $\quad t = 0.693\,\tau.$ **Ans.**

19. The effective circuit is shown in figure.

Resistance of wires, $R_{12} = R_{13} = R_{34} = R_{24} = r$

and $R_{15} = R_{25} = R_{36} = R_{46} = \dfrac{r}{\sqrt{2}}.$

The heat liberated per unit time,

$$Q_{12} = \frac{V^2}{r}.$$

From Ohm's law, we can get current through the conductor 3 – 4 :

$$i_{34} = \frac{V}{r(\sqrt{2}+3)}.$$

Thus $\quad Q_{34} = i_{34}^2 \, r = \dfrac{V^2}{r(\sqrt{2}+3)^2}.$

Therefore required ratio is :

$$\frac{Q_{12}}{Q_{34}} = (\sqrt{2}+3)^2 = 11 + 6\sqrt{2}. \text{ Ans.}$$

20. (a, b)

The power of the circuit $P = i^2 R + \xi i$

or $\quad 50 = 1^2 \times 2 + \xi \times 1$

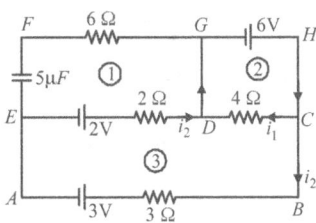

∴ $\quad \xi = 48\,V.$

Thus p.d. between A and B,

$V_{AB} = 48 + 1 \times 2 = 50\,V.$ **Ans.**

21. At steady state, there will be no current in the capacitor. The current distribution is shown in diagram. In loop (2),

$$i_1 = \frac{6}{4} = 1.5\,A$$

In loop (3),

$+2 - 2i_2 + 4i_1 - 3i_2 - 3 = 0$

∴ $\quad i_2 = 1A.$

The p.d. across the capacitor,

$V_{EG} = 2 - 2i_2 = 2 - 2 \times 1 = 0$

∴ $\quad U = \dfrac{1}{2} C V_{EG}^2 = 0$ **Ans.**

22. Using Kirchoff's loop rule in loop (1), (2) and (3), we have

$100 - 10i_1 - 10(i_1 - i_3) - 10(i_1 - i_2) = 0 \quad$ ...(i)

$10(i_3 - i_2) - 50 + 10(i_1 - i_2) = 0 \quad$ ...(ii)

and $-10i_3 - 10(i_3 - i_2) + 10(i_1 - i_3) = 0 \quad$ ...(iii)

After solving above equations, we get

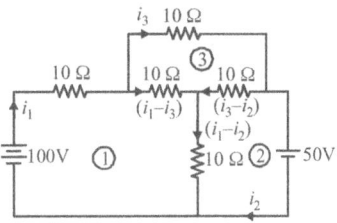

$i_1 = 3.75\,A, \; i_2 = 0, \; i_3 = 1.25\,A$ **Ans.**

23. The current distribution in different branches of the circuit is shown in the diagram.

By using Kirchoff's loop rape in four loops, we can get

$$i_2 = 1.85\,A.$$

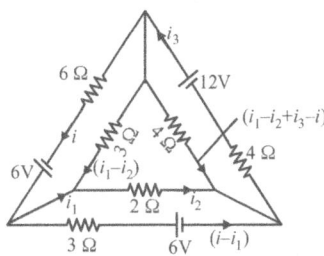

24. At steady state, there is no current in the capacitor, so the effective circuit is as follows :

If V_1 and V_2 are the p.d. across $4\,\Omega$ and $8\,\Omega$ respectively, then

$$V_1 + V_2 = 24$$

and $\quad \dfrac{V_1}{4} = \dfrac{V_2}{8}$

∴ $\quad V_1 = 8\,V$ and $V_2 = 16\,V$

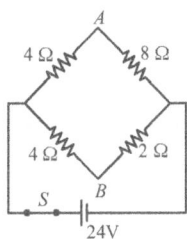

Similarly if V_3 and V_4 are the p.d. across $4\,\Omega$ and $2\,\Omega$ respectively, then

$$V_3 + V_4 = 24$$

and $\quad \dfrac{V_3}{4} = \dfrac{V_4}{2}$

∴ $\quad V_3 = 16\,V$ and $V_4 = 8\,V.$

Thus p.d. across capacitor

$V_A - V_B = V_3 - V_1 = 8\,V.$ **Ans.**

The discharged circuit is shown in figure.

The effective resistance, $R = \dfrac{8 \times 10}{8 + 10} = \dfrac{40}{9}\,\Omega.$

∴ Current $\quad i = \dfrac{V_A - V_B}{R}$

$= \dfrac{8}{\dfrac{40}{9}} = 1.8\ A.$ **Ans.**

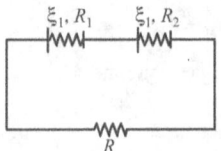

25. During the time interval from 0 to t_0, the voltage across the capacitor is zero, the charge on it is also zero, there is no current through it and hence V_{CD} is zero. From t_0 to $2t_0$, the voltage across the capacitor, and hence the charge on its plates increases linearly and hence a current passes through it. This means that voltage V_{CD} becomes constant. During time interval $2t_0$ to $3t_0$ the voltage across the capacitor does not change. Hence current does not flow, and V_{CD} is zero. Finally from $3t_0$ to $5t_0$, the capacitor is discharged the current through the resistor is negative and constant, and its magnitude is half the value of the current during t_0 to $2t_0$.

26. For balanced bridge,

$$\dfrac{R_{AJ}}{R_{JB}} = \dfrac{0.6\rho}{0.4\rho} = \dfrac{12}{x}$$

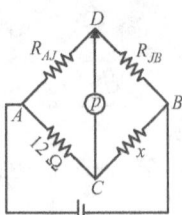

∴ $\quad x = 8\ \Omega.$ **Ans.**

27. Suppose the linear charge density of the cylinder is λ. Take an element of length dx on the surface of the cylinder, the charge on it is, $dq = \lambda dx$. The electric field at a point on the surface of the cylinder is

$$E = \dfrac{\lambda}{2\pi\epsilon_0\ a}.$$

∴ $\quad \lambda = 2\pi\epsilon_0\ aE$

and $\quad dq = 2\pi\epsilon_0\ aE(dx)$

Thus current, $\quad i = \dfrac{dq}{dt} = 2\pi\epsilon_0\ aE\left(\dfrac{dx}{dt}\right)$

or $\quad i = 2\pi\epsilon_0\ aEv.$ **Ans.**

28. The leakage current $\quad i = \dfrac{V}{R} = \dfrac{V}{\rho\dfrac{d}{A}}.$

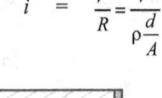

We know that, $\quad C = \dfrac{\epsilon_0\epsilon\ A}{d}$

∴ $\quad \dfrac{d}{A} = \dfrac{\epsilon_0\epsilon}{C}$

Now $\quad i = \dfrac{V}{\rho\dfrac{\epsilon_0\epsilon}{C}} = \dfrac{VC}{\rho\epsilon\epsilon_0}.$ **Ans.**

29. The current in the circuit,

$$i = \dfrac{2\xi_1}{R_1 + R_2 + R}.$$

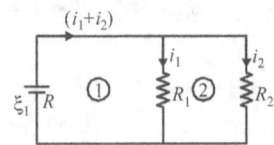

The p.d. across any source is, $V = \epsilon_1 - ir$.

As $r = R_2$ is greater, so p.d. across this cell becomes zero. Thus

$$0 = \dfrac{\xi - 2\xi}{(R_1 + R_2 + R)} \times R_2$$

or $\quad R = R_2 - R_1.$

30. Using Kirchoff's loop rule in loops (1) and (2), we have

$$\xi - R(i_1 + i_2) - i_1 R_1 = 0$$

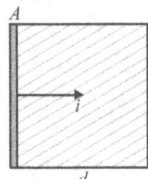

and $\quad -i_1 R_1 + i_2 R_2 = 0$

After solving above equations, and substituting the known values, we get

$i_1 = 1.2\ A$ and $i_2 = 0.8\ A.$

31. In closed loop 123451, $\xi_2 - iR_2 - iR_1 - \xi_1 = 0$

or $\quad i = \left[\dfrac{\xi_2 - \xi_1}{R_1 + R_2}\right]$

Now in close loop 12361, we have

$$\xi_2 - iR_2 + V_{AB} - \xi_1 = 0$$

∴ $\quad V_{AB} = (\xi_1 - \xi_2) + iR_2$

$= \dfrac{(\xi_1 - \xi_2)R_1}{R_1 + R_2} = -0.5\ V.$

32. (a) The current, $\quad i = \dfrac{n\xi}{nR} = \dfrac{\xi}{R}$

$= \dfrac{\alpha R}{R} = \alpha.$ **Ans.**

(b) The circuit can be redrawn as :
For upper close loop, we have

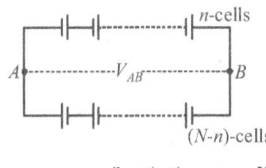

$$n\xi - i(nR) = V_{AB}$$
or $$n(\alpha R) - \alpha(nR) = V_{AB}$$
∴ $$V_{AB} = 0. \quad \textbf{Ans.}$$

33. The resistance of x length of the potentiometer wire is
$$R_x = \frac{R_0 x}{\ell}, \text{ and } R_{\ell-x} = \frac{R_0(\ell-x)}{\ell}$$

The total resistance of the circuit
$$R_T = \frac{\left(\frac{R_0 x}{\ell}\right)R}{\frac{R_0 x}{\ell}+R} + \frac{R_0(\ell-x)}{\ell}$$
$$= \left[\frac{\ell-x}{\ell} + \frac{xR}{\ell R + xR_0}\right]R_0.$$

The circuit current, $$i = \frac{V_0}{\left[\frac{\ell-x}{\ell} + \frac{xR}{\ell R + xR_0}\right]R_0}$$

The voltage, $$V = i\left[\frac{R_x R}{R_x + R}\right].$$

After substituting the values, we get
$$V = \left[\frac{V_0 R_x}{R\ell + R_0(\ell-x)\frac{x}{\ell}}\right]. \quad \textbf{Ans.}$$

34. (a) We have, $V_A - V_B = 6$ V.
As $V_B = 0$, ∴ $V_A = 6$V
$V_C = V_A - 4V = 6 - 4 = 2$V.

(b) The current in the potentiometer wire,
$$i = \left[\frac{6}{R_{AB}}\right].$$
If x is the required length, then
$$V_{AD} = iR_{AD}$$
or $$4 = \frac{6}{R_{AB}} \times \frac{R_{AB} x}{100}$$
∴ $$x = 66.7 \text{ cm}. \quad \textbf{Ans.}$$

(c) As $V_D = V_C$, so $V_D - V_C = 0$, therefore no current through it.
(d) Do as above.

35. By Kirchoff's I law $i = i_1 + i_2$.
Using Kirchoff's loop rule in loops (1) and (2), we have
$$\xi_2 - i_1 R_2 + \xi_1 + i_2 R_1 = 0$$
and $$-i_2 R_1 - \xi_1 - iR = 0$$
After substituting the values, and solving, we get,
$$i = 0.02 \text{ A}. \quad \textbf{Ans.}$$

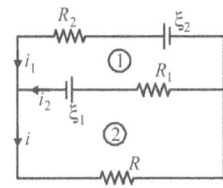

36. The circuit current $$i = \left[\frac{\xi_1 - \xi_2}{R_1 + R_2}\right].$$

The p.d. $$V_A - V_B = \xi_1 - i_1 R_1$$

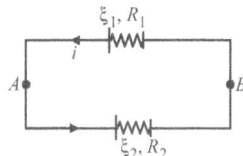

$$= \xi_1 - \left[\frac{\xi_1 - \xi_2}{R_1 + R_2}\right]R_1$$
$$= \left[\frac{\xi_1 R_2 + \xi_2 R_1}{R_1 + R_2}\right]. \quad \textbf{Ans.}$$

37.

Applying Kirchoff's junction rule, we have
$$i_0 = i_1 + i_2 \quad ...(i)$$
and $$i_1 = i_3 + i_4 \quad ...(ii)$$
Now in the loop 12781,
$$\xi_0 + i_2 R_1 = 0 \quad ...(iii)$$
In loop 1236781,
$$-i_3 R_3 - i_1 R_2 - \xi_0 = 0 \quad ...(iv)$$
and in loop 34563,
$$-i_4 R + \xi_1 + i_3 R_3 = 0 \quad ...(v)$$
After solving above equations, we get
$$i_4 = \left[\frac{\xi(R_2 + R_3) + \xi_0 R_3}{R(R_2 + R_3) + R_2 R_3}\right]. \quad \textbf{Ans.}$$

38. The current in different branches is shown in diagram.
In close loops (1) and (2), we have,

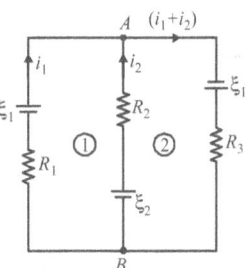

$$-i_1 R_1 + \xi_1 + i_2 R_2 - \xi_2 = 0$$
and $$\xi_2 - i_2 R_2 + \xi_1 + (i_1 + i_2)R_3 = 0$$
After solving above equations, and substituting the values, we get
$$i_1 = 0.06 \text{ A}.$$

39. Suppose q is the charge on the capacitor at any instant, and i_2 is the current, then
$$i_2 = \frac{dq}{dt}.$$

By Kirchoff's first law,

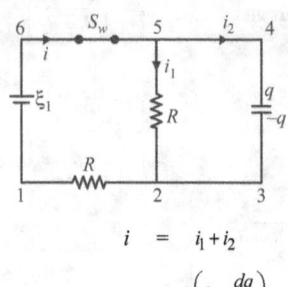

$$i = i_1 + i_2$$
$$= \left(i_1 + \frac{dq}{dt}\right)$$

In close loop 1-2-3-4-5-6-1,
$$ir + \frac{q}{C} - \xi = 0$$
or
$$\left(i_1 + \frac{dq}{dt}\right)R + \frac{q}{C} - \xi = 0 \quad ...(i)$$

In close loop 2-3-4-5-2,
$$\frac{q}{C} - i_1 R = 0 \quad ...(ii)$$

From equations (i) and (ii), we get
$$\frac{dq}{dt}R = \left(\xi - \frac{2q}{C}\right)$$

or
$$\int_0^q \frac{dq}{\left(\xi - \frac{2q}{C}\right)} = \int_0^t \frac{dt}{R}$$

or
$$q = \frac{C\xi}{2}\left(1 - e^{-\frac{2t}{RC}}\right)$$

$$\therefore \quad V = \frac{q}{C} = \frac{\xi}{2}\left(1 - e^{-2t/RC}\right) \quad \textbf{Ans.}$$

40. The current distribution is shown in figure.

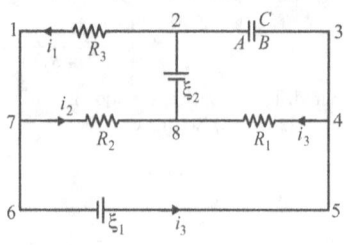

In close loop 1-2-8-7-1,
$$+i_1 R_3 - \xi_2 + i_2 R_2 = 0, \quad ...(i)$$
and in close loop 4-5-6-7-8-4,
$$-\xi_1 - i_2 R_2 + i_3 R_1 = 0 \quad ...(ii)$$

At junction 7, we have
$$i_1 = i_2 + i_3 \quad ...(iii)$$

After solving above equations, we get
$$i_3 = \left[\frac{\xi_1 (R_2 + R_3) + \xi_2 R_2}{R_1 R_2 + R_2 R_3 + R_3 R_1}\right]$$

Potential difference, $V_A - V_B = \xi_2 - i_3 R_1$
$$= \left[\frac{\xi_2 R_3 (R_1 + R_2) - \xi_1 R_1 (R_2 + R_3)}{R_1 R_2 + R_2 R_3 + R_3 R_1}\right] \cdot \textbf{Ans.}$$

41. The current distribution is shown in figure.
In closed loop A-6-5-4-B-C-D-A,
$$-i_2 R_3 - (i_2 + i_3) R_4 + V = 0 \quad ...(i)$$
In closed loop 1-2-3-4-5-6-1,
$$-i_1 R_1 - (i_1 - i_3) R_2 + (i_2 + i_3) R_4 + i_2 R_3 = 0 \quad ...(ii)$$

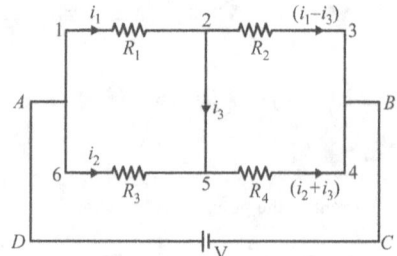

and closed loop 1-2-5-6-1,
$$-i_1 R_1 + i_2 R_3 = 0 \quad ....(iii)$$

After substituting the values and simplifying, we get
$$i = 1 \text{ A.} \quad \textbf{Ans.}$$

★ ★ ★

CHAPTER 4

Thermal & Chemical Effects of Current
(307-338)

4.1	THERMAL EFFECT OF CURRENT : JOULE'S LAW	
4.2	ELECTRICAL APPLIANCES	
4.3	SEEBECK EFFECT	
4.4	PELTIER EFFECT	
4.5	THOMSON EFFECT	
4.6	CHEMICAL EFFECT OF CURRENT	
4.7	FARADAY'S LAW OF ELECTROLYSIS	

REVIEW OF FORMULAE AND IMPORTANT POINTS

EXERCISE 4.1

EXERCISE 4.2

EXERCISE 4.3

EXERCISE 4.4

EXERCISE 4.5

EXERCISE 4.6

HINTS & SOLUTIONS

4.1 THERMAL EFFECT OF CURRENT : JOULE'S LAW

Consider a part of circuit, carrying current i. If dq charge flows between two points differing in potential by V in time dt, then work done by the electric field

$$dW = V\, dq$$
$$= V\, i\, dt$$

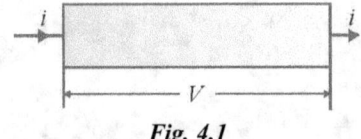

Fig. 4.1

The rate at which energy enters in this part of the circuit

i.e., Power, $\qquad P = \dfrac{dW}{dt} = Vi$

The SI unit of power is J/s. 1 J/s = 1 W.

The power dissipated in the resistor

If the portion of the circuit is a resistor, the potential difference is given by $V = iR$ and

$$P = Vi = i^2 R = \dfrac{V^2}{R}$$

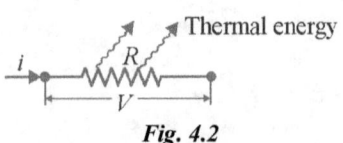

Fig. 4.2

The power enters in the resistor appears as thermal energy. On a microscopic scale the transfer of power in the form of thermal energy can be understood as : Collisions between the electrons and lattice of ions increase the amplitude of the thermal vibrations of the lattice and this corresponds to increase in temperature of resistor. This effect is often called **Joule heating effect.**

Power output of a source

Consider a source of emf ξ and internal resistance r, connected to an external circuit. The current i flows out from the source. The power input into the external circuit,

$$P = Vi$$

We have, $\qquad V = \xi - ir,$

and hence, $\qquad P = (\xi - ir)\, i$

$$= \xi i - i^2 r$$

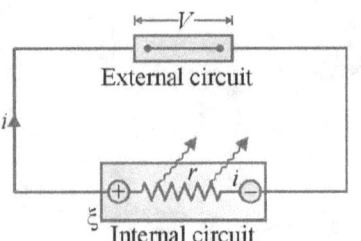

Fig. 4.3

The product ξi is the rate at which work is done on the source. The term $i^2 r$ is the rate at which energy is dissipated in the internal resistance of the source. The power output of the source is the power input to the remaining part of the circuit. Therefore

$$P_{out} = \xi i - i^2 r$$

Power input to a source

Let us consider the source of emf ξ and internal resistance r. The current i is flowing into the source. The power input into the source

$$P = Vi.$$

Here we have $\qquad V = \xi + ir$

Therefore $\qquad P_{in} = (\xi + ir)\, i$

or $\qquad P_{in} = \xi i + i^2 r$

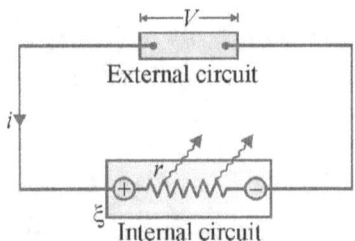

Fig. 4.4

Loss of power in transmission lines and cables

When electrical power is transmitted from the generator to the point where it is used, there is always a loss of energy due to the resistance of the transmission wires owing to the Joule heating effect.

The power used in home is measured by the product of current i and voltage V between the power lines, as they enter the home output power $P_O = Vi$. If the total resistance of the wires from generator to the home is R, then power lost $= i^2 R$. Hence the input power to the home is $P_i = Vi + i^2 R$, and the voltage at the generator must be $V + iR$. The electrical efficiency

$$\eta = \dfrac{P_O}{P_i}$$

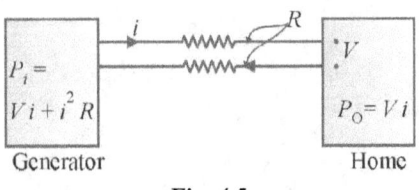

Fig. 4.5

or $\qquad \eta = \left(\dfrac{Vi}{Vi + i^2 R}\right)$

THERMAL AND CHEMICAL EFFECT OF CURRENT

Note: To keep losses minimum, the power is always supplied at high potential, and so to keep the current in the power lines as low as possible

$$i = \frac{(P_{required})}{V}$$

and $$P_{loss} = i^2 R = \frac{(P_{required})^2}{V^2} R.$$

From the above equation, it is clear that, $P_{loss} \propto \frac{1}{V}$.

The supply voltage from the generator may be 33000 V or more.

Maximum power theorem

Consider a battery of emf ξ and internal resistance r is used in a circuit with a variable external resistance R. The value of R for which the power consumed in R is maximum;

The current in the resistor R is $\quad i = \dfrac{\xi}{R+r}$

The power consumed in R is

$$P = i^2 R = \frac{\xi^2 R}{(R+r)^2}$$

P to be maximum $\dfrac{dP}{dR} = 0$,

or $$\frac{dP}{dR} = \frac{\xi^2 (R+r)^2 - 2R(R+r)}{(R+r)^4} = 0$$

which gives $\quad R = r$

and $$P_{max} = \frac{\xi^2 R}{(R+r)^2} = \frac{\xi^2 r}{(r+r)^2}$$

or $$P_{max} = \frac{\xi^2}{4r}.$$

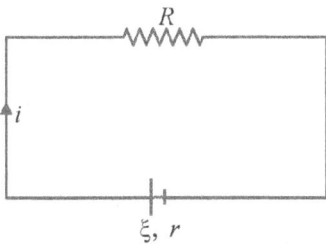

Fig. 4.6

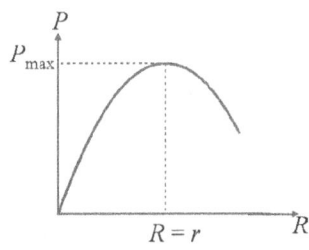

Fig. 4.7

Kilowatt-hour

It is the commercial unit of electrical energy. It is knows as 1 unit.

Thus $1\text{kW-h} = 1000 \times 3600\,\text{J}$
$\qquad = 3.6 \times 10^6\,\text{J}$

Number of units consumed $= \dfrac{\text{total power }(W) \times \text{time}(h)}{1000}$.

Ex. 1 Consider following circuit, find power generated in the resistor R.

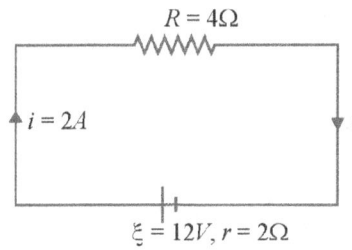

Fig. 4.8

Sol. The power input in the source (electrical power produced)
$$P_{in} = \xi i$$
$$= 12 \times 2 = 24\,W$$
The power dissipated in the source
$$= i^2 r = 2^2 \times 2$$
$$= 8\,W$$
The power output of the source
$$P_{out} = 24 - 8 = 16\,W$$
The power generated in resistor $= 16\,W$

4.2 Electrical appliances

1. **Filament of electrical bulb** : It is made of tungsten which has low resistivity and high melting point.
2. **Filament of heating devices** : It is made of nichrome which has high resistivity and high melting point.
3. **Standard resistances (Resistance box)** : Standard resistances are made of manganin or constantan. These materials have moderate resistivity and very low temperature coefficient of resistance.
4. **Fuse wire** : It is made of tin-lead alloy. It has low resistivity and low melting point.

Rated or design values :

Some of the values like; wattage, voltage etc. are printed on the electrical appliances are called rated or design values. These values give the informations about resistance and allowable current etc. For a bulb of 100 W and 200 V,
Its resistance can be obtained by

$$R = \frac{V_{design}^2}{P_{design}};$$

or $$R \propto \frac{1}{P_{design}}$$

where V_{design} and P_{design} are the design voltage and power of the bulb.

100 W, 220V

Fig. 4.9

$$\therefore \quad R = \frac{220^2}{100}$$
$$= 484 \; \Omega$$

[Assuming this resistance constant for all values of supply voltage V]

Allowable current $$i = \frac{P_{design}}{V_{design}}$$

$$= \frac{100}{220} = \frac{5}{11} A$$

Note: All electrical appliances are design for same voltage; i.e., 220 V.

Power consumed

Power consumed depend on the supply voltage which may be different from rated power.

$$P_{consumed} = \frac{V_{supply}^2}{R}$$

For $V_{supply} = V_{design}$; $\quad P_{consumed} = P_{design}$
Let us now consider two bulbs of wattage P_1 and P_2 :
For $V_{supply} = V_{design} = V$

Resistance of first bulb $$R_1 = \frac{V^2}{P_1}$$

and resistance of second bulb $$R_2 = \frac{V^2}{P_2}$$

THERMAL AND CHEMICAL EFFECT OF CURRENT

1. **Bulbs connected in series :** In series both the bulbs have same current.

$$\therefore \quad \frac{(P_1)_{consumed}}{(P_2)_{consumed}} = \frac{i^2 R_1}{i^2 R_2} = \frac{R_1}{R_2}$$

If $P_1 > P_2$ then $R_1 < R_2$,

$\therefore (P_1)_{consumed} < (P_2)_{consumed}$.

Thus in series low wattage bulb glows brighter than high wattage bulb.

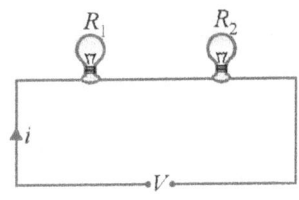

Fig. 4.10

Total power consumed

$$P_{consumed} = \frac{V^2}{R_{total}} = \frac{V^2}{R_1 + R_2}$$

$$= \frac{V^2}{\frac{V^2}{P_1} + \frac{V^2}{P_2}}$$

or $$\frac{1}{P_{consumed}} = \frac{1}{P_1} + \frac{1}{P_2}$$

2. **Bulbs connected in parallel :** In parallel the voltage across them is same.

$$\therefore \quad \frac{(P_1)_{consumed}}{(P_2)_{consumed}} = \frac{\frac{V^2}{R_1}}{\frac{V^2}{R_2}}$$

$$= \frac{R_2}{R_1}$$

If $P_1 > P_2$ then $R_1 < R_2$,

$\therefore (P_1)_{consumed} > (P_2)_{consumed}$

Thus in parallel high wattage bulb glows brighter than less wattage bulb.

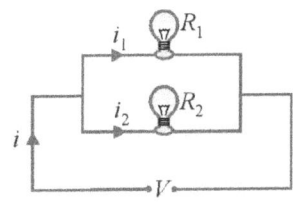

Fig. 4.11

Total power consumed, $P_{consumed} = \frac{V^2}{R_{total}} = \frac{V^2}{\left(\frac{R_1 R_2}{R_1 + R_2}\right)}$

where $R_1 = \frac{V^2}{P_1}$ and $R_2 = \frac{V^2}{P_2}$

$\therefore \quad P_{consumed} = P_1 + P_2$.

Fuse : It is used in series with the circuit to prevent the electrical appliances from burning by melting itself to open the circuit.
Let R is the resistance of the fuse wire, then

$$R = \frac{\rho \ell}{\pi r^2}$$

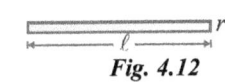

Fig. 4.12

The heat produced in fuse wire $\quad H = i^2 R = \frac{i^2 \rho \ell}{\pi r^2}$

If h is the heat loss per unit surface area of fuse wire, then heat radiated per second

$$= h \times 2\pi r \ell$$

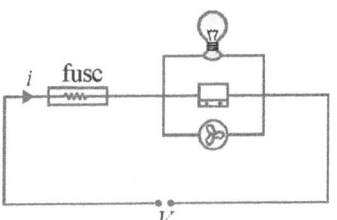

Fig. 4.13

At thermal equilibrium
$$\frac{i^2 \rho \ell}{\pi r^2} = h \times 2\pi r \ell$$

or
$$h = \frac{i^2 \rho}{2\pi^2 r^3}$$

According to Newton's law of cooling
$$h = C\Delta\theta$$
[where $\Delta\theta$ is the temperature of fuse wire above surrounding, and C is a constant]

$\therefore$
$$\frac{i^2 \rho}{2\pi^2 r^3} = C\Delta\theta$$

or
$$\Delta\theta = \frac{i^2 \rho}{2\pi^2 r^3 C}$$

The above expression is free from length of the fuse wire. Hence the function of fuse is independent of its length provided i remains constant.
For given material of fuse wire
$$i^2 \propto r^3.$$

An important explanation

In houses all electrical appliances are connected in parallel with the supply line. Hence each of them has same potential. But because of resistance of current carrying wires, the potential across each of them is different. It is common experience that when any high voltage appliance is switched on, the other get affected (bulb glows less brighter). It is due to current carrying cables. To understand more clearly consider a simple circuit having a bulb and a heater connected in paralled with a source.

When only bulb is switched on
$$i = \frac{200}{50+100} = \frac{4}{3} A$$

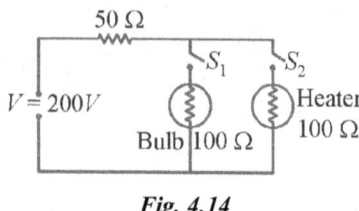

Fig. 4.14

The power consumed by bulb
$$P = i^2 R = \left(\frac{4}{3}\right)^2 \times 100 = \frac{1600}{9} W = 177.8 W$$

Now heater is also switched on, then net current supply
$$i = \frac{200}{\left(50 + \frac{100 \times 100}{100+100}\right)} = 2A$$

The current flows in the bulb = 1A
The power consumed by the bulb $P' = i^2 R$
$$= 1^2 \times 100 = 100 \text{ W}$$

It is clear from above calculations that when heater in parallel is switched on, bulb consumes less power, and therefore becomes dim. If the resistance of current carrying wire becomes zero, there will no such effect occur.

THERMAL AND CHEMICAL EFFECT OF CURRENT

Ex. 2 Two bulbs rated 25 W-200 V and 100 W-200 V are connected in series to a 400 V supply. Show with necessary calculations, which bulb if any will fuse ? What should happen if the two bulbs were connected in parallel to the same supply ?

Sol.

Resistances of the bulbs:

$$R_1 = \frac{V^2}{P_1} = \frac{200^2}{25} = 1600 \, \Omega$$

and $\quad R_2 = \frac{V^2}{P_2} = \frac{200^2}{100} = 400 \, \Omega$

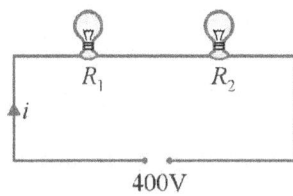

Fig. 4.15

Allowable currents: $\quad i_1 = \frac{P_1}{V} = \frac{25}{200} = \frac{1}{8} A$

and $\quad i_2 = \frac{P_2}{V} = \frac{100}{200} = \frac{1}{2} A$

(i) When they are connected in series, both have same current

$$\therefore \quad i = \frac{V_{supply}}{R_1 + R_2} = \frac{400}{1600 + 400} = \frac{1}{5} A$$

$$> i_1$$
$$< i_2$$

It means 25 W bulb will fuse in series.

(ii) When bulbs are connected in parallel, both the bulb will have same voltage. Thus

$$i'_1 = \frac{V_{supply}}{R_1}$$

$$= \frac{400}{1600} = \frac{1}{4} A$$

$$> i_1$$

and $\quad i'_2 = \frac{V_{supply}}{R_2}$

$$= \frac{400}{400} = 1 A$$

$$> i_2$$

The currents in both the bulbs are greater than their allowable currents. Therefore both bulbs will fuse in parallel.

Ex. 3 An electric kettle has two heating elements. One brings it to boil water in time t_1 and the other in time t_2. Find the time t taken by water to boil in kettle when
(i) heating filaments are connected in series.
(ii) heating filaments are connected in parallel.

Sol.
Let H is the heat required to boil the water, then for first coil

$$H = \frac{V^2}{R_1} t_1 \quad \Rightarrow R_1 = \frac{V^2 t_1}{H}$$

and for second coil $\quad R_2 = \frac{V^2 t_2}{H}$

(i) When both the filaments are connected in series

$$H = \frac{V^2}{R_{total}} t = \frac{V^2}{R_1 + R_2} t$$

$$= \frac{V^2}{\left(\frac{V^2 t_1}{H} + \frac{V^2 t_2}{H}\right)} t$$

$$\therefore \quad t = t_1 + t_2$$

(ii) When both the filaments are connected in parallel

$$H = \frac{V^2}{R_{total}} t = \frac{V^2}{\left(\frac{R_1 R_2}{R_1 + R_2}\right)} t$$

After substituting values of R_1 and R_2, we get

$$\frac{1}{t} = \frac{1}{t_1} + \frac{1}{t_2}.$$

Ex. 4 A cell of emf ξ and internal resistance r supplies currents for the same time t through external resistance R_1 and R_2 separately. If the heat developed in the external resistance in the two cases is the same, then what should be the internal resistance ?

Sol.

In first case $\quad i_1 = \frac{\xi}{R_1 + r}$

and heat produced in R_1

$$H_1 = i_1^2 R_1 t = \left(\frac{\xi}{R_1 + r}\right)^2 R_1 t$$

In second case $\quad i_2 = \frac{\xi}{R_2 + r}$

and heat produced in R_2

$$H_2 = i_2^2 R_2 t = \left(\frac{\xi}{R_2 + r}\right)^2 R_2 t$$

For the condition given,
$$H_1 = H_2$$

or $\quad \left(\frac{\xi}{R_1 + r}\right)^2 R_1 t = \left(\frac{\xi}{R_2 + r}\right)^2 R_2 t$

After solving, we get

$$r = \sqrt{R_1 R_2} . \qquad \text{Ans.}$$

Ex. 5 What amount of heat will be generated in a coil of resistance R due to a charge q passing through it if the current in the coil
(a) decreases down to zero uniformly during a time interval Δt.
(b) decreases down to zero halving its value every Δt seconds?

Sol.
(a) As the current decreases uniformly, its value at any time t, assuming initial current i_0

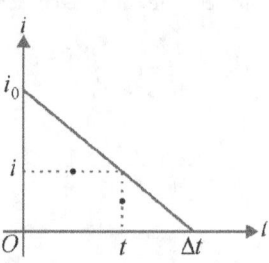

Fig. 4.17

$$i = i_0 - \frac{i_0}{\Delta t} t = i_0 \left(1 - \frac{t}{\Delta t}\right)$$

Thus $$q = \int_0^{\Delta t} i\, dt = i_0 \int_0^{\Delta t} \left(1 - \frac{t}{\Delta t}\right) dt$$

$$= i_0 \left| t - \frac{t^2}{2\Delta t} \right|_0^{\Delta t} = \frac{i_0 \Delta t}{2}$$

or $$i_0 = \frac{2q}{\Delta t}$$

Hence $$i = i_0 \left(1 - \frac{t}{\Delta t}\right) = \frac{2q}{\Delta t}\left(1 - \frac{t}{\Delta t}\right)$$

The heat generated

$$H = \int_0^{\Delta t} i^2 R\, dt = \int_0^{\Delta t} \left[\frac{2q}{\Delta t}\left(1 - \frac{t}{\Delta t}\right)\right]^2 R\, dt$$

$$= -\frac{4q^2 R}{3\Delta t}\left|\left(1 - \frac{t}{\Delta t}\right)^3\right|_0^{\Delta t}$$

$$= \frac{4q^2 R}{3\Delta t} \qquad \text{Ans.}$$

(b) According to given condition

$$i = i_0 \left(\frac{1}{2}\right)^{t/\Delta t}$$

When current decreases according to above equation it becomes zero at $t = \infty$. Therefore charge will flow till infinite time.

The charge $$q = \int_0^\infty i\, dt = \int_0^\infty i_0 \left(\frac{1}{2}\right)^{t/\Delta t} dt$$

$$= i_0 \int_0^\infty 2^{-t/\Delta t}\, dt \qquad \ldots (i)$$

Substituting $2^{-t/\Delta t} = z$

or $$\frac{-t}{\Delta t} \ln 2 = \ln z$$

Differentiating above equation, we have

$$\frac{d}{dt}\left[\frac{-t}{\Delta t}\ln 2\right] = \frac{d\ln z}{dt}$$

or $$\frac{-\ln 2}{\Delta t} = \frac{1}{z}\frac{dz}{dt}$$

or $$dt = \left(-\frac{\Delta t}{\ln 2}\right)\cdot \frac{dz}{z}$$

Substituting these values in equation (i), we get

$$q = i_0 \int_0^\infty z \times \left(\frac{-\Delta t}{\ln 2}\right)\frac{dz}{z}$$

$$= \frac{i_0(-\Delta t)|z|_0^\infty}{\ln 2}$$

$$= \frac{i_0(-\Delta t)}{\ln 2}\left|2^{-t/\Delta t}\right|_0^\infty$$

$$= \frac{i_0 \Delta t}{\ln 2}$$

Thus we have $$i_0 = \frac{q\ln 2}{\Delta t} \text{ and } i = \frac{q\ln 2}{\Delta t}\left(\frac{1}{2}\right)^{t/\Delta t}$$

The heat generated in the time interval 0 to ∞

$$H = \int_0^\infty i^2 R\, dt$$

$$= \int_0^\infty \left[\frac{q\ln 2}{\Delta t}\left(\frac{1}{2}\right)^{t/\Delta t}\right]^2 R\, dt$$

$$= -\frac{q^2 \times 2R}{2\Delta t}\left[2^{-2t/\Delta t}\right]_0^\infty$$

$$= \frac{q^2 R}{\Delta t}. \qquad \text{Ans.}$$

Ex. 6 A conductor has a temperature independent resistance and a total heat capacity C. At the moment $t = 0$ is connected to a dc voltage V. Find the time dependance of the conductor's temperature T assuming that thermal power dissipated into surrounding space to vary as $q = k(T - T_0)$, where k is a constant, T_0 is the environment temperature (equal to the conductor's temperature at the initial moment).

Sol.

The rate of heat evolved by the resistance
= rate of absorption of heat + power dissipated into surrounding

or $\quad \dfrac{V^2}{R} = \dfrac{CdT}{dt} + k(T-T_0)$

or $\quad \dfrac{V^2}{R} - k(T-T_0) = \dfrac{CdT}{dt}$

or $\quad \displaystyle\int_{T_0}^{T} \dfrac{dT}{\left[\dfrac{V^2}{R} - k(T-T_0)\right]} = \int_0^t \dfrac{dt}{C}$

$\quad \dfrac{\left|\ln\left[\dfrac{V^2}{R} - k(T-T_0)\right]\right|_{T_0}^{T}}{-k} = \dfrac{t}{C}$

$\ln\left[\dfrac{V^2}{R} - k(T-T_0)\right] - \ln\left[\dfrac{V^2}{R} - k(T_0-T_0)\right] = -\dfrac{kt}{C}$

$\ln\left[\dfrac{\dfrac{V^2}{R} - k(T-T_0)}{\dfrac{V^2}{R}}\right] = -\dfrac{kt}{C}$

$\ln\left[1 - \dfrac{k}{(V^2/R)}(T-T_0)\right] = -\dfrac{kt}{C}$

or $\quad 1 - \dfrac{k(T-T_0)}{(V^2/R)} = e^{-kt/C}$

or $\quad k(T-T_0) = \dfrac{V^2}{R}\left(1 - e^{-kt/C}\right)$

or $\quad T = T_0 + \dfrac{V^2}{kR}\left(1 - e^{-kt/C}\right).$ **Ans.**

4.3 SEEBECK EFFECT

The conversion of electrical energy from thermal energy was discovered by Seebeck in 1826. According to him if the junctions of two different metals are kept at different temperatures, then there is an electric current in the circuit. This effect is called Seebeck effect. The emf produced across the junctions is called thermo-emf and the resulting current is called thermo-electric current, the pair of metals is called a thermo-couple.

Thermoelectric series

Seebeck arranged different metals in a specific order which gives the thermo-electric series, and showed that when any two metals of the series are used with junctions at different temperatures, current flows from the metal earlier in the series to the metal later in the series through the cold junction. Also, the series gives an idea of the relative magnitude of emf for different thermocouples. Farther apart two metals lie in the series, larger is the emf produced. The thermo-electric series is as :
Antimony, Fe, Cd, Zn, Ag, Au, Rb, Mo, Cr, Sn, Pb, Hg, Mn, Cu, Pt, Ni, constantan, bismuth.
Take as an example, a thermocouple madeup of copper and iron. The current will be from iron to copper at the cold junction. The largest emf will generate in a thermocouple made of antimony and bismuth.

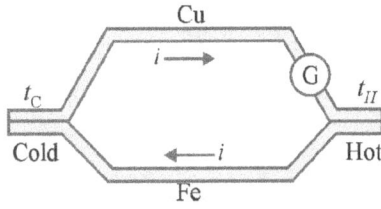

Fig. 4.18 *Thermocouple made of Cu-Fe.*

Variation of emf with temperature

Suppose a thermocouple is made up of two metals A and B, and the thermo-emf produced is ξ_{AB}. Figure shows graphically the variation in thermo-emf as the temperature of the hot junction changes.
If t_C, t_n and t_i denote the temperature of the cold junction, the neutral temperature and the inversion temperature respectively, then

$$t_n - t_C = t_i - t_n$$

or $\quad t_n = \dfrac{t_C + t_i}{2} \quad \ldots(1)$

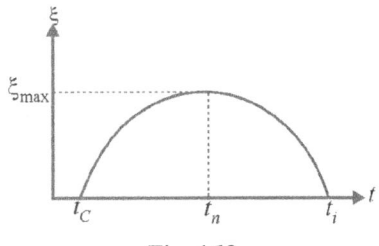

Fig. 4.19

If the cold junction is kept in ice (0°C) and the hot junction at $t(°C)$, then the thermo-emf depends on the temperature as

$$\xi_{AB} = a_{AB}t + \dfrac{b_{AB}}{2}t^2. \quad \ldots(2)$$

where a_{AB} and b_{AB} are constants for a pair of metals A and B. It should be remembered that the parabolic variation is obtained in the case when either of a and b is negative.

Neutral and inversion temperature

The temperature of the hot junction at which the thermo-emf is maximum is called the neutral temperature and the temperature at which the thermo-emf changes in sign is called the inversion temperature.

Thus for ξ_{AB} to be maximum,

$$\frac{d\xi}{dt} = 0$$

or

$$\frac{d}{dt}\left(at + \frac{bt^2}{2}\right) = 0$$

or

$$a + bt = 0$$

$$\therefore \quad t = t_n = -\frac{a}{b}. \quad \ldots(3)$$

As both a and b are constants for a thermo-couple and so neutral temperature is constant for any thermo-couple. The quantity $\frac{d\xi}{dt}$ is called thermoelectric power or seebeck coefficient.

The maximum value of thermo-emf

$$\xi_{max} = a\left(\frac{-a}{b}\right) + \frac{b}{2}\left(\frac{-a}{b}\right)^2$$

or

$$\xi_{max} = -\frac{a^2}{b}. \quad \ldots(4)$$

Coefficients a and b for thermocouple

Metal with Pb	a (µV/°C)	b (µV/°C^2)
Al	−0.47	0.003
Bi	−43.7	−0.47
Cu	2.76	0.012
Au	2.9	0.0093
Fe	16.6	−0.030
Ni	19.1	−0.030
Pt	−1.79	−0.035
Ag	2.5	0.012
Steel	10.8	−0.016

Law of intermediate metal

Suppose ξ_{AB}, ξ_{AC} and ξ_{BC} are the thermo emfs across the thermo-couples made of A, B; A, C; and B, C respectively. If the temperature difference across the junctions of all the thermocouples are the same, then

$$\xi_{AC} = \xi_{AB} + \xi_{BC} \qquad \ldots(5)$$

Law of intermediate temperature

Let $[\xi_{AB}]_{t_1}^{t_2}$ denotes the thermo-emf of a thermocouple made of metals A and B when the temperatures of the junctions are t_1 and t_2. Then

$$[\xi_{AB}]_{t_1}^{t_2} = [\xi_{AB}]_{t_1}^{t_3} + [\xi_{AB}]_{t_3}^{t_2} \qquad \ldots(6)$$

This is known as the law of intermediate metals.

Ex. 7 The cold junction of a thermocouple is maintained at 20°C. No thermo-emf is developed when the hot junction is at 540°C. Find the neutral temperature.

Sol. Given $t_c = 20°C$, $t_i = 540°C$

$$\therefore \quad t_n = \frac{t_c + t_i}{2}$$

$$= \frac{20 + 540}{2} = 280°C. \qquad \text{Ans.}$$

Ex. 8 The expression for thermo emf in a thermocouple is given by the relation $\xi = 40\theta - \frac{\theta^2}{20}$, where θ is the temperature difference of two junctions. What is the neutral temperature?

Sol. Given $\xi = 40\theta - \frac{\theta^2}{20}$

For maximum value of ξ,

$$\frac{d\xi}{d\theta} = 0$$

or $\quad \frac{d}{d\theta}\left(40\theta - \frac{\theta^2}{20}\right) = 0$

or $\quad 40 - \frac{2\theta}{20} = 0$

Which on solving gives

$$\theta = 400°C$$

Thus neutral temperature is 400°C. **Ans.**

Ex. 9 Find the emf of a Cu – Fe thermocouple when temperature of hot junction is 100°C and that of cold junction is 0°C.

Sol. We know that

$$\xi = at + \frac{bt^2}{2}$$

By law of intermediate metals, we have

$$\xi_{Cu,Fe} = \xi_{Cu,Pb} + \xi_{Pb,Fe} = \xi_{Cu,Pb} - \xi_{Fe,Pb}$$

$$= \left[a_{Cu}t + b_{Cu}\frac{t^2}{2}\right]_{Pb} - \left[a_{Fe}t + b_{Fe}\frac{t^2}{2}\right]_{Pb}$$

$$= [a_{Cu} - a_{Fe}]_{Pb} t + \frac{1}{2}[b_{Cu} - b_{Fe}]_{Pb} t^2$$

$$= (2.76 - 16.65) \times 100 + \frac{1}{2}(0.012 + 0.030) \times 100^2$$

$$= -1.179 \, mV \qquad \text{Ans.}$$

4.4 Peltier effect

In 1834, Peltier discovered that if a current is allowed to pass through the junction of two different metals, heat is either evolved or absorbed at the junctions. That means the junction is either heated or cooled. This effect is known as Peltier effect and the heat evolved or absorbed is knwon as Peltier heat. Experiments has shown that the peltier heat transferred at any junction is proportional to the amount of current crossing the junction and changes its sign when reversing the direction of current. Thus Peltier effect is reversible. If ΔH is the amount of heat evolved or absorbed when a charge ΔQ is passed through the junction, then we define Peltier coefficient (Peltier emf) as :

$$\Pi = \frac{\text{Peltier heat}}{\text{charge transferred}} = \frac{\Delta H}{\Delta Q}$$

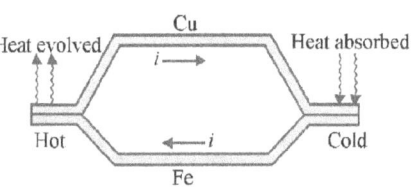

Fig. 4.20 Peltier effect

4.5 Thomson effect

If a metal has a nonuniform temperature and a current is passed through it, heat is absorbed or evolved in different sections of the metal. This heat is over and above the Joule's heat. This effect is called Thomson effect. If a charge ΔQ is passed through a small section of the metal wire having temperature difference Δt between the ends, the

Thomson coefficient $\sigma = \dfrac{\Delta H}{\Delta Q \Delta t}$.

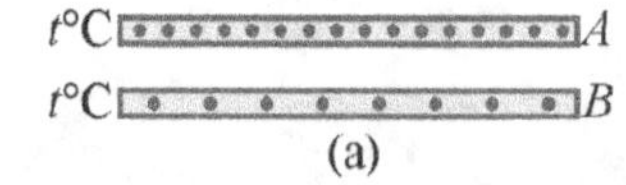

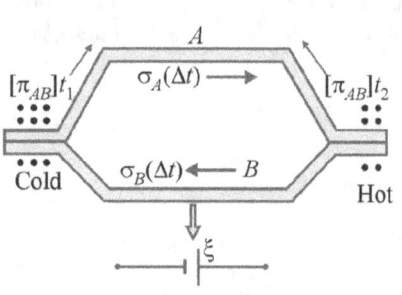

Fig. 4.21 (a) Two metals at same temperature

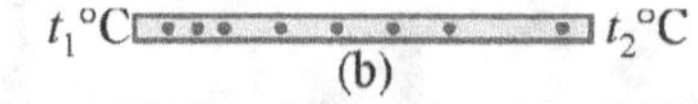

Fig. 4.21 (b) A metals with different temperature

Explanation of Seebeck, Peltier and Thomson effects

We know that the density of free electrons is different in different metals at same temperature. Thus when two different metals are joined together, the electrons tend to diffuse from the side with higher concentration to the side with lower concentration. Also the density of free electrons varies inside the same metal, if temperature of metal is not uniform everywhere. Thus electrons tend to diffuse from the higher concentration to the lower concentration region. So if the junctions are kept at different temperatures, an emf is developed across the junctions.

It can be easily understand that at the cold junction the electron density is more than the electron density at the hot junction. It will cause the p.d. between the junctions. Thus, if $[\Pi_{AB}]_{t_1}$, $[\Pi_{AB}]_{t_2}$ be the emf's at the cold and hot junctions respectively, then thermo-emf will be $[\Pi_{AB}] = [\Pi_{AB}]_{t_2} - [\Pi_{AB}]_{t_1}$.

It is clear from the above explanation that Seebeck emf is a combination of Peltier emf and Thomson emf. Thus

$$\xi_{AB} = [\Pi_{AB}]_{t_2} - [\Pi_{AB}]_{t_1} + \Delta t(\sigma_A - \sigma_B).$$

Fig. 4.22

Difference between Peltier effect and Joule's effect

Peltier effect	Joule's effect
1. It is a reversible effect.	1. It is an irreversible effect.
2. It takes place at the junctions.	2. It takes place across the entire metal.
3. It may be heating or a cooling effect.	3. It always be a heating effect.
4. Peltier heat is proportional to the current: $H_{\text{Peltier}} \propto i$.	4. Joule heat is proportional to the square of the current: $H_{\text{Joule}} \propto i^2$.

4.6 Chemical effect of current

Electrolyte : The liquid which dissociates into its ions on passing current through it is called electrolyte.

Electrolysis : The process of decomposition of electrolyte solution into ions on passing current through it is called electrolysis.

Electroplating : The article to be electroplated is made as the cathode and the metal to be deposited is made as the anode. A solution of the metal is taken as the electrolyte. If gold is to be coated then auric chloride is used as electrolyte. In case of ornament of silver, electroplating is to be done by $AgNO_3$. The Ag^+ ions move to the cathode and receives an electron from the cathode to become neutral Ag atom and deposited on the cathode.

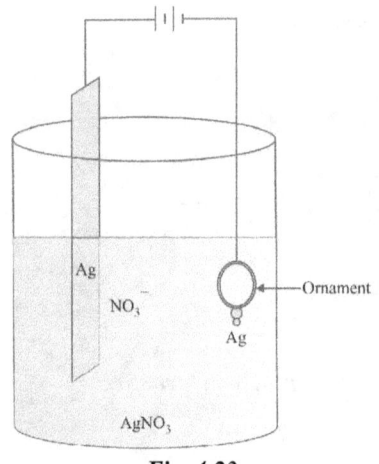

Fig. 4.23

THERMAL AND CHEMICAL EFFECT OF CURRENT

$$Ag^+ + e^- = Ag.$$

The NO_3^- ion moves to the anode and gives its extra electrons to it. The NO_3^- ion is converted to NO_3,

$$NO_3^- = NO_3 + e.$$

The NO_3 so formed reacts with a silver atom of the anode to form $AgNO_3$ which gets dissolved in the solution. This way, silver anode slowly dissolved in the solution. Thus, silver anode slowly dissolves and deposited on the cathode with the concentration of the electrolyte remaining unchanged.

4.7 FARADAY'S LAW OF ELECTROLYSIS

First law : The mass of a substance liberated at an electrode is proportional to the amount of the charge passing through the electrolyte. Thus

$$m = zQ$$

If an electric current of constant magnitude i is passed through an electrolyte for a time t, then

$$Q = it$$
$$\therefore \quad m = zit$$

where z is a constant called electrochemical equivalent (ECE) of the substance. The SI unit of ECE is kg/C.

Second law : The mass of a substance liberated at an electrolyte by a given amount of charge is proportional to the chemical equivalent of the substance. The chemical equivalent of a substance is

$$W = \frac{\text{atomic mass}}{\text{valency}}$$

If W_1 and W_2 are the chemical equivalent of two substances, then from Faraday is II law

$$\frac{m_1}{m_2} = \frac{W_1}{W_2} \quad \ldots(i)$$

Also from I law

$$\frac{m_1}{m_2} = \frac{z_1}{z_2} \quad \ldots(ii)$$

From (i) and (ii)

$$\frac{W_1}{W_2} = \frac{z_1}{z_2}$$

or

$$\frac{W_1}{z_1} = \frac{W_2}{z_2} = \text{constant (F)}$$

or

$$\frac{W}{z} = F$$

F is the proportionality constant called Faraday's constant. $1F = 96500$ C/eq.

Ex. 10 A brass plate having surface area 200 cm² on one side is electroplated with 0.10 mm thick silver layers on both sides using a 15A current. Find the time taken to do the job. The specific gravity of silver is 10.5 and its atomic weight is 107.9 g/mol.

Sol. The volume of silver deposited

$$V = 2 \times \text{vol. of silver deposited on one side}$$
$$= 2(200 \times 10^{-4} \times 0.1 \times 10^{-3}) \text{ m}^3$$
$$= 4 \times 10^{-6} \text{ m}^3$$

The mass of silver needed

$$m = \rho V = 10.5 \times 10^3 \times 4 \times 10^{-6}$$
$$= 42 \times 10^{-3} \text{ kg} = 42 \text{ g}$$

Chemical equivalent of silver

$$W = \frac{107}{1} = 107 \text{ g}$$

$$\therefore \quad z = \frac{W}{F} = \frac{107}{96500}$$

If t is the required time, then by Faraday I law

$$z i t = m$$

$$\therefore \quad t = \frac{m}{zi} = \frac{42}{\frac{107}{96500} \times 15} = \frac{42 \times 96500}{107 \times 15}$$

$$= 42 \text{ minute} \qquad \text{Ans.}$$

Ex. 11 A current of 1A is passed through a dilute solution of sulphuric acid for some time to liberate 1g of oxygen. How much hydrogen is liberated during this period ? How long was the current passed? Faraday constant = 96500 C/mole.

Sol. Chemical equivalent of oxygen

$$W = \frac{\text{Atomic mass}}{\text{valency}} = \frac{16}{2} = 8.$$

Chemical equivalent of hydrogen = 1

By Faraday II law

$$\frac{m_O}{m_H} = \frac{W_O}{W_H} = \frac{8}{1}$$

or $\quad m_H = \frac{m_O}{8} = \frac{1}{8} g$

We have 1g of oxygen = $\frac{1}{8}$ gram – equivalent of hydrogen

We know that for liberation of 1 gram - equivalent weight, it requires 96500C of charge. Thus for $\frac{1}{8}$ gram-equivalent, it requires a charge

$$= \frac{96500}{8} = 1.12 \times 10^4 C.$$

If t is the required time, then

$$t = \frac{Q}{i} = \frac{1.12 \times 10^4}{1}$$
$$= 1.2 \times 10^4 \text{ s}$$
$$= 3 \text{ hour } 20 \text{ min} \qquad \text{Ans.}$$

Review of formulae & Important Points

1. The rate of energy transfer is called power in an electrical device with a potential difference V is
$$P = Vi.$$
If the device is a resistor, then we can write
$$P = i^2 R = \frac{V^2}{R}.$$

2. Thermal energy produced in time t
$$Q = Pi = Vit.$$
In a resistor, electrical potential energy is converted to internal thermal energy via collisions between charge carriers and atoms.

3. **kW-h :** It is the commercial unit of electrical energy.
$$1 \text{kW-h} = 3.6 \times 10^6 \text{ J}.$$
1 kW-h is known as 1 unit of electrical energy.

$$\text{Number of units} = \left[\frac{\text{power}(W) \times \text{time}(h)}{1000} \right]$$

Cost of electricity = number of units × cost of one unit

4. **Maximum power theorem :**
Power generated in the resistor R

$$P = \left(\frac{\xi}{R+r} \right)^2 R.$$

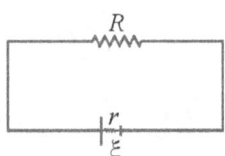

For maximum power

$$r = R \text{ and } P_{max} = \frac{\xi^2}{4R}$$

5. **Electrical appliances :**
The resistance of any electrical appliance of power P_{design} and V_{design} can be obtained by

$$R = \frac{V_{design}^2}{P_{design}}$$

The allowable current

$$i = \frac{P_{design}}{V_{design}}$$

6. In houses the electrical appliances are connected in parallel. If appliances of powers $P_1, P_2, \ldots$ are connected in parallel across the design voltage V, then total power consumed
$$P = P_1 + P_2 + \ldots$$
In series :
$$\frac{1}{P} = \frac{1}{P_1} + \frac{1}{P_2} + \ldots$$

7. **Fuse wire :** In a fuse wire, the change in its temperature $\Delta\theta$ for the constant current i is given by
$$\Delta\theta = \frac{i^2 \rho}{2\pi^2 r^3 C}$$
For the given material of fuse wire $i^2 \propto r^3$.

8. **Chemical effect of direct current :**
   (i) Faraday's I law : The amount of substance deposited or liberated on any electrode is proportional to the charge flows in the electrolyte solution. Thus
   $$m = zq = z\,it,$$
   where z is called electrochemical equivalent.
   (ii) Faraday's II law : If same amount of charge flows in two different electrolyte solutions, then the ratio of amounts of substances deposited is proportional to their chemical equivalent. Thus
   $$\frac{m_1}{m_2} = \frac{W_1}{W_2}$$

9. **Faraday constant :**
$$\frac{W}{Z} = F \qquad \text{(Faraday constant)}$$
$$1F = 96500 \text{ C/eq.}$$

10. **Seebeck effect :** The conversion of thermal energy into electrical energy is known as Seebeck effect.
The emf across the junctions of two different metals is given by
$$\xi = at + \frac{bt^2}{2},$$
where a and b are Seebeck's constants.

11. **Neutral temperature :** It is constant for any thermocouple. Neutral temperature
$$t_n = \frac{t_c + t_i}{2}$$
Also $\qquad t_n = -\frac{a}{b}.$

The maximum value of ξ will occur at t_n, which is
$$\xi_{max} = -\frac{a^2}{b}.$$

12. **Law of intermediate metal :** For thermocouples made of $A, B; B, C$ and A, C
$$\xi_{AB} + \xi_{BC} = \xi_{AC}$$

13. **Law of intermediate temperature :** For any thermocouple
$$\left[\xi_{AB}\right]_{t_1}^{t_3} + \left[\xi_{AB}\right]_{t_3}^{t_2} = \left[\xi_{AB}\right]_{t_1}^{t_2}$$

14. **Thermoelectric power or Seebeck coefficient**
$$S = \frac{d\xi}{dt} = a + bt.$$

15. **Peltier coefficient :**
$$\pi = \frac{\Delta H}{\Delta Q} = T\left(\frac{d\xi}{dt}\right).$$

16. **Thomson coefficient :**
$$\sigma = \frac{\Delta H}{\Delta Q \Delta t} = -T\left(\frac{dS}{dt}\right)$$

★★★

Electricity — MCQ Type 1 — Exercise 4.1

LEVEL - 1

Only one option correct

1. Which of the following plots may represent the thermal energy produced in a resistor in a given time as a function of the electric current?

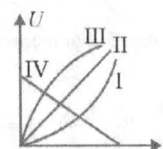

(a) I (b) II
(c) III (d) IV

2. Two resistors R and $2R$ are connected in series in the circuit. The thermal energy developed in R and $2R$ are in the ratio
(a) 1 : 2 (b) 2 : 1
(c) 1 : 4 (d) 4 : 1

3. Two resistors R and $2R$ are connected in parallel in the circuit. The thermal energy developed in R and $2R$ are in the ratio
(1) 1 : 2 (b) 2 : 1
(c) 1 : 4 (d) 4 : 1

4. Forty electric bulbs are connected in series across a 220 V supply. After one bulb is fused, the remaining 39 are connected again in series across the same supply. The illumination will be
(a) more with 40 bulbs than with 39
(b) more with 39 bulbs than with 40
(c) equal in both the cases
(d) in the ratio of $49^2 : 39^2$

5. A heater coil is cut into two parts of equal length and one of them is used in the heater. The ratio of the heat produced by this half coil to that by the original coil is
(a) 2 : 1 (b) 1 : 2
(c) 1 : 4 (d) 4 : 1

6. What is immaterial for an electric fuse wire?
(a) Its specific resistance (b) Its radius
(c) Its length (d) Current flowing through it

7. An electric bulb is rated 220 volt and 100 watt. Power consumed by it when operated on 110 volt is
(a) 50 watt (b) 75 watt
(c) 90 watt (d) 25 watt

8. Two heater wires of equal length are first connected in series and then in parallel. The ratio of heat produced in the two cases is
(a) 2 : 1 (b) 1 : 2
(c) 4 : 1 (d) 1 : 4

9. A battery of e.m.f. 10 V and internal resistance 0.5 ohm is connected across a variable resistance R. The value of R for which the power delivered in it is maximum is given by
(a) 2.0 ohm (b) 0.25 ohm
(c) 1.0 ohm (d) 0.5 ohm

10. An electric bulb is designed to draw power P_0 at voltage V_0. If the voltage is V it draws a power P. Then

(a) $P = \left(\dfrac{V_0}{V}\right)^2 P_0$ (b) $P = \left(\dfrac{V}{V_0}\right)^2 P_0$

(c) $P = \left(\dfrac{V}{V_0}\right) P_0$ (d) $P = \left(\dfrac{V_0}{V}\right) P_0$

11. The three resistances of equal value are arranged in the different combinations shown below. Arrange them in increasing order of power dissipation

(I)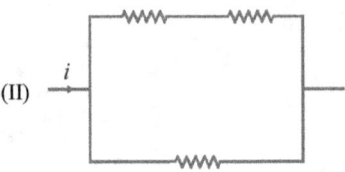

(II)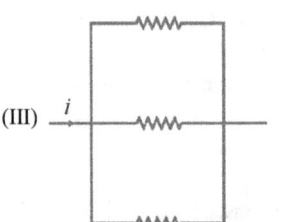

(III)

(IV)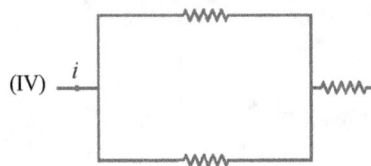

(a) III < II < IV < I (b) II < III < IV < I
(c) I < IV < III < II (d) I < III < II < IV

Answer Key (Sol. from page 333)

| 1 | (a) | 2 | (a) | 3 | (b) | 4 | (b) | 5 | (a) | 6 | (c) |
| 7 | (d) | 8 | (d) | 9 | (d) | 10 | (b) | 11 | (a) | | |

12. A 100 W bulb B_1, and two 60 W bulbs B_2 and B_3, are connected to a 250 V source, as shown in the figure. Now W_1, W_2 and W_3 are the output powers of the bulbs B_1, B_2 and B_3, respectively. Then

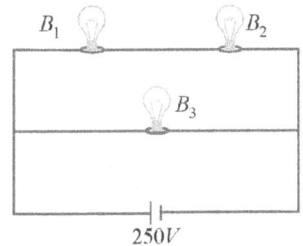

(a) $W_1 > W_2 = W_3$
(b) $W_1 > W_2 > W_3$
(b) $W_1 < W_2 = W_3$
(d) $W_1 < W_2 < W_3$

13. A 1000 W heating unit is designed to operate on a 120 V line. The line voltage drops to 110 V. The percentage of heat output drops by :
(a) 9 %
(b) 27 %
(c) 16 %
(d) 30 %

14. Three electric bulbs of 200 W, 200 W and 400 W are shown in figure. The resultant power of the combination is

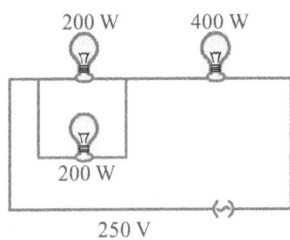

(a) 800 W
(b) 400 W
(c) 200 W
(d) 600 W

15. An electric bulb rated 220 V, 100 W is connected in series with another bulb rated 220 V, 60 W. If the voltage across the combination is 220 V, the power consumed by the 100 W bulb will about
(a) 25 W
(b) 14 W
(c) 60 W
(d) 100 W

16. (1) The product of a volt and a coulomb is a joule.
(2) The product of a volt and an ampere is a joule/second.
(3) The product of volt and watt is horse power.
(4) Watt-hour can be measured in terms of electron volt.
State if
(a) All four are correct
(b) (1), (2) and (4) are correct
(c) (1) and (3) are correct
(d) (3) and (4) are correct

17. Two bulbs are working in parallel order. Bulb A is brighter than bulb B. If R_A and R_B are their resistance respectively then
(a) $R_A > R_B$
(b) $R_A < R_B$
(c) $R_A = R_B$
(d) None of these

18. A bulb rated at (100W – 200 V) is used on a 100 V line. The current in the bulb is
(a) $\frac{1}{4}$ amp
(b) 4 amp
(c) $\frac{1}{2}$ amp
(d) 2 amp

19. Two electrolytic cells containing $CuSO_4$ and $AgNO_3$ respectively are connected in series and a current is passed through them until 1 mg of copper is deposited in the first cell. The amount of silver deposited in the second cell during this time is approximately [Atomic weight of copper and silver are respectively 63.57 and 107.88]
(a) 1.7 mg
(b) 3.4 mg
(c) 5.1 mg
(d) 6.8 mg

20. How much current should be passed through acidified water for 100s to liberate 0.224 litre of H_2.
(a) 22.4 A
(b) 19.3 A
(c) 9.65 A
(d) 1 A

21. One junction of certain thermoelectric couple is at a fixed temperature T_r and the other junction is at temperature T. The thermo electromotive force for this is expressed by $E = K(T - T_r)\left[T_0 - \frac{1}{2}(T + T_r)\right]$. At temperature $T = \frac{1}{2}T_0$, the thermoelectric power is
(a) $\frac{1}{2}KT_0$
(b) KT_0
(c) $\frac{1}{2}KT_0^2$
(d) $\frac{1}{2}K(T_0 - T_r)^2$

22. For ensuring dissipation of same energy in all three resistors (R_1, R_2, R_3) connected as shown in figure, their values must be related as

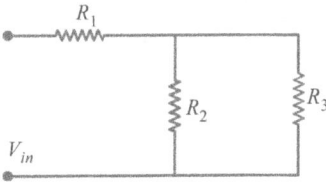

(a) $R_1 = R_2 = R_3$
(b) $R_2 = R_3$ and $R_1 = 4R_2$
(c) $R_2 = R_3$ and $R_1 = \frac{1}{4}R_2$
(d) $R_1 = R_2 + R_3$

23. Each of three resistors having a resistance R can dissipate maximum power P. What is maximum power the circuit comprising of three resistors can dissipate?
(a) 3 P
(b) 2 P
(c) 1.5 P
(d) 2.5 P

Answer Key	12	(d)	13	(c)	14	(c)	15	(b)	16	(b)	17	(b)
Sol. from page 333	18	(a)	19	(b)	20	(b)	21	(a)	22	(c)	23	(a)

24. Consider the following two statements.
    1. Free-electron density is different in different metals.
    2. Free-electron density in a metal depends on temperature.
    Seebeck effect is caused
    (a) due to both statements 1 and 2
    (b) due to 1 but not due to 2
    (c) due to 2 but not due to 1
    (d) neither due to 1 nor due to 2.

25. For a copper-iron thermocouple the values of the various temperatures are given below : $T_0 = 0°C$, $T_N = 275°C$ and $Ti = 550°C$. If T_0 is changed to $10°C$, the new value of T_N and T_i will be respectively
    (a) $275°C$ and $560°C$
    (b) $275°C$ and $540°C$
    (c) $285°C$ and $540°C$
    (d) $285°C$ and $560°C$

26. The emf of a thermocouple, one junction of which is at $0°C$ is given by $E = at + bt^2$. The Peltier coefficient is given by (T is in kelvin) :
    (a) $T(2at + b)$
    (b) $T(2a + bt)$
    (c) $T(a + bt)$
    (d) $T(a + 2bt)$

27. In an electrolysis experiment, a current i passes through two different cells in series, one containing a solution of $CuSO_4$ and the other a solution of $AgNO_3$. The rate of increase of the weight of the cathodes in the two cells will be
    (a) in the ratio of the densities of Cu and Ag
    (b) in the ratio of the atomic weight of Cu and Ag
    (c) in the ratio of half the atomic weight of Cu to the atomic weight of Ag
    (d) in the ratio of half the atomic weight of Cu to half the atomic weight of Ag

28. The electrochemical equivalent of a metal is 3.3×10^{-7} kg/coulomb. The mass of the metal liberated at the cathode when a 3 A current is passed for 2 second will be
    (a) 19.8×10^{-7} kg
    (b) 9.39×10^{-7} kg
    (c) 6.6×10^{-7} kg
    (d) 1.1×10^{-7} kg

29. In Seebeck series Sb appears before Bi. In a Sb-Bi thermocouple current flows from
    (a) Sb to Bi at the hot junction
    (b) Sb to Bi at the cold junction
    (c) Bi to Sb at the cold junction
    (d) none of the above

30. Two different metals are joined end to end. One end is kept at constant temperature and the other end is heated to a very high temperature. The graph depicting the thermo e.m.f. is

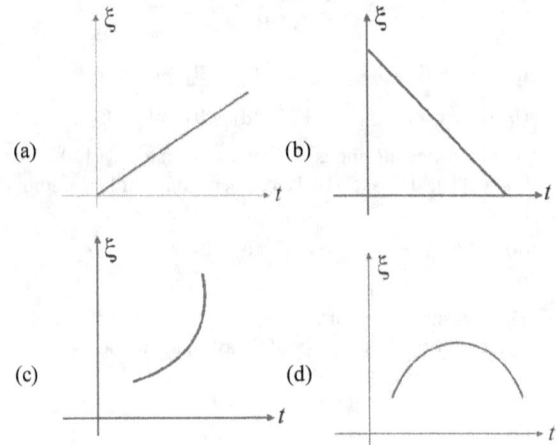

31. The negative Zn pole of a Daniel cell, sending a constant current through a circuit, decreases in mass by 0.13 g in 30 minutes. If the electrochemical equivalent of Zn and Cu are 32.5 and 31.5 respectively, the increase in the mass of the positive Cu pole in this time is
    (a) 0.242 g
    (b) 0.190 g
    (c) 0.141 g
    (d) 0.126 g

32. Thomson coefficient of a conductor is $10\mu V/K$. The two ends of it are kept at $50°C$ and $60°C$ respectively. Amount of heat absorbed by the conductor when a charge of 10 C flows through it is
    (a) 1000 J
    (b) 100 J
    (c) 100 mJ
    (d) 1 mJ

Answer Key	24	(a)	25	(b)	26	(d)	27	(c)	28	(a)
Sol. from page 333	29	(b)	30	(d)	31	(d)	32	(d)		

LEVEL -2

Only one option correct

1. Figure shows three resistor configuration R_1, R_2 and R_3 connected to $3V$ battery. If the power dissipated by the configuration R_1, R_2 and R_3 is P_1, P_2 and P_3 respectively, then

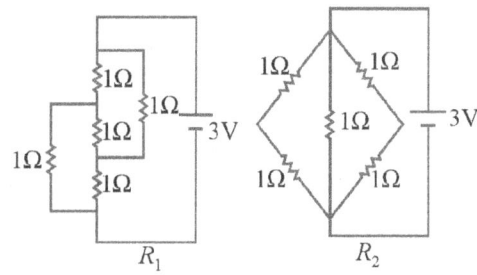

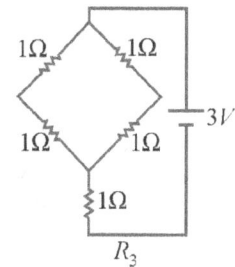

(a) $P_1 > P_2 > P_3$
(b) $P_1 > P_3 > P_2$
(c) $P_2 > P_1 > P_3$
(d) $P_3 > P_2 > P_1$

2. Find the power of the circuit

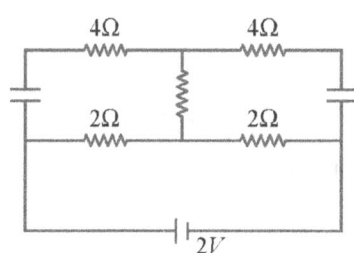

(a) $1.5\ W$
(b) $2\ W$
(c) $1\ W$
(d) None of these

3. Water of volume 2 litre in a container is heated with a coil of 1 kW at 27 °C. The lid of the container is open and energy dissipates at rate of 160 J/s. In how much time temperature will rise from 27°C to 77°C [Given specific heat of water is 4.2 kJ/kg]

(a) 8 min 20 s
(b) 6 min 2 s
(c) 7 min
(d) 14 min

4. A constant current i is passed through a resistor. Taking the temperature coefficient of resistance into account, indicate which of the plots shown in figure best represents the rate of production of thermal energy in the resistor

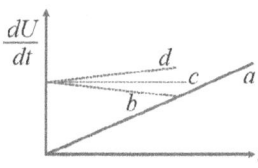

(a) a
(b) b
(c) c
(d) d

5. The charge flowing through a resistor R varies as $Q(t) = \alpha t - \beta t^2$. The total heat produced is R is :

(a) $\dfrac{\alpha^3 R}{\beta}$
(b) $\dfrac{\alpha^3 R}{2\beta}$
(c) $\dfrac{\alpha^3 R}{3\beta}$
(d) $\dfrac{\alpha^3 R}{6\beta}$

6. Consider four circuits shown in the figure below. In which circuit power dissipated is greatest (neglect the internal resistance of the power supply)

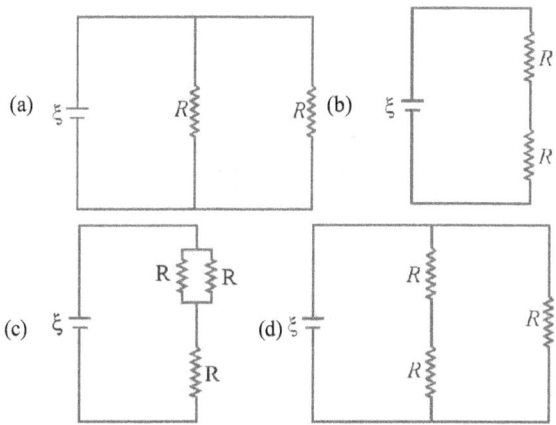

7. A torch bulb rated as $4.5\ W$, $1.5\ V$ is connected as shown in the figure. The e.m.f. of the cell needed to make the bulb glow at full intensity is

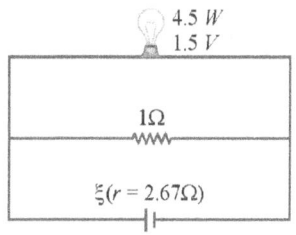

(a) $4.5\ V$
(b) $1.5\ V$
(c) $2.67\ V$
(d) $13.5\ V$

Answer Key

Sol. from page 334

1	(c)	2	(c)	3	(a)	4	(d)
5	(d)	6	(a)	7	(d)		

8. A battery of internal resistance 4Ω is connected to the network of resistances as shown. In order to give the maximum power to the network, the value of R (in Ω) should be

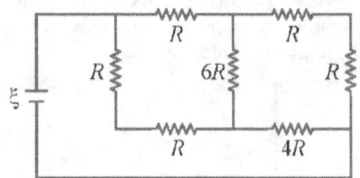

(a) 4/9 (b) 8/9
(c) 2   (d) 18

9. Consider a wire of non-uniform cross-section. If the area of cross-section at point A is double of the area of cross-section at point B. What is ratio of heat energy dissipated in a unit volume at points A and B?

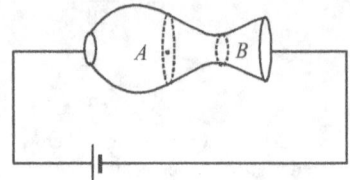

(a) $\dfrac{1}{2}$ (b) $\dfrac{2}{1}$
(c) $\dfrac{1}{4}$ (d) $\dfrac{4}{1}$

10. In the circuit shown in figure, the internal resistances of the sources are negligible. What is maximum power that can be generated in resistance R?

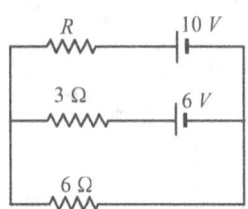

(a) 4 W   (b) 4.5 W
(c) 2 W   (d) 2.5 W

11. Two voltameters, one of copper and another of silver, are joined in parallel. When a total charge q flows through the voltameters, equal amount of metals are deposited. If the electrochemical equivalents of copper and silver are z_1 and z_2 respectively the charge which flows through the silver voltameter is

(a) $q\dfrac{z_1}{z_2}$ (b) $q\dfrac{z_2}{z_1}$

(c) $\dfrac{q}{1+\dfrac{z_1}{z_2}}$ (d) $\dfrac{q}{1+\dfrac{z_2}{z_1}}$

12. In the circuit shown in figure, the heat produced in 5 ohm resistance is 10 cal/s. The heat produced in 4Ω resistance is

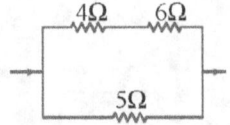

(a) 1 cal/s   (b) 2 cal/s
(c) 3 cal/s   (d) 4 cal/s

13. Silver and copper voltameter are connected in parallel with a battery of e.m.f. 12 V. In 30 minutes, 1 gm of silver and 1.8 gm of copper are liberated. The power supplied by the battery is
(a) 24.13 J/s   (b) 2.413 J/s
(b) 0.2413 J/s (d) 2413 J/s
($Z_{Cu} = 6.6 \times 10^{-4}$ gm/C and $Z_{Ag} = 11.2 \times 10^{-4}$ gm/C)

14. The thermo e.m.f. of a thermo-couple is $25\mu V/°C$ at room temperature. A galvanometer of 40 ohm resistance, capable of detecting current as low as 10^{-5} A, is connected with the thermocouple. The smallest temperature difference that can be detected by this system is
(a) 20° C   (b) 16° C
(c) 12° C   (d) 8° C

15. The thermo e.m.f. of a thermocouple varies with the temperature θ of the hot junction as $E = a\theta + b\theta^2$ in volt where the ratio a/b is 700°C. If the cold junction is kept at 0°C, then the neutral temperature is
(a) 700° C
(b) 350° C
(c) 1400° C
(d) no neutral temperature is possible for this thermocouple

Answer Key	8	(c)	9	(c)	10	(b)	11	(d)
Sol. from page 334	12	(b)	13	(a)	14	(b)	15	(d)

Electricity — MCQ Type 2 — Exercise 4.2

Multiple correct options

1. For the circuit shown in the figure

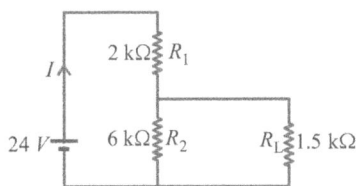

   (a) the current I through the battery is 7.5 mA
   (b) the potential difference across R_L is 18 V
   (c) ratio of powers dissipated in R_1 and R_2 is 3
   (d) if R_1 and R_2 are interchanged, magnitude of the power dissipated in R_L will decrease by a factor of 9

2. Two bulbs : 10 W and 200 W are connected in parallel. Then :
   (a) The voltage through each bulb is same
   (b) The current in each bulb is same
   (c) The current in 100 W bulb is smaller than current in 200 W bulbs
   (d) The voltage across 200 W is greater

3. Three identical bulbs are connected as shown in figure.

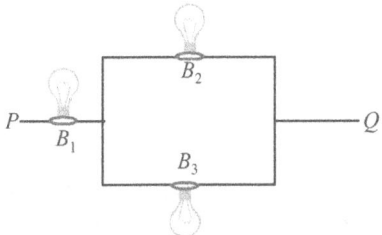

   Each bulb dissipate a maximum power P. Then :
   (a) The total power dissipate of the circuit is $3P$.
   (b) The total power dissipate of the circuit is $\dfrac{3P}{2}$.
   (c) The current in each resistor is same
   (d) The current in bulbs B_1, B_2 and B_3 are in ratio $2:3:1$.

4. A cell of emf 6 V and internal resistance 1 Ω is connected across resistor $R = 2\ \Omega$. Then :

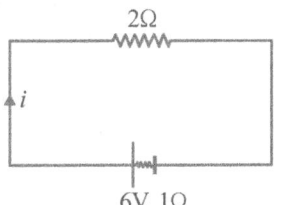

   (a) Power dissipate in the source is 4 W.
   (b) Chemical energy dissipated at the rate of 12 W.
   (c) Power output of the source is 8 W.
   (d) Power output of the source is 12 W.

5. The constants a and b for the pair silver-lead are 2.50 µV/C and 0.012 µV/C² respectively. For a silver-lead thermocouple with colder junction at 0°C,
   (a) there will be no neutral temperature
   (b) there will be no inversion temperature
   (c) there will not be any thermo-emf even if the junctions are kept at different temperatures
   (d) there will be no current in the thermocouple even if the functions are kept at different temperatures.

Answer Key Sol. from page 335	1	(a, d)	2	(a, c)	3	(b, d)	4	(a, b, c)
	5	(a, b)						

Electricity — Statement Questions — Exercise 4.3

Read the two statements carefully to mark the correct option out of the options given below:
(a) If both the statements are true and the *statement - 2* is the correct explanation of *statement - 1*.
(b) If both the statements are true but *statement - 2* is not the correct explanation of the *statement - 1*.
(c) If *statement - 1* true but *statement - 2* is false.
(d) If *statement - 1* is false but *statement - 2* is true.

1. **Statement 1**
   If a constant potential difference is applied across a bulb, the current slightly decreases as time passes and then becomes constant.
   Statement 2
   The resistance of the metal increases with temperature.

2. **Statement 1**
   The 200 W bulb glows more brightly than 100 W bulb.
   Statement 2
   The resistance of 200 W bulb is less than the 100 W bulb.

3. **Statement 1**
   Fuse wire must have low resistance and low melting point.
   Statement 2
   Fuse is used for small current only.

4. **Statement 1**
   A domestic electrical appliance, working on a three pin will continue working even if the top pin is removed.
   Statement 2
   The third pin is used only as a safety device.

5. **Statement 1**
   A laser beam 0.2 W power can drill holes through a metal sheet, whereas 1000 W torchlight cannot.
   Statement 2
   The frequency of laser light is much higher than that of torch light.

6. **Statement 1**
   Electric appliances with metallic body; e.g. heaters, presses etc. have three pin connections, whereas an electric bulb has a two pin connection.
   Statement 2
   Three pin connections reduce heating of connecting cables.

7. **Statement 1**
   Neutral temperature of any thermocouple is a basic characteristic.
   Statement 2
   All the thermocouples have a neutral temperature.

8. **Statement 1**
   The neutral temperature does not depend on the temperature of the cold junction.
   Statement 2
   The inversion temperature does not depend on the temperature of the cold junction.

9. **Statement 1**
   The possibility of an electric bulb fusing is higher at the time of switching ON and OFF
   Statement 2
   Inductive effects produce a surge at the time of switch ON and OFF

10. **Statement 1**
    In the given circuit if lamp B or C fuses then light emitted by lamp A decreases.

    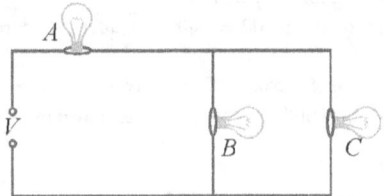

    Statement 2
    Voltage on A decreases.

11. **Statement - 1**
    In an electrolyte, the positive ions move from left to right and the negative ions from right to left, so there is no net current flows in an electrolyte.
    Statement - 2
    The current flows from cathode to anode in an electrolyte.

12. **Statement - 1**
    The thermal power generated in a resistor is given by $P = i^2R$ and so it is proportional to i^2.
    Statement - 2
    The thermal power generated in a resistor is given by $P = Vi$ and so it is proportion to i.

13. **Statement - 1**
    In each electrical circuit, the thermal power generated is equal to the rate of work done by battery.
    Statement - 2
    The rate of work done by the battery is equal to the power delivered to the circuit.

Answer Key (Sol. from page 336)

1	2	3	4	5	6	7
(a)	(a)	(c)	(a)	(c)	(c)	(c)

8	9	10	11	12	13
(c)	(a)	(a)	(d)	(c)	(d)

Electricity — Passage & Matrix — Exercise 4.4

PASSAGES

Passage for Q. 1 to Q. 3

The internal resistance of a dry cell increases gradually with age, even though the cell is not used. The emf, however, remains fairly constant at about 1.5 V. Dry cells may be tested for age at the time of purchase by connecting an ammeter directly across the terminals of the cell and reading the current. The resistance of the ammeter is so small that the cell is practically short circuited.

1. The short circuit current of the cell is about 30 A. The internal resistance of the cell approximately is :
   (a) $0.01\,\Omega$ (b) $0.02\,\Omega$
   (c) $0.05\,\Omega$ (d) $0.1\,\Omega$

2. The power generated by the internal resistance is :
   (a) $45\,W$ (b) $60\,W$
   (c) $90\,W$ (d) $100\,W$

3. The power generated in the circuit is :
   (a) $45\,W$ (b) $60\,W$
   (c) greater than $45\,W$ (d) less than $45\,W$

Passage for Q. 4 to Q. 6

The current in a charging capacitor(C) is given by $i = i_0 e^{-t/RC}$, where $i_0 = \dfrac{\xi}{R}$. For instantaneous potential V of the capacitor, power is given by $P = Vi$.

4. Total energy supplied by the battery is :
   (a) $\dfrac{1}{2}C\xi^2$ (b) $C\xi^2$
   (c) $2C\xi^2$ (d) zero

5. The instantaneous power dissipated in the resistor is i^2R. The total energy dissipated in the resistor is

   (a) $\dfrac{1}{2}C\xi^2$ (b) $C\xi^2$
   (c) $2C\xi^2$ (d) none of them

6. Maximum energy stored in the capacitor
   (a) $\dfrac{1}{2}C\xi^2$ (b) $C\xi^2$
   (c) $2C\xi^2$ (d) Infinite.

Passage for Q. 7 to Q. 9

Two batteries $(2\xi, r)$ and $(\xi, 2r)$ are connected as shown in diagram the resistance R (external load) is variable, which can be adjusted using rheostat, carefully answer the questions for this given situation.

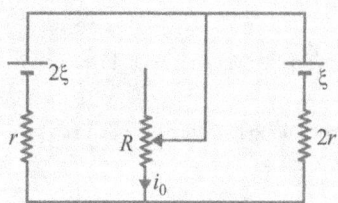

7. Value of R for which power across the load (R) is maximum is
   (a) $\dfrac{3r}{2}$ (b) $\dfrac{2r}{3}$
   (c) r (d) none of these

8. Maximum power dissipation in the circuit is
   (a) $\dfrac{2\xi^2}{3r}$ (b) $\dfrac{3\xi^2}{2r}$
   (c) $\dfrac{2\xi^3}{6r}$ (d) none of these

9. Maximum value of i_0 is
   (a) $\dfrac{\xi}{2r}$ (b) $\dfrac{\xi}{r}$
   (c) $\dfrac{5\xi}{2r}$ (d) $\dfrac{\xi}{3r}$

Answer Key (Sol. from page 336)

1	(c)	2	(a)	3	(c)	4	(b)	5	(a)
6	(a)	7	(b)	8	(d)	9	(c)		

330 ELECTRICITY & MAGNETISM

MATRIX MATCHING

10. Match the Column I with the Column II from the combination shown. In the left side (Column I) there are four different conditions and in the right side (Column II), there are ratios of heat produced in each resistance of each condition :

	Column I		Column II
A.	Two wires of same resistance are connected in series and same current is passed through them	(p)	1 : 2
B.	Two wires of resistance R and $2R$ ohm are connected in series and same potential difference is applied across them	(q)	4 : 1
C.	Two wires of same resistance are connected in parallel and same current is flowing through them	(r)	1 : 1
D.	Two wires of resistances in the ratio 1 : 2 are connected in parallel and current i is across them	(s)	2 : 1

11. A cell of e.m.f ξ and internal resistance r is connected across a variable load resistance R. Match the statements given in column I to conductions gives in column II.

	Column I		Column II
A.	Thermal power generated in the load resistance is less than $\dfrac{E^2}{4r}$	(p)	$R = r$
B.	Potential difference across load is more than $\dfrac{E}{2}$	(q)	$R = 0$
C.	Thermal power generated in the cell is $\dfrac{E^2}{r}$	(r)	$r = \dfrac{R}{4}$
D.	Work done by battery is positive	(s)	$r = \dfrac{3R}{2}$
		(t)	$r = \dfrac{R}{2}$

12. n cell are connected in a closed loop. Emf of the cells are $1V, 2V, 3V ....nV$, here n is even. Internal resistance of the cell are $0.5\,\Omega, 1.0\,\Omega, 1.5\,\Omega, 2\,\Omega ..... \dfrac{n}{2}\Omega$. Based on above facts, match column I with column II.

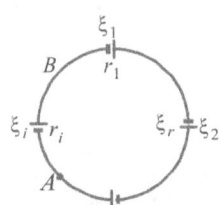

	Column I		Column II
A.	Zero	(p)	Current through each cell
B.	Equal	(q)	Terminal voltage of each cell
C.	Unequal	(r)	Potential difference between any two points
D.	Non-zero	(s)	A and B on the circuit
		(t)	Current through each cell if alternate cells are connected with reverse polarity

---

Answer Key (Sol. from page 336)

10	A-r ; B-s ; C-r ; D-s	11	A-r, s, t ; B-r, t ; C-q ; D-p, q, r, s
12	A-q, r ; B-q, r, t ; C-s ; D-p, s, t		

Electricity — Subjective Integer Type — Exercise 4.5

Solution from page 337

1. An immersion heater rated 1000 W, 220 V is used to heat 0.01 m^3 of water. Assuming that the power is supplied at 220 V and 60 % of the power supplied is used to heat the water, how long will it take to increase the temperature of the water from $15°C$ to $40°C$?

   Ans. 29 min.

2. Four resistances carrying a current as shown in the diagram are immersed in a box containing ice at 0°C. How much ice must be put in the box every 10 minute to keep the average quantity of ice in the box constant? Latent heat of ice = 80 cal/g.

   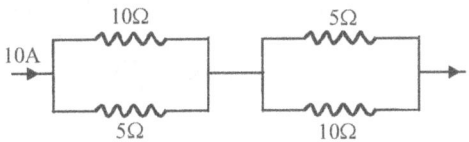

   Ans. 1190 g.

3. In circuit shown in figure the heat produced in 5 Ω resistor due to current flowing through it is 10 calorie per second. The heat generated in 4 Ω resistor is :

   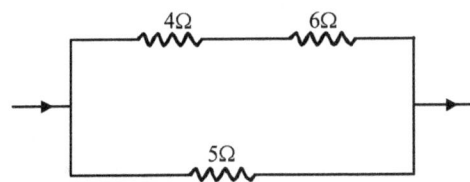

   Ans. 2 cal/s.

4. A heater is designed to operate with a power of 1000 W in 100 V line. It is connected to two resistances of 10 Ω and R as shown in figure. If the heater is now given a power of 62.5 W, calculate the value of resistance R.

   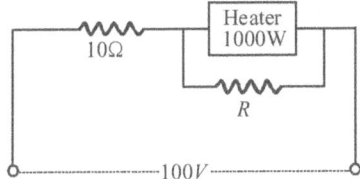

   Ans. R = 5 Ω.

5. A charged capacitor of 5×10^{-2} F capacity is discharged through a resistor R of 20 Ω and a copper voltmeter of internal resistance 30 Ω connected in series. If 4.62×10^{-6} kg copper is deposited, calculate the heat generated in the resistor R. (Electrochemical equivalent of copper is 3.3×10^{-7} kg/C).

   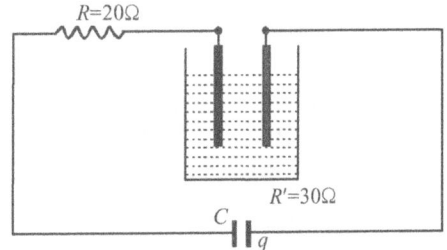

   Ans. 784 J.

6. Find the time required to liberate 1.0 litre of hydrogen at STP in an electrolytic cell by a current of 5.0 A.

   Ans. 29 min.

7. The potential difference across the terminals of a battery of emf 12 V and internal resistance 2 Ω drops to 10 V when it is connected to a silver voltmeter. Find the silver deposited at the cathode in half an hour. Atomic weight of silver is 107.9 g/mole.

   Ans. 2g.

Electricity — Subjective

Exercise 4.6

Solution from page 338

1. The 2.0 Ω resistor shown in figure is dipped into a calorimeter containing water. The heat capacity of the calorimeter together with water is 2000 J/K.
   (a) If the circuit is active for 15 minutes, What would be the rise in the temperature of the water?
   (b) Suppose the 6.0 Ω resistor gets burnt. What would be the rise in the temperature of the water in the next 15 minutes?

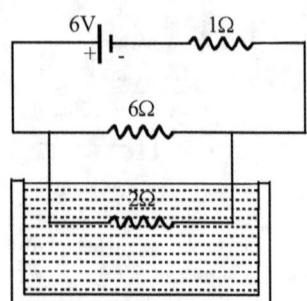

Ans. (a) 2.9°C (b) 3.6°C.

2. A battery of internal resistance 4Ω is connected to the network of resistances as shown in figure. What must be the value of R so that maximum power is delivered to the network? What is the maximum power?

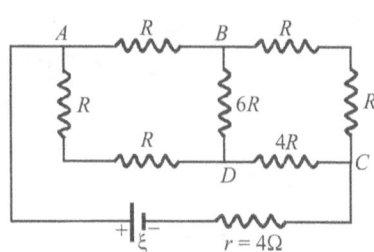

Ans. 2 Ω, $\xi^2/16$.

3. An electric kettle has two coils. When one coil is switched on, it takes 15 minute to boil water and when the second coil is switched on, it takes 30 minute. How long will it take to boil water and when both the coils are used in (i) series and (ii) parallel?

Ans. (i) 45 min. (ii) 10 min.

4. The temperatures of the junctions of a bismuth–silver thermocouple are maintained at 0°C and 0.001°C. Find the thermo–emf (Seebeck emf) developed. For bismuth–silver, $a = -46 \times 10^{-6}$ V/°C and $b = -0.48 \times 10^{-6}$ V/°C².

Ans. -4.6×10^{-8} V.

5. A piece of metal weighing 20 g is to be electroplated with 5% of its weight in gold. If the strength of the available current is 2 A, how long would it take to deposit the required amount of gold ECE of $H = 0.1044 \times 10^{-4}$, atomic weight of gold = 197.1, atomic weight of hydrogen = 1.008.

Ans. 4 min. 27.9 s.

6. Figure shows an electrolyte of AgCl through which a current is passed. It is observed that 2.68 g of silver is deposited in 10 minutes on the cathode. Find the heat developed in the 20 Ω resistor during this period. Atomic weight of silver is 107.9 g/mol.

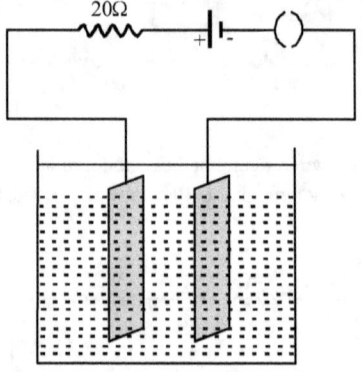

Ans. 190 kJ.

7. A copper wire having cross–sectional area 0.5 mm² and a length of 0.1 m is initially at 25°C and is thermally insulated from the surrounding. If a current of 10 A is set up in this wire.
   (i) Find the time in which the wire will start melting. The change of resistance with the temperature of the wire may be neglected.
   (ii) What will be the time taken if length of the wire is doubled?
   Given for copper wire, density = 9×10^3 kg/m³, specific heat = 9×10^{-2} kcal/kg-°C, melting point = 1075°C, specific resistance 1.6×10^{-8} Ω–m.

Ans. (i) 558 s, (ii) 558 s.

8. A plate of area 10 cm² is to be electroplated with copper (density 9000 kg/m³) to a thickness of 10 micrometre on both sides, using a cell of 12 V. Calculate the energy spent by the cell in the process of deposition. If this energy is used to heat 100 g of water, calculate the rise in the temperature of the water. ECE of copper = 3×10^{-7} kg/C and specific heat capacity of water = 4200 J/kg-K.

Ans. 7.2 kJ, 17 K.

9. Find the amount of silver liberated at cathode of 0.500 A of current is passed through AgNO₃ electrolyte for 1 hour. Atomic weight of silver is 107.9 g/mol.

Ans. 2.01 g.

THERMAL AND CHEMICAL EFFECT OF CURRENT

Hints & Solutions

Solutions EXERCISE 4.1 LEVEL-1

1. (a) Thermal energy, $U = i^2Rt$, and so $U \propto i^2$, it represents a parabola between U and i.

2. (a) In series, current in both the resistors is same and so
$$\frac{U_1}{U_2} = \frac{i^2Rt}{i^2(2R)t} = \frac{1}{2}.$$

3. (b) In parallel, potential difference across both the resistors is same and so
$$\frac{U_1}{U_2} = \frac{(V^2/R)t}{(V^2/2R)t} = \frac{2}{1}$$

4. (b) When one bulb is fused, the resistance of rest 39 bulb becomes smaller and so current in the bulbs will increase, which result increase in illumination.

5. (a) The resistance of half coil, $R' = \frac{R}{2}$.

   So, ratio of heat produced, $\frac{H'}{H} = \frac{V^2/R'}{V^2/R} = \frac{R}{R'} = 2.$

6. (c)

7. (d) Resistance of the bulb, $R = \frac{V^2}{P} = \frac{220^2}{100}$.

   Power consumed with 110 V, $P = \frac{V^2_{supply}}{R}$

   $= \frac{110^2}{220^2/100} = 25\ W.$

8. (d) $\frac{H_1}{H_2} = \frac{V^2/2R}{V^2/(R/2)} = \frac{1}{4}$

9. (d) For maximum power, $R = r = 0.5\ \Omega$.

10. (b) $\frac{P^2}{P_0^2} = \frac{V^2}{V_0^2}$

11. (a) If each resistance is of value R, then
    $R_1 = 3R$, $R_2 = \frac{2R \times R}{2R+R} = \frac{2R}{3}$, $R_3 = \frac{R}{3}$, $R_4 = \frac{R}{2} + R = \frac{3R}{2}$.
    As $R_1 > R_4 > R_2 > R_3$, so power $P_1 > P_4 > P_2 > P_3$.

12. (d) Resistance, $R_1 < R_2$, also $R_2 = R_3$.
    So, in series, $W_1 < W_2$.
    Current in B_3 will be greater than current in bulb B_2 and so $W_3 > W_2$.

13. (c) $P_1 = \frac{120^2}{R}$ and $P_2 = \frac{110^2}{R}$

    $\therefore \frac{P_1 - P_2}{P_1} \times 100 = \frac{120^2 - 110^2}{120^2} = 16\%$

14. (c) The total power of bulbs in parallel = 400 W

    Now $\frac{1}{P} = \frac{1}{400} + \frac{1}{400}$, and so $P = 200$ W

15. (b) $R_1 = \frac{V^2}{P_1} = \frac{220^2}{100} = 484\Omega$

    and $R_2 = \frac{V^2}{P_2} = \frac{220^2}{60} = 806.7\ \Omega$

    Current, $i = \left[\frac{220}{484 + 806.7}\right] = 0.17\ A$

    Now, $P_1 = i^2 R_1 = 0.17^2 \times 484 = 14$ W.

16. (b)
17. (b)

18. (a) Resistance of the bulb, $R = \frac{V^2}{P} = \frac{200^2}{100} = 400\Omega$

    Now, current $i = \frac{V}{R} = \frac{100}{400} = \frac{1}{4} A$

19. (b) $\frac{m_1}{m_2} = \frac{W_1}{W_2}$

    $\therefore m_2 = m_1 \frac{W_2}{W_1}$

    $= 1 \times \left(\frac{107.88}{\frac{63.57}{2}}\right)$

    = 3.4 mg

20. (b) To liberate $\left(\frac{22.4}{2}\right)$ litre of H_2, the charge needed = 96500C

    $\therefore$ to liberate 0.224 litre of H_2, the charge needed

    $= \frac{96500 \times 2}{100} C$

    = 1930 C

    Current needed, $i = \frac{q}{t} = \frac{1930}{100} = 1930\ A$

21. (a) We know that $S = \frac{dE}{dT}$.

    Given $E = k(T - T_r)\left[T_0 - \frac{(T + T_r)}{2}\right]$.

    On differentiating E w.r.t. T and putting, $T = \frac{T_0}{2}$, we get

    $S = \frac{kT_0}{2}$.

22. (c) For same energy dissipation in all the resistors, $R_2 = R_3$. If i is the current in R_1, then it will divide equally in R_2 and R_3, so

$$i^2 R_1 = \left(\frac{i}{2}\right)^2 R_2$$

$$\therefore R_1 = \frac{R_2}{4}.$$

23. (a) For maximum power, all the three resistors must be placed in parallel and so, $P_{total} = 3 \times P = 3P.$

24. (a)

25. (b) We know that, $T_N = \frac{T_0 + T_i}{2}$,

$\therefore T_i = 2T_N - T_0 = 2 \times 275 - 10 = 540°$ C

26. (d) Peltier coefficient, $\pi = T\left(\frac{dE}{dt}\right) = T \times \frac{d}{dt}(at + bt^2)$

$= T(a + 2bt).$

27. (c) $\frac{m_{cu}}{m_{Ag}} = \frac{W_{cu}}{W_{Ag}} = \frac{(A_{cu}/2)}{A_{Ag}}$

28. (a) $m = Zit = 3.3 \times 10^{-7} \times 3 \times 2 = 19.8 \times 10^{-7}$ kg.

29. (b)

30. (d)

31. (d) $\frac{m_1}{m_2} = \frac{Z_1}{Z_2}$

$\therefore m_2 = \frac{Z_2}{Z_1} m_1 = \frac{31.5}{32.5} \times 0.13$

$= 0.126$ g

32. (d) $\Delta H = \sigma(\Delta Q)\Delta t$

$= (10 \times 10^{-6}) \times 10 \times (60 - 50)$

$= 10^{-3}$ J

Solutions Exercise 4.1 Level -2

1. (c) $R_1 = 1\Omega$, $R_2 = \frac{1}{2}\Omega$ and $R_3 = 2\Omega$.

Now, $P_1 = \frac{V^2}{R_1} = \frac{V^2}{1}, P_2 = \frac{V^2}{(1/2)}, P_3 = \frac{V^2}{2}$

$\therefore P_2 > P_1 > P_3$.

2. (c) The only current in 2Ω resistors, $i = \frac{2}{4} = \frac{1}{2} A$

Now, power $P = i^2 R = \left(\frac{1}{2}\right)^2 \times 4 = 1 W$

3. (a) Energy required to raise the temperature of water from 27° to 77°C.

$Q = mC\Delta T + $ loss

or $1000t = 2 \times 4200 \times (77 - 27) + 160 \times t$

or $t = 500$ s
$= 8$ min 20 s

4. (d) Power, $P = \frac{dU}{dt} = i^2 R$

$= i^2 [R_0(1 + \alpha t)]$.

It represents a straight line in P and t with positive slope.

5. (d) Current through a resistor,

$i = \frac{dQ}{dt} = \frac{d}{dt}(\alpha t - \beta t^2)$

$= \alpha - 2\beta t$.

The time upto current flows,

$i = \alpha - 2\beta t = 0$

or $t = \frac{\alpha}{2\beta}$.

Total heat produced, $H = \int_0^t i^2 R dt$

$= \int_0^{\alpha/2\beta} (\alpha - 2\beta t)^2 R dt$

$= \frac{\alpha^3 R}{6\beta}$.

6. (a) Resistance of the circuits are :

$R_1 = \frac{R}{2}, R_2 = 2R, R_3 = \frac{3R}{2},$ and $R_4 = \frac{2R}{3}$

$P_{greatest} = \frac{V^2}{R_{least}} = \frac{V^2}{R/2} = \frac{2V^2}{R}$.

7. (d) Allowable current in the bulb, $i_1 = \frac{P}{V} = \frac{4.5}{1.5} = 3A$

Current in 1Ω resistor, $i_2 = \frac{1.5}{1} = 1.5 A$

Total circuit current $i = i_1 + i_2 = 4.5 A$

Now, $\varepsilon = V + ir$
$= 1.5 + 4.5 \times 2.67$
$= 13.5$ V

8. (c) The effective circuit is shown in figure.

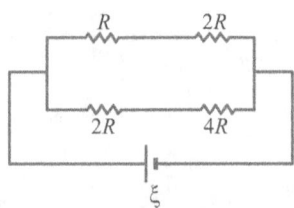

The equivalent resistance across the battery.

$R_{eq} = \left(\frac{3 \times 6}{3 + 6}\right) R$

$= 2R.$

THERMAL AND CHEMICAL EFFECT OF CURRENT

For maximum power,

$R_{eq} = r$

or $2R = 4$

∴ $R = 2\,\Omega$

9. (c)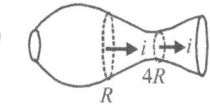

$\dfrac{H_1}{H_2} = \dfrac{i^2 R_1}{i^2 R_2} = \dfrac{R}{4R} = \dfrac{1}{4}$

10. (b)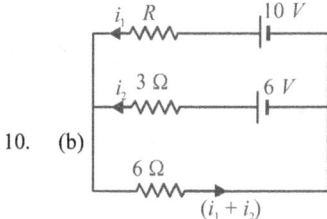

$i_1 R - 10 + 6 - 3i_2 = 0$
or $i_1 R - 3i_2 = 4$ ...(i)
and $3i_2 - 6 + 6(i_1 + i_2) = 0$
or $6i_1 + 9i_2 = 6$ ...(ii)
Solving above equations, we get

$i_1 = \dfrac{18}{6+3R} = \left[\dfrac{6}{2+R}\right]$

Power in R,

$P = i_1^2 R$

$= \left[\dfrac{6}{2+R}\right]^2 R$

P to be maximum, $\dfrac{dP}{dR} = 0$

or $\dfrac{d}{dR}\left[\dfrac{6^2}{(2+R)^2}\right] R = 0$

∴ $R = 2\,\Omega$

Now $P_{max} = \left[\dfrac{6}{2+2}\right]^2 \times 2$

$= 4.5\,\Omega$

11. (d) Given $m_{cu} = m_{si}$
or $Z_1 q_1 = Z_2 q_2$
Also, $q_1 + q_2 = q$

∴ $q_2 = \dfrac{q Z_1}{Z_1 + Z_2} = \dfrac{q}{\left(1 + \dfrac{Z_2}{Z_1}\right)}$

12. (b) As $P = \dfrac{V^2}{R}$, ∴ $V = \sqrt{PR} = \sqrt{10 \times 5}$ volt $= \sqrt{50}$ volt

Now, current in 4Ω resistor, $i = \dfrac{\sqrt{50}}{10}\,A$.

Power generated in 4Ω resistor, $= i^2 R$

$= \dfrac{50}{100} \times 4 = 2$ cal/s

13. (a) $m = Zq$, ∴ $q = \dfrac{m}{Z}$

Now, $q_1 = \dfrac{1}{11.2 \times 10^{-4}} C = 0.89 \times 10^3 C$

$q_2 = \dfrac{1.8}{6.6 \times 10^{-4}} = 2.73 \times 10^3 C$

Total charge,

$q = q_1 + q_2 = (0.89 + 2.73) \times 10^3 C = 3.62 \times 10^3 C$.

Power supplied by battery, $P = (Vq)/t$

$= \dfrac{12 \times 3.62 \times 10^3}{30 \times 60}$ J/s

$= 24.13$ J/s

14. (b) The p.d. across galvanometer,
$V = iR = 10^{-5} \times 40 = 40 \times 10^{-5}$ volt
The temperature difference that can be detected,

$\Delta T = \dfrac{40 \times 10^{-5}}{25 \times 10^{-6}} = 16°C$

15. (d) Given, $E = a\theta + b\theta^2$.

For neutral temperature, $\dfrac{dE}{d\theta} = 0$,

or $\dfrac{d}{d\theta}(a\theta + b\theta^2) = 0$

or $a + 2b\theta = 0$,

or $\theta = -\dfrac{a}{2b} = -\dfrac{700}{2} = -350\,C$ (not possible)

Solutions EXERCISE 4.2

1. (a, d) Total resistance of the circuit

$R = 2 + \dfrac{6 \times 1.5}{6 + 1.5} = 4.2\,k\Omega$

Now $I = \dfrac{24}{4.2 \times 10^3} = 7.5 \times 10^{-3}\,A$

Current in R_L, $i_1 = \dfrac{7.5 \times 10^{-3} \times 6}{(6+1.5)} = 6 \times 10^{-3}\,A$

Power, $P_1 = i_1^2 \times 1.5 = (6 \times 10^{-3})^2 \times 1.5 \times 10^3$

$= 54 \times 10^{-3}$ J

After interchanged, total resistance

$R = 6 + \dfrac{2 \times 1.5}{2 + 1.5} = 6.86\,k\Omega$

Total current, $I = \dfrac{24}{6.86 \times 10^3} = 3.5 \times 10^{-3}\,A$

Now current in $R_L = \dfrac{3.5 \times 10^{-3} \times 2}{(2+1.5)} = 2 \times 10^{-3} A$

Power, $P_1' = (2 \times 10^{-3})^2 \times 1.5 \times 10^3$
$= 6 \times 10^{-3} J$

Clearly $P_1 : P_1' = 9$.

2. (a,c) Resistance of 100 W bulb is greater and in parallel, both the bulbs have same potential, and so current in 100 W bulb will be smaller.

3. (b,d) If i in the current in bulb B_1, then it will divide equally in bulbs B_2 and B_3. Also
$P = i^2 R$.

Power dissipate in bulb B_2 or B_3,

$$P' = \left(\dfrac{i}{2}\right)^2 R = \dfrac{P}{4}.$$

Thus total power $= P + \dfrac{P}{4} + \dfrac{P}{4} = \dfrac{3P}{2}$.

4. (a,b,c) Current, $i = \dfrac{6}{2+1} = 2A$.

Electric power produced in the source $= \varepsilon i = 6 \times 2 = 12$ W.
Power dissipate in the source $= i^2 r = 2^2 \times 1 = 4$ W.

5. (a, b) For neutral and inversion temperature, either of a or b must be negative.

Solutions EXERCISE 4.3

1. (a) With increase in temperature of filament, its resistance will increase and so current will decrease.
2. (a) Power consumed by 200 W bulb will be twice that of 100 W bulb. Also $R \propto \dfrac{1}{p}$.
3. (c) Fuse wire has low resistance and low melting point, so it will melt easily due to excessive heat.
4. (a) Statement -2 is the correct explanation of statement-1.
5. (c) The energy of laser light is focused to small area but that of bulb, it spread on larger area.
6. (c) In case of short circuit third pin passes the extra current.
7. (c) Netural temperature is the characteristics of metals used in the thermocouple. Only few thermocouple has neutral temperature.

8. (c) Netural temperature is the characteristics of metals used in the thermocouple. As $t_i = 2t_n - t_c$, so inversion temperature depends on cold junction temperature.
9. (a) The change in current at the time of switch ON or OFF is greater.
10. (a) If either of bulbs B or C fuses, the effective resistance of circuit increases and so current and p.d. across bulb A will decreases.
11. (d) Both types of ions constitute the current.
12. (c) In $P = Vi$, V also depends on i, $V = iR$, and so $P \propto i^2$.
13. (d) Some power is dissipated by the battery itself due to internal resistance.

Solutions EXERCISE 4.4

Passage Q.1 to Q.3

1. (c) $r = \dfrac{\xi}{i} = \dfrac{1.5}{30} = 0.05 \Omega$

2. (a) Power generated by internal resistance,
$P = i^2 r = 30^2 \times 0.05 = 45$ W

3. (c) The power generated in the circuit is the sum of power generated in external and internal circuit, so it must be greater than 45 W.

Passage of Q.4 to Q.6

4. (b) Total energy supplied by the battery $= \xi q = \xi(C\xi) = C\xi^2$.

5. (a) Half the work done by battery will store in electrical energy of the capacitor, $U = \dfrac{1}{2}C\xi^2$ and rest half converts into the heat energy.

6. (a) The maximum energy stored in the capacitor, $U = \dfrac{1}{2}C\xi^2$.

Passage of Q.7 to Q.9

The equivalent circuit is shown in figure.

$\xi_{net} = \dfrac{2\xi \times 2r + \xi \times r}{2r + r} = \dfrac{5\xi}{3}$

$r_{net} = \dfrac{2r \times r}{2r + r} = \dfrac{2r}{3}$

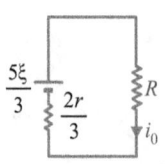

7. (b) For maximum power,
$R = r_{net}$
or $R = \dfrac{2r}{3}$.

8. (d) $i = \dfrac{\xi_{net}}{R_{total}} = \dfrac{5\xi/3}{R + r_{net}} = \dfrac{5\xi/3}{2 \times 2r/3} = \dfrac{5\xi}{4r}$

$P_{max} = i^2 R_{total} = \left(\dfrac{5\xi}{4r}\right)^2 \times \left(\dfrac{4r}{3}\right) = \dfrac{25\xi^2}{12r}$

9. (c) Maximum value of i_0;

$i_0 = \dfrac{\xi_{net}}{R_{min}} = \dfrac{5\xi/3}{2r/3} = \dfrac{5\xi}{2r}$ [R = 0]

10. A-r : When same current is passed through them,
$H_1 = i^2 R$ and $H_2 = i^2 R$, and so $H_1/H_2 = 1:1$.

B -s : $\dfrac{H_1}{H_2} = \dfrac{V^2/R}{V^2/2R} = 2$.

C-r : $\dfrac{H_1}{H_2} = \dfrac{i^2 R}{i^2 R} = 1$

D-q : $\dfrac{H_1}{H_2} = \dfrac{i_1^2 R_1}{i_2^2 R_2} = \dfrac{(2i/3)^2 R}{(2i/3)^2 \times 2R} = 2$.

THERMAL AND CHEMICAL EFFECT OF CURRENT

11. A-r, s, t : The maximum power across external circuit generated when $R = r$. For any other value of r, the power generated will be less than maximum.
    B-r,t : For $V > \xi/2$, the value of r should be less than R.
    C- q : If $R = 0$, then $P = \dfrac{\xi^2}{r}$.
    D- p, q, r, s : W.d. by battery in each case is positive.

12. A-q, r : Current in the circuit,
    $$i = \dfrac{\xi_1 + \xi_2 + ... + \xi_n}{r_1 + r_2 + ... + r_n} = \left[\dfrac{1+2+.....+n}{0.5+1+...+n/2}\right]$$
    $$= 2$$
    p.d. across any cell $V = \xi - ir$
    $$= 1 - 2 \times 0.5 = 0$$
    B- q, r, t : As all the cells are connected in series and so current in each cell will be same in both the cases.
    C- s :

Solutions EXERCISE-4.5

1. Mass of the water, $m = \rho V = 1000 \times 0.01$
   $$= 10 \text{ kg}.$$
   The amount of heat required to raise the temperature of water,
   $$H = mC\Delta T$$
   $$= 10 \times 4200 \times (40 - 15)$$
   $$= 1.05 \times 10^6 \text{ J}.$$
   If t be the required time, then
   $$0.60\, Pt = H$$
   or $t = \dfrac{H}{0.60\, P} = \dfrac{1.05 \times 10^6}{0.6 \times 1000}$
   $$\approx 29 \text{ min}. \quad \text{Ans.}$$

2. The equivalent resistance of the circuit
   $$R = 2\dfrac{10 \times 5}{10 + 5} = 6.67\, \Omega.$$
   The heat evolved in 10 minute,
   $$H = i^2 Rt = 10^2 \times 6.67 \times (10 \times 60)$$
   $$= 4 \times 10^5 \text{ J}.$$
   $$= 95238 \text{ Cal}.$$
   The amount of ice required
   $$m = \dfrac{H}{L} = \dfrac{95238}{80}$$
   $$= 1190 \text{ g} \quad \text{Ans.}$$

3. If V is the p.d. across $5\,\Omega$ resistor, then
   $$P = \dfrac{V^2}{R}$$
   $$\therefore \quad V = \sqrt{PR} = \sqrt{10 \times 5} = \sqrt{50}$$

   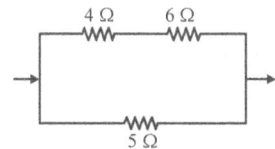

   The current in $4\,\Omega$ resister,
   $$i = \dfrac{V}{4+6} = \dfrac{\sqrt{50}}{10}.$$
   Thus heat generated in $4\,\Omega$ resistor,
   $$H = i^2 \times 4 = \left(\dfrac{\sqrt{50}}{10}\right)^2 \times 4 = 2 \text{ cal}. \text{ Ans.}$$

4. The resistance of heater, $R = \dfrac{V^2}{P} = \dfrac{100^2}{1000} = 10\,\Omega$
   If i is the current in heater, then
   $$i_1 = \sqrt{\dfrac{P}{R}}$$
   $$= \sqrt{\dfrac{62.5}{10}} = 2.5 \text{ A}$$
   The current in resistor R, $i_2 = \dfrac{2.5 \times 10}{R} = \dfrac{25}{R}.$
   The total current, $i = i_1 + i_2$
   $$= \left(2.5 + \dfrac{25}{R}\right)$$
   Thus $i \times R_{\text{Total}} = 100$
   or $\left(2.5 + \dfrac{25}{R}\right)\left[\dfrac{10R}{10+R} + 10\right] = 100$
   After solving, we get $R = 5\,\Omega.$ Ans.

5. By Faraday law, we have $m = zq$
   $$\therefore \quad q = \dfrac{m}{z} = \dfrac{4.62 \times 10^{-6}}{3.3 \times 10^{-7}} = 14 \text{ C}$$
   The total heat generated $H = \dfrac{q^2}{2C} = \dfrac{14^2}{2 \times 5 \times 10^{-2}} = 1960 \text{ J}.$
   If H_1 and H_2 are the heat generated in $20\,\Omega$ and $30\,\Omega$ resistors, then
   $$H_1 + H_2 = 1960 \quad ...(i)$$
   Also $\dfrac{H_1}{H_2} = \dfrac{i^2 \times 20}{i^2 \times 30} = \dfrac{2}{3} \quad ...(ii)$
   After solving above equations, we get
   $$H_1 = 784 \text{ J}. \quad \text{Ans.}$$

6. Charge required to liberate 22.4 litre of hydrogen
   $$= 2 \times 96500 \text{ C}$$
   $\therefore$ Charge required to liberate 1 litre of hydrogen
   $$q = \dfrac{2 \times 96500}{22.4} \text{ C}.$$
   If t is the required time, then
   $$t = \dfrac{q}{i} = \dfrac{2 \times 96500 / 22.4}{5}$$
   $$= 29 \text{ min}. \quad \text{Ans.}$$

7. If i be the current in the circuit, then
   $$V = \xi - ir$$
   or $10 = 12 - i \times 2$
   $\therefore \quad i = 1 \text{ A}.$
   The charge flows in half hour,
   $$q = it = 1 \times 1800 = 1800 \text{ C}.$$
   The charge required to liberate 107.9 g of silver
   $$= 96500 \text{ C}$$
   $\therefore$ 1800 C will liberate, $= \dfrac{107.9 \times 1800}{96500}$
   $$= 2 \text{ g}. \quad \text{Ans.}$$

Solutions Exercise-4.6

1. The total resistance of the circuit
$$R = \frac{2 \times 6}{2+6} + 1 = \frac{5}{2}\,\Omega$$
   The current drawn from the battery
$$i = \frac{V}{R} = \frac{6}{5/2} = 2.4\,A.$$
   The current in $2\,\Omega$ resistor, $i' = 2.4 \times \frac{6}{(6+2)} = 1.8\,A.$
   The heat produced through $2\,\Omega$ resistor in 15 minute is,
$$H = i^2 Rt = 1.8^2 \times 2 \times (15 \times 60)$$
$$= 5832\,J$$
   (a) If ΔT be the size in temperature of water, then
$$\Delta T = \frac{H}{C} = \frac{5832}{2000} = 2.9°C. \quad Ans.$$
   (b) If $6\,\Omega$ resistor gets burnt, then current in $2\,\Omega$ resistor,
$$i = \frac{6}{2+1} = 2\,A$$
   The heat produced in it in 15 minute
$$H = 2^2 \times 2 \times (15 \times 60) = 7200\,J.$$
   The rise in temperature $\Delta T = \frac{7200}{2000} = 3.6°C.$ **Ans.**

2. The given circuit is balanced wheat stone bridge type, so its resistance
$$R_t = \frac{3R \times 6R}{3R + 6R} = 2R.$$
   For the maximum power, $R_t = r$
$$2R = 4$$
$$\therefore \quad R = 2\,\Omega.$$
   The maximum power, $P = \frac{\xi^2}{4R_t} = \frac{\xi^2}{4 \times 4} = \frac{\xi^2}{16}.$ **Ans.**

3. (i) In series, time taken to boil water
$$t = t_1 + t_2 = 15 + 30 = 45\text{ minute}$$
   (ii) In parallel, time taken to boil water
$$t = \left[\frac{t_1 t_2}{t_1 + t_2}\right] = \frac{15 \times 30}{15 + 30} = 10\text{ minute}.$$

4. Given, $t = 0.001 - 0 = 0.001°C$
   The Seebeck emf, $e = at + \frac{b}{2}t^2$
$$= (-46 \times 10^{-6}) \times (0.001) + \left(\frac{-0.48 \times 10^{-6}}{2}\right)(0.001^2)$$
$$= -4.6 \times 10^{-8}\,V. \quad Ans.$$

5. Mass of gold required, $m = \frac{5}{100} \times 20 = 1\,g.$
   We know that $\frac{Z_{Au}}{Z_H} = \frac{W_{Au}}{W_H}$
$$\therefore \quad Z_{Au} = \frac{W_{Au}}{W_H} \times Z_H = \frac{197.1}{1.008} \times 0.1044 \times 10^{-4}$$
$$= 20.41 \times 10^{-4}$$
   We know that, $m = Z_{Au}\,i\,t$
$$\therefore \quad t = \frac{m}{Z_{Au} i} = \frac{1 \times 10^{-3}}{20.41 \times 10^{-7} \times 2}$$
$$\approx 4\text{ min.} \quad Ans.$$

6. The charge needed to deposit 107.9 g (1 mol) of silver
$$= 96500\,C$$
   $\therefore$ Charge needed to deposit 2.68 g
$$q = \frac{96500 \times 2.68}{107.9} = 2397\,C.$$
   The current in the resistor $i = \frac{q}{t} = \frac{2397}{10 \times 60} = 4A$
   The heat produced, $H = i^2 Rt$
$$= 4^2 \times 20 \times (10 \times 60)$$
$$= 192\,kJ. \quad Ans.$$

7. Mass of the wire, $m = \rho A \ell$
$$= 9 \times 10^3 \times 0.5 \times 10^{-6} \times 0.1$$
$$= 0.45 \times 10^{-3}\,kg$$
   Resistance of the wire, $R = \frac{\rho \ell}{A}$
$$= \frac{(1.6 \times 10^{-8}) \times (0.1)}{0.5 \times 10^{-6}}$$
$$= 0.32 \times 10^{-2}\,\Omega$$
   The amount of heat needed to melt the wire
$$H = mC\Delta T$$
$$= (0.45 \times 10^{-3}) \times (9 \times 10^{-2} \times 4200) \times (1075 - 25)$$
$$= 178.6\,J$$
   (i) If t is the required time, then
$$i^2 R t = H$$
   or $10^2 \times 0.32 \times 10^{-2} \times t = 178.6$
$$\therefore \quad t = 558\,s.$$
   (ii) If mass of the wire is doubled, the heat required becomes zH and resistance of wire becomes zR, so the time required will be same.

8. The mass of copper needed for electroplating,
$$m = 2(\rho A t)$$
$$= 2 \times 9000 \times 10 \times 10^{-4} \times 10 \times 10^{-6}$$
$$= 18 \times 10^{-5}\,kg$$
   Charge required to deposit copper
$$q = \frac{m}{z} = \frac{18 \times 10^{-5}}{3 \times 10^{-7}} = 600\,C$$
   The energy spent by the cell
$$H = Vq = 12 \times 600$$
$$= 7.2\,kJ \quad Ans.$$
   If ΔT be the rise in temperature, then
$$H = mC\Delta T$$
   or $\Delta T = \frac{H}{mC} = \frac{7.2 \times 10^3}{(100 \times 10^{-3} \times 4200)}$
$$= 17\,K. \quad Ans.$$

9. The charge flows in one hour
$$q = it = 0.5 \times 3600$$
$$= 1800\,C.$$
   96500 C of charge liberates the silver
$$= 107.9\,g$$
   $\therefore$ 1800 C of charge liberate
$$= \frac{107.9 \times 1800}{96500} = 2.01\,g \quad Ans.$$

★★★

www.ingramcontent.com/pod-product-compliance
Lightning Source LLC
LaVergne TN
LVHW061937070526
838199LV00060B/3853